A Law of Her Own

A Law of Her Own

The Reasonable Woman
as a Measure of Man

Caroline A. Forell and
Donna M. Matthews

Foreword by Barbara Y. Welke

NEW YORK UNIVERSITY PRESS

New York and London

NEW YORK UNIVERSITY PRESS
New York and London

Library of Congress Cataloging-in-Publication Data
Forell, Caroline A.
A law of her own : the reasonable woman as a measure of man /
Caroline A. Forell and Donna M. Matthews.
p.   cm.
Includes bibliographical references and index.
1. Sex crimes–United States. 2. Criminal liability—United
States. 3. Defense (Criminal procedure)—United States.
4. Sexual abuse victims—Legal status, laws, etc.—United States.
5. Women—Legal status, laws, etc.—United States.   I. Matthews,
Donna M. (Donna Meredith). II. Title.
KF9325.F67 1999
345.73'04—dc21   99-6811
                             CIP

New York University Press books are printed on acid-free paper,
and their binding materials are chosen for strength and durability.

Manufactured in the United States of America

10 9 8 7 6 5 4 3 2 1

For Mum, Dick, Ian, and Emily —C.F.
For Kevin, Rusty, and my parents —D.M.

Imagine if you will a world of law in which women are the predominant players and where the male is the exception to the norm.

—Judge Francis X. Hennessy,
Connecticut Court of Appeals

Contents

Foreword

A fundamental tenet of the American legal system is uniform application of the laws based on an objective standard. But, as this disturbing, even haunting narrative makes clear, a single nongendered standard of reasonable conduct—the "reasonable person"—remains as elusive as ever.

Through case after case involving hostile environment sexual harassment, domestic homicide, stalking, and rape, Forell and Matthews reveal a harrowing truth: "the reasonable person" is little more than a mask for "the reasonable man" it replaced. Man remains the measure of woman and as a result the law continues to condone men's victimization of women. Taking to heart another fundamental tenet of law— that law is a system of values—the authors propose a radical departure: if we truly believe in rights to bodily integrity, individual agency, and autonomy, why not make woman the measure of man?

The authors' proposal that a reasonable woman standard should apply in all cases of sexual harassment, stalking, domestic homicide, and rape is uncompromising and provocative—a frontal challenge to the male standard that remains deeply embedded in American law. Whether or not the reader embraces their proposal, there is no turning back from the legal reality their narrative so baldly exposes.

Barbara Y. Welke
Professor, Department of History
University of Minnesota

Acknowledgments

Thanks to our families, friends, and colleagues for their support and patience. We couldn't have done it without you.

Many readers provided valuable assistance by reviewing drafts throughout the evolution of this book. Particular thanks to Nancy Adess, Dan Fletcher, Leslie Harris, Lisa Kloppenberg, Margie Paris, Peggy Pascoe, Ken Pendelton, Jamie Ross, and Merle Weiner for reading and commenting on drafts. The Law Research Interest Group of the University of Oregon's Center for the Study of Women in Society both gave us helpful feedback on a few chapters of the book and an opportunity to "go public" for the first time. The students in Caroline Forell's 1999 Women and the Law seminar read the introductory chapters—the second time to "go public"—and made helpful comments.

Thanks for providing us with contacts go to Mary Forell Davis and Jennifer Freyd. We are also grateful to the people who provided us with prepublication reviews for our cover: Martha Chamallas, Barbara Ehrenreich, Susan Estrich, Alison Jaggar, and Gloria Steinem. We are especially grateful to Barbara Welke for her wonderful foreword. Anna Quindlen and Carol Sanger also provided us with support and ideas for promoting the book.

Nancy Farmer kept the system going with her great administrative support, and lent her eagle eye to proofread the manuscript page proofs. Research assistance was provided by Rebecca Hotchkiss, Ellen Theordorson, Sandy Gorman, Melanie Smith, Meredeth Allen, and Tim Bennett, students at the University of Oregon School of Law.

Special thanks to Suzanne Lewis for taking our photograph and for her good humor through the process.

Our editor, Niko Pfund, through his extraordinary e-mail responses, was always instantly available to us. His humor and constant support made a huge difference to our morale and determination to make the most of the opportunity that NYU Press gave us to get our ideas out through our first book.

Finally we acknowledge each other and the wonderful way in which our abilities and interests complemented each other. It was truly a joint effort throughout with none of the strife that can accompany such effort. We both improved as writers and editors through working together. This was collaboration at its best.

Introduction

This book is intended for people concerned about how the law treats women. Despite the apparent progress in women's legal status, the law remains profoundly male. We believe the law's fundamental paradigm must change because superficial changes serve primarily to mask the continuing, pervasive violence and injustice against women. The spectrum of violence and disregard of women is most evident and problematic in the law of sexual harassment, stalking, rape, and domestic homicide—all areas in which acquaintances or intimates usually inflict the injury. Men harass, beat, stalk, rape, and kill women, yet the law still minimizes, or even denies, these injuries. We therefore propose a method by which the law can better redress the injuries women experience.

We advocate that courts apply a "reasonable woman" standard *to the conduct of men* in certain legal settings—where men's and women's life experiences and views on sex and aggression diverge and women are overwhelmingly the injured parties. Such a woman-based legal standard would make currently acceptable or excusable conduct unacceptable and inexcusable by focusing on respect for bodily integrity, agency, and autonomy. It would help rectify the imbalance in how society and its legal system view sexual and gender-based harassment, rape, stalking, and domestic imprisonment, violence, and death. This "reasonable woman," based to the extent possible on the experiences and expectations of most women, would become the standard by which men's behavior is measured. When women are the aggressors, their conduct would also be held to the reasonable woman standard.

Our proposal is radical. The reasonable woman standard is intended to make a difference by affecting both the head and the gut. In certain contexts, this paradigm shift will entirely change the outcome in women's lives and in legal cases. It is based on the premise that human beings have great ability to learn, empathize, adapt, and to control their own behavior. Men who batter or kill their intimates, who harass, stalk, or rape, *can change*. The rare women who behave similarly can change also. And they must.

We place men into three broad groups with regard to these issues. First are the "good guys"—men who already "get it," who respect and value the personhood, physical integrity, and safety of women and of other men. Happily, many men are good guys and already behave according to the reasonable woman standard. The second group we call the "redeemables"—men who are willing and able to change their beliefs and behavior once they are induced to reconsider their attitudes toward gender roles. The reasonable woman standard will assist such men in changing both their perceptions and their behaviors. In the third group are the "diehards"—men who will not change their beliefs, who will always blame the target for their own rage and aggression. It is highly unlikely that the reasonable woman standard will affect the diehards' worldview. However, application of this standard will force them to stop their violence against women, although the threat of either economic, social, or legal consequences or by lengthy incarceration.

Sexual harassment, stalking, rape, and domestic violence are choices—voluntary acts. To those men who try to impose their will on women, we want the law to say "Change or else!" We believe that once they understand women's perspectives and experiences, many men who engage in such conduct—the redeemables—will change of their own accord. Many of those who are unwilling to change their beliefs—the diehards—can still learn to conform their behavior to the law, stemming their violence against and subordination of women. But if they continue to harass, to hit, to stalk, to kill, to rape, the legal consequences must be swift, harsh, and certain. Such men must be made to take responsibility for and recognize the wrongfulness of their own acts. The law must no longer support rationalizations such as "She led me on" or "I beat/killed her because she provoked me."

At present, law is a warrior code that sympathizes with and accommodates violence that derives from sexual jealousy, wounded pride, and the desire to dominate another. For women, the most common forms of such violence involve intimates or former intimates. But, even though women are by far the most common victims of intimate violence, men's intimate violence injures themselves as well, both interpersonally and physically. A particularly grim example is domestic homicide. In many cases, men who kill their wives also kill themselves, and some women kill their batterers in response to extreme violence and threats. Thus, demanding that batterers behave like reasonable women will save the batterers' lives too. Furthermore, because the reasonable woman standard would apply to the conduct of both men and women, regardless of the parties' gender, women who harass or kill men would also be held to this more respectful and antiviolence standard of conduct.

We believe that deliberate use of the reasonable woman standard in areas involving sex, sexism, and aggression, with careful explanation of what the standard means, will elicit greater empathy for women's experiences from society in general and from legal decision makers in particular. Humans have a great capacity both to empathize and to modify their behavior based on better understanding of another's experiences. Studies have demonstrated, for example, that many men and women have divergent perceptions about what conduct constitutes rape—about what kinds of words and conduct indicate nonconsent. However, according to a study by Hatterly Freetly and Kane, men who know rape survivors have views that are much like those of women. That is, men personally acquainted with a rape survivor share with most women a similar perception, recognizing that sex with someone who says "no" is rape. The law, by adopting a reasonable woman standard that incorporates and explains women's values and experience, can similarly increase empathy. It can thereby help decision makers—male and female—identify with the injured party in assessing the injuring conduct.

For the reasonable woman standard to be effective, it must be given substantive content. Unlike some versions of the reasonable woman standard that make women into either victims or pseudomen, our standard seeks to achieve meaningful equality by emphasizing that reasonable women want and demand respect, personal autonomy, agency, and bodily integrity. These values must be effectively communicated to avoid simply putting another name onto male values and perspectives. Therefore, our standard should be fleshed out in jury instructions, clearly explaining that a reasonable woman expects these personal qualities to be honored, and that behavior violating these aspects of a woman's humanity is legally unacceptable. Such instructions would enhance decision-maker empathy, require judges and juries to treat women with respect, and subvert the inherent bias in the law. Courts and other lawmakers would also be encouraged to find new ways to put a human face on the reasonable woman standard, for example, through expert testimony refuting myths about women and by admitting evidence of a perpetrator's earlier instances of violence and aggression toward women.

As Ruth Colker put it, our law should first ask whether the particular behavior "respect[s] women's well-being, as seen from women's perspective." Explicitly holding men to a reasonable woman standard in areas where male prerogatives have traditionally defined what is right and lawful will challenge the systematic subordination of women and the largely unexamined biases in the law. Specifically, law must change so that it stops holding women responsible for the violent and aggressive conduct of men.

For example, men who kill their former or current "intimates" often claim that the victim provoked the killing by her behavior, which almost invariably involves the entirely emotional "provocation" of her infidelity or leaving. Like O. J. Simpson, these men explain: "Let's say I committed this crime. Even if I did do this, it would have to have been because I loved her very much, right?" Wrong! Yet, under current law, the basic assumption that a woman *makes* a "reasonable" man uncontrollably jealous, *causing* his violent rage and loss of control so that he kills her out of love, is almost never adequately scrutinized. As a result, the law treats a killing that is "provoked" by a woman's infidelity or leaving less seriously than other forms of killing.

Under our standard, decision makers would judge the killer in terms of whether a reasonable woman would have lost control and killed in the circumstances. Only secondarily would they consider the victim's "provocatory" conduct, and then only in terms of whether it would have provoked a reasonable woman to lose control and kill. Thus, for example, the decision maker would be asked whether a reasonable woman, on discovering that her husband was unfaithful, or knowing that her ex-husband was seeing someone new, would react with deadly violence. The decision maker would also consider whether a husband's unfaithfulness or an ex-husband's dating behavior would provoke a reasonable woman to be violent. As a result of applying our reasonable woman standard, provocation would most likely disappear as a mitigating factor except in response to threatened or actual violence.

As current rape law demonstrates, certain applications of a reasonable woman standard are not in women's interests. In rape claims, the reasonable woman standard has been used to judge, in essence, whether the target "asked for it," by asking how *men* think "reasonable" women ought to behave or demonstrate nonconsent. Our proposed reasonable woman standard would turn current rape law on its head: consent would not be determined by whether the target resisted enough to demonstrate nonconsent (protecting her virtue unto death, if necessary, as some men choose to believe a "reasonable woman" would if she didn't *really* want sex). Instead, the culpability of the accused rapist would be measured by whether, in the same circumstances, a reasonable woman would have believed consent existed and behaved similarly to the *accused—not* the target. In assessing the *target's* conduct in the rape context, the reasonable woman standard would be used only to the extent that conduct may have indicated consent to a reasonable woman under the circumstances.

We do not believe that men and women are different in the sense that women are fragile, needing special protection in order to be equal. Rather, recognition of women's viewpoints and experience in areas where women are primarily on the receiving end of violence aids in achieving equality: the perceptions and conduct generally associated with women—*gendered* female—in our culture are simply better for everyone in addressing these areas. Women are disproportionately injured, terrorized, and killed as a result of male dominance and aggression. Holding women to the present male standard and therefore permitting them to "equally" injure, terrorize, and kill men is not an equality that would serve anyone well. In contrast, holding everyone to a reasonable woman standard of behavior when it comes to assessing violence against acquaintances and intimates could be transformative and foster meaningful and positive equality. Thus, we advocate that *everyone* be held to this more respectful standard of conduct associated with, and expected of, women in our culture.

By applying these gendered perspectives and viewing certain behavior in context of women's experience, we may begin to achieve true equality of the sexes. If such a rebalancing occurs, then, over time, society will evolve sufficiently so that a reasonable *person* comes to mean not just a man in disguise but instead incorporates the positive values of both genders. When that time arrives, the reasonable woman standard will no longer be necessary to ensure justice.

The book is organized into sections. Part 1 gives an overview of the issues and of our argument. The other parts examine four major areas of law and conduct that continue to injure, silence, and disempower women—sexual harassment, stalking, domestic homicide, and rape. We believe and argue that applying our proposed reasonable woman standard in these contexts would effectuate positive change for women in particular, and for people in general. We do not examine the law of domestic violence as such, although it is conduct that injures, silences, and disempowers vast numbers of women. However, stalking, domestic homicide, and acquaintance rape intersect many domestic violence issues. Battered women are the most common victims of stalking; rape is most frequently committed by intimates or former intimates; and domestic homicide is the most violent and extreme outcome of domestic violence and stalking.

Each substantive part begins with an overview of the applicable legal framework and the current legal standard for the area of law at issue; the parts can be read independently and in any order. We examine the bias of the "reasonable person" through legal cases described in news articles and judicial opinions. Appellate and trial decisions tell stories about real people and demonstrate how the legal system succeeds or fails in achieving justice. These legal cases illustrate the differences between how men and women experience male violence and sexual conduct as well as how the law perceives that conduct. Challenging the basic assumptions in these cases, we show how the existing legal framework distorts the woman's voice and sometimes erases her story—reducing her to a provoker, a bad woman who tempted the man to harassment or violence—and how a woman-based standard would change the outcome.

A Note on Sources and Citation

Readers will notice that we do not include footnotes or in-text references. Instead, when we refer to a particular work, we cite the author or title in the text. We decided to write the book this way to make it easier to read while still giving appropriate credit. The "References" section at the end of the book includes the full citation for each work referred to in the text, as well as additional books and articles that we consider useful and that have formed a more general basis for our theories and analysis. Anyone interested in referring to the source material from which we drew quotes or other facts can do so by finding the author and work listed in the references.

PART I

The Idea and the Reality

The public and the private worlds are inseparably connected; . . .
the tyrannies and servilities of the one are the tyrannies and servilities of the other. —Virginia Woolf, *Three Guineas*

1

Locked In and Locked Out

I thought how unpleasant it is to be locked out; and I thought
how it is worse perhaps to be locked in; and . . . of the safety and
prosperity of the one sex and the poverty and insecurity of the
other.   —Virginia Woolf, *A Room of One's Own*

The status of women has changed significantly since the
time of Virginia Woolf. But in many ways, it has not. In Woolf's time,
women were almost wholly locked out of public and professional life
and locked in the private sphere, subjugated to husband, father, or
other male "guardian." While this is no longer true, many women continue to be marginalized as workers and dominated by their male partners, who are supported by our social and legal institutions.

Until very recently, women were considered unfit for the rigors of law,
diplomacy, and politics. They were deemed inherently more fit to be
wives, models, nurses, stewardesses, secretaries, and schoolteachers than
artists, doctors, pilots, business executives, and professors. Women remain mostly locked out of certain jobs, from construction and combat to
engineering and the "hard" sciences, and, thanks to the glass ceiling, to
the upper strata of business, law, diplomacy, and politics. Today women,
along with their children, comprise the majority of the poor. Even worse,
many women are still locked into violent relationships and homes by men
who promise to kill them if they leave. And some of these battered women
are literally locked in—in prison or in death—because they killed to escape or were murdered in the attempt to escape.

Law plays a significant role in both locking women out and locking
them in. Because law is based on male experience, it "understands"
men. Thus, courts apply male values to conclude that sexual and sexist
workplace conduct is merely annoying, that fear of a stalker is unjusti-
fied, and that sex against a woman's will is seduction. These largely

unexamined, male-centered values serve also to mitigate the seriousness of the crime when men kill "their" women who leave, or try to, and to condemn women who kill their batterers in self-defense. Where gender structures societal expectations and affects perception and experience, the law defines what is lawful in terms of traditional male rights and conduct. Consequently, in these legal contexts the system fails women.

Within the "private" realm of the home, and where women enter the "public" realm of the traditionally male workplace or justice system, gender bias permeates both the lived reality and the law. What is considered legally reasonable behavior in these realms stems from a long history in which male aggression and sexuality defined the rights and relationships between "persons," and in which all "persons" were male.

The Legal Status of Women

For hundreds of years the law scoffed at the idea that a woman could reason. Women had no legal personhood; they were viewed as incompetent, akin to children. Women were forbidden from entering into contracts or writing wills. Until the mid–nineteenth century, a woman couldn't own property; instead, she *was* property. Marriage traditions such as the father "giving away" his daughter to her husband, whose name she then takes, are remnants of the not-too-distant past when fathers owned daughters, whom they bartered away to husbands. Consigned to the private rule of a man, and under unregulated and often violent domestic "law" with minimal recourse in the courts, women submitted. Both inside and outside the home, the only work they were permitted involved various forms of caretaking of men and children.

The U.S. Constitution begins "We the People," and the Declaration of Independence says, "We hold these truths to be self-evident, that all Men are created equal." This "we" has been mythologized to mean all Americans—including women, the poor, and people of color—as if both genders and all classes and races had a voice from the beginning. In fact, when the United States was founded the "we" was male, white, and of the propertied class. Not until one hundred years later did the Fifteenth Amendment give black men the right to vote. It took another fifty years for women to get the vote in 1920. Yet voting was only the barest beginning of inclusion in the political process and of legal and social equality. Not until *Reed v. Reed* in 1971 did the U.S. Supreme Court declare that women were entitled to equal protection under the Fourteenth Amendment. Since then, the Court has decided a number of cases in which it found that discrimination based on gender violates the Constitution, most of which, ironically, involved purported gender discrimination against men.

Although women are now legal persons and officially allowed access to many professions and workplaces, the law remains male biased beneath a veneer of gender neutrality. It is therefore inevitable that in certain contexts, society's and the law's supposedly generic "we" and "persons" mean "men." As Catharine MacKinnon points out in *Feminism Unmodified*, despite years of struggle and progress, under the law as in life man remains the standard by which women are measured:

> Men's physiology defines most sports, their needs define auto and health insurance coverage, their socially designed biographies define workplace expectations and successful career patterns, their perspectives and concerns define quality in scholarship, their experiences and obsessions define merit, their objectification of life defines art, their military service defines citizenship, their presence defines family, their inability to get along with each other—their wars and rulerships—defines history, their image defines god, and their genitals define sex.

These often hidden, male-biased presumptions can have devastating effects on women's lives. Even when the sexism is benevolent—as when a woman is treated "like a lady"—it harms women. As Justice William Brennan noted more than twenty-five years ago in *Frontiero v. Richardson*, this "attitude of 'romantic paternalism' . . . in practical effect, put[s] women, not on a pedestal, but in a cage." Rather than attaining empowerment and respect in the workplace and the home, women are expected to "fit in" to the existing legal and work structure, without any fundamental redefinition of rights or norms. Asking for more—or for something different—is criticized as radical feminist bitching or demands for special treatment.

The Reasonable Person and the Status Quo

Law plays a role in maintaining the gender status quo through how it determines whether conduct is unreasonable and therefore wrongful.

Nancy Ehrenreich calls the reasonableness standard the "expression of the law's fairness and objectivity" deemed necessary for justice. In determining culpability for an injury, the legal system traditionally asked whether the actor behaved like a reasonable man, a standard that was supposed to abstractly represent the values and expectations of the community as a whole, and which was usually applied regardless of the actor's gender. Considering the different roles of men and women in the nineteenth century, it is not surprising that the standard was intentionally gendered. Until the twentieth century, the people who engaged in activities likely to injure others—such as operating trains or carriages and using heavy machinery or firearms—were almost exclusively male, so men actually were usually the people whose conduct was judged by the reasonable man standard.

Apologists might argue that *man* in the phrase "reasonable man" included both sexes, but that is simply not true. Courts adopted the reasonable man standard when virtually all judges, jurors, lawyers, legislators, and law professors were men, and women had virtually no independent public, economic, or legal identity. In fact, courts even interpreted *non*gendered terms to cover only men. For example, the courts, including the U.S. Supreme Court in *Bradwell v. Illinois*, upheld statutes excluding qualified women from practicing law by construing the phrase "any attorney" to mean "any male attorney." As Barbara Welke's work demonstrates, the maleness of the reasonable man was highlighted by the occasional use of a reasonable woman standard to enable women victims, injured in accidents, to recover damages despite what might have been, for a man, contributory negligence.

During the past twenty-five years, most courts have rephrased the normative standard as the "reasonable person," which sounds, and sometimes is, more neutral and fair than the reasonable man. However, when the reasonable person is applied, it often exemplifies what Riva Seigel calls "preservation-through-transformation." Just as the Jim Crow separate-but-equal regime succeeded slavery and spousal immunity replaced the right of domestic "chastisement," changing the reasonable man to the reasonable person didn't change the underlying reality. In specific contexts the changed terminology simply glosses over fundamental differences between the perceptions and experiences of men and women.

A reasonableness standard is intended to define a minimum standard of behavior and to impose liability for injuries stemming from what society views as substandard conduct. Thus, if society deemed it unreasonable to persist in sexually touching someone after she said to stop, a person would be held liable even if he sincerely believed it was seduction. In practice, the reasonable person has all the attributes of the original reasonable man. The law describes him as the "average guy"—the man who mows the lawn in his shirtsleeves or who rides a commuter bus. Despite the middle-class male imagery it evokes, for most injuries, such as auto accidents and slip-and-fall cases, the reasonable person is the appropriate standard. Using the term *person* when assessing most injurious conduct helps us realize and acknowledge the common traits, interests, and perceptions among men and women that exist in most areas. Furthermore, in many situations the risk of stereotyping created by a reasonable woman standard outweighs any symbolic or actual benefit it might produce. (For example, think about how the term "woman driver" is used.)

However, in certain contexts, the interests of men and women conflict and their perceptions and experiences differ. As discussed in greater detail in the chapters that follow, empirical research has shown, for example, markedly different perceptions by men and women of what constitutes sexual harassment, rape, and stalking. Similarly, the studies discussed in part 4, "Domestic Homicide," have demonstrated that the reasons most men and most women kill their intimates also differ dramatically: men kill out of jealousy and need to control; women kill in self-defense. In addition, conduct that demeans and disempowers women often has the opposite effect on men. Women frequently view aggressive sexual conduct toward them as unwanted and harmful. In contrast, many men view the effect of such conduct on women as harmless and believe they would welcome it if the tables were turned. Often, when a woman feels raped by an acquaintance, he sees it as seduction.

When decision makers are asked to apply a reasonable person standard in cases of sexual harassment, rape, stalking, and domestic homicide, they generally adopt either a male or a female perspective. In our still-patriarchal society, absent explicit instructions to apply a woman-based standard, men's interests and values automatically apply and trump women's whenever they conflict. Regardless of the decision makers' gender, they are most likely to adopt a male perspective, especially when, as is typical, the accused is male. Judging the accused by a woman-based standard simply will not occur unless the decision maker is explicitly instructed to do so.

2

The Meaning of Equality

How do we end the inequality of the sexes?
What kind of equality do we want?
—U.S. Circuit Court Judge Guido Calabresi

Women's intellectual freedom, as Virginia Woolf observed seventy years ago, requires material things, such as a room of one's own and an adequate income. Women's freedom of movement, physical safety, and full personhood require less tangible but no less essential things. Just as a poet must have a room of her own in order to write, a woman must have a law that explicitly includes and values her—a law of her own—in order to be truly free and equal, to exist as a complete, legally recognized "person." Such a law would esteem behavior associated with women in our society and take into account the gendered nature of experience. Harms women suffer would be taken seriously. Violence would be less tolerated, and dignitary injuries would be treated as serious harms. Expected relations among all persons would be more empathetic and respectful.

Our society and legal system continue to view women as lesser than men. Thus, injuries to them—particularly by "their" men—are considered lesser. As Catharine MacKinnon wrote in *Feminism Unmodified*: "When [men] are hit, a person is assaulted. When they are sexually violated, it is not simply tolerated . . . or defended as the necessary structure of the family." In contrast, when women are hit in their homes, it's just a domestic spat. When women are pursued by men whose sexual attention is unwanted, it's just seduction. And when a woman who "sleeps around" or wears a short skirt or walks alone at night is sexually assaulted, it's just that she asked for it.

By adopting a reasonable woman standard of care defined from a woman's perspective, the law would explicitly acknowledge that women are entitled to respect, dignity, personal autonomy, and safety from intimates. Further, when sex or aggression is involved, the reasonable woman should be the standard for anyone claiming injury—man or woman, heterosexual or homosexual, of any race, color, or creed—because all persons should be treated with respect and freed from violence in the home, on the street, and in the workplace.

Difference as a Double Bind

The reasonable woman standard intentionally highlights difference. We maintain that to achieve real gender equality the law must demand that men conform to woman-based norms concerning sex and violence. Our focus on difference involves some risk. Because society defines what is normal as what is male, the issue of difference and sameness creates a double-bind for women: to be different from men often means to be lesser. Thus, some argue that highlighting gender differences concerning sex and aggression does not empower women but instead turns them into victims by reinforcing the negative stereotypes of women as weak, overly sensitive, and less able to cope than men.

However, if we ignore certain differences, we unquestionably accept men's values, for to be treated "the same" means to be treated the same *as men*. In theory, that is how legal equality now operates. When it comes to sex and aggression, women can do whatever they want, as long as they act like men: women can kill out of jealousy or hurt pride, like men; women can refuse to take no for an answer, like men; and women in power can sexualize relationships with subordinates, like men. In the context of sex and aggression, failure to acknowledge difference means that men's views and values prevail. This male-centered "equality" is especially unfair because of how the rare women who *do* act like men in these contexts are *actually* viewed and treated. All too often both society and law view such a woman as "unnatural" or aberrant, her behavior as less excusable than if she had been a man. Women are just not similarly situated when it comes to sexual and violent conduct.

Consider society's outrage and bewilderment about Mary Kay Letourneau bearing two children by her fourteen-year-old student, *especially* because she was married with children. Letourneau is currently serving seven and a half years in prison for rape. Posit instead the more common scenario of a female student bearing children by her married male teacher. It is impossible, through simple role reversal, to make the parties similarly situated because it's the student, not the teacher, who bears the children. Surely that would harm a female student more. Nevertheless, communities often accept "traditional" male-teacher–female-student sexual relationships, as long as they marry. It would likely be rationalized even for a married male teacher as long as he divorced his wife and married the student. It certainly would not—and does not—make national news.

Compare the treatment of Letourneau with the policy in Orange County, California. According to columnist Ellen Goodman, during 1996 "a 22-year-old man arrested for having sex with a 14-year-old girl was given court permission to marry her [and] a pregnant 13-year-old legally wed her 20-year-old boyfriend/child molester." Imagine a court giving a pregnant twenty-year-old permission to marry her fourteen-year-old boyfriend—it just sounds absurd. However, if the reasonable woman standard were applied to the conduct of an adult man impregnating a fourteen-year-old girl, marriage would not be an acceptable alternative in this case either; it, too, would sound absurd.

Law's reasonable person/man, which theoretically views and treats women like men, ignores the harm women suffer as the "persons" almost always on the receiving end of all this supposedly equal sexual and aggressive behavior. And on the rare occasions when women are the aggressors, they are viewed as more dangerous than similarly situated men. In short, women are damned if they do and damned if they don't.

In crimes and civil injuries where women are disproportionately victimized, such as sexual harassment, rape, stalking, domestic violence, and domestic homicide, the present methodology usually focuses on both the actor's and the target's behavior from the male perspective. From that perspective, one sees the woman target as blameworthy. She wanted, provoked, or even deserved what happened, and therefore the male perpetrator behaved as a reasonable man would have behaved under the circumstances. Her conduct was unreasonable because she was friendly or not, because she resisted or didn't, because she said "yes" or "no," because she left or stayed. Women are held responsible for how men treat them.

A man may repeatedly ask a female work subordinate to remove change from his front pants pocket or comment on her body or her sex life, but he is not harassing her if she acquiesces, laughs nervously, or ignores him. After all, unless she tells him to stop, how is he to know she doesn't like it? Even today, in many cases involving acquaintances—especially if they were intimate previously—a man may force sexual intercourse on a woman although she repeatedly says no, cries, begs him to stop, or tries to escape. If she doesn't have bruises or torn clothing, it's not rape because she didn't demonstrate adequate nonconsent. Anyway, since she went out with him, invited him up to her room, kissed him, or had sex with him before, she had given some kind of irrevocable consent. A man may repeatedly intrude into a woman's life by phone, letters, e-mail, or in person, but even if she asks him to stop, unless the law views his actions as physically threatening, she can only be irritated, certainly not frightened. In other words, under the present male standard, if targets act as women are acculturated to act, by being "nice," by not fighting back, or by feeling scared, the law views their conduct as justifying male aggression and denies the profound injuries women experience.

This catch-22 is most pronounced in the context of domestic homicide. Men kill women they know for reasons different from those of women who kill men they know. When a woman is killed because she left or tried to leave her partner or because she simply "made him" jealous, she is considered to have provoked him to kill her. But when a woman kills her batterer believing—as a reasonable woman would—that he was going to seriously injure or kill her or her children, she must explain why she didn't leave him. Either way, it's her conduct that matters, and it's her fault.

As we discuss in detail in chapter 9, studies indicate that most men who kill their female intimates do so in reaction to the woman's leaving or deciding to leave; women almost never behave similarly. Men who kill their wives not infrequently also commit suicide or kill other people, particularly their children and their wives' lovers; women rarely do so. Men who kill their intimates often kill in response to revelations of infidelity or the woman's attempt to separate; for many, the homicide follows a lengthy period of coercive abuse and assaults of the victim. In contrast, many women who kill their intimates have suffered years of abuse, and kill only after they have exhausted meager and often ineffective sources of assistance, when they feel there is no escape, and because they fear for their own or their children's lives.

Because the law applies a male standard to these different reasons for killing, it tends to view men who kill intimates as more reasonable than women who do. If, instead, the law applied a reasonable woman standard to domestic homicides, "heat of passion" would no longer make a man killing a woman less serious, and a woman killing to save her and her childrens' lives and end years of torture would be considered justifiable homicide.

As we would apply it, the reasonable woman standard could potentially free women from the equality paradigm's double bind of "be a victim" or "be a man" by recognizing women's differences *and* explicitly making women's views and values the standard by which *men's* conduct is measured. Under this new paradigm, women's differences from men form a basis for condemning and reducing gendered violence and abuse of power, rather than for excusing it. This use of difference stops the victimization of women by requiring that they be treated not as acted-upon objects but as powerful subjects, whose perceptions and experiences of sex and aggression matter and define permissible behavior of both men and women. This woman-based standard incorporates the core values of respect for women's bodily integrity, human dignity, personal agency, and autonomy. If the law, in determining the reasonableness of sexual and aggressive conduct, took these values seriously, women would become men's equals on their own terms.

The Sources of Difference

Accepting that the way men and women view and experience sex and aggression crucially differs, what is the origin of this difference? The source of gendered differences has been, and continues to be, hotly debated. Are they biological or socially created? How malleable are they? These questions have no definitive answers.

Sociobiologists assert that gendered perspectives emerged from evolutionary development to maximize reproductive success. Kingsley Browne cites typical sociobiologists as saying that "[f]or very fundamental reasons, the sexes have differing views of sexuality. Where a man might see 'opportunity,' a woman sees 'danger.' These differences flow in turn from differences in relative parental investment and they run very deep." As Dale Peterson and Richard Wrangham assert: "Patriarchy is worldwide and history-wide. . . . It serves the reproductive purposes of men who maintain the system. . . . [I]t emerges from men's temperaments, out of their evolutionarily derived efforts to control women and at the same time have solidarity with fellow men in competition against outsiders." It should be noted, however, that even if sociobiologists are correct, it does not follow that men must prevail when their interests conflict with those of women, nor that men are justified in behaving badly.

At the other end of the spectrum from sociobiologists are those who believe that difference is entirely socially constructed. As Simone de Beauvoir so aptly put it in *The Second Sex*: "One is not born, but rather becomes a woman. No biological, psychological, or economic fate determines the figure that the human female presents in society: it is civilization as a whole that produces this creature intermediate between male and eunuch."

Or as Catharine MacKinnon argues in *Feminism Unmodified*: "Inequality comes first; differences come after." In her view, it is *because* women are dominated by men that they are different. Thus, MacKinnon objects to identifying those values associated with women, such as caring and connectedness, as belonging to women. In "A Conversation" she rightly asks: "*Why* do women become these people, more than men, who represent *these* values?" MacKinnon answers by saying that men subordinate women—women have been made victims, *so their values are the values of victims.*

This leaves unanswered the even more fundamental question of why men dominate women. In *Three Guineas*, Virginia Woolf asks: "Is dominance craving for submission? And, most persistent and difficult of all the questions . . . , what possible satisfaction can dominance give the dominator?" Professor J. C. Smith also asks the question, which he then answers, saying: "The pathological need of males to dominate females stems from a deep seated unconscious hostility towards women which ranges from the mere resentment or fear of the female to hatred. An unconscious misogyny and gynophobia is part of the psyche of the male of the species."

Regardless of why men dominate women, it is likely that in most, and possibly all, societies it has served men's interests (whether biological or social) to establish systems that subordinate women through their greater physical strength. These patriarchies relegate women to the role of serving men, who hold the monopoly on the public sphere where social and legal policy is made.

In the United States, until the mid–twentieth century, men's voices were the only ones heard in the halls of power, and thus their values and desires were the only ones reflected in the law. Even laws protecting women were created from a male perspective of protecting his women. This "protection" was usually from other men and guarded each man's investment in his female property. Such protection assured him that his wife would be available to serve his needs, including bearing and raising his children and keeping his home, and that his daughters' value as marriage partners was preserved.

As the many women-generated changes in law during the late twentieth century demonstrate, legal and social gender domination is not inevitable. Those who are physically dominant do not invariably make the law, or make it in their own image when they do. Furthermore, legal and social paradigms do not have to remain static. And it certainly doesn't follow that because men have certain biological drives they can't help behaving badly. There are numerous examples of men's (and women's) altering their behavior when confronted with societal or legal expectations or penalties.

Equality on Women's Terms

We believe gender differences cannot be entirely attributed to either nature or nurture. As Carol Gilligan wrote: "these differences arise in a social context where factors of social status and power combine with reproductive biology to shape the experiences of males and females and the relations between the sexes." Regardless of why, the lived experience of women differs from that of men. Further, the difference in perception echoes and amplifies a gendered difference in experience. Thus, when courts apply the purportedly neutral reasonable person standard where the male experience defines neutrality—but where consensus and commonality between men and women simply do not exist—the law systematically excludes women's experiences and punishes women because they are not men. No matter what they do, women are deemed responsible for most male sexual and violent conduct against them. In these areas of systematic disadvantage and exclusion, women need a "law of their own."

By arguing for a reasonable woman standard, we walk a fine line between what we, like MacKinnon, see as the values of victims—be nice or suffer—and the qualities we believe women want and are entitled to as powerful actors, such as respect, dignity, compassion, and autonomy through being treated as equals. Historical research by Barbara Welke demonstrates that a reasonable woman standard was used originally in the nineteenth century to mitigate the harshness of applying contributory negligence rules to women who suffered serious physical injuries. That reasonable woman standard combined benign sexism and real differences (ranging from corsets to pregnancy) to make it less likely that women's own conduct would bar them from recovering against the person or entity who injured them. Generally, these women's injuries arose from using public transportation while wearing their cumbersome and confining clothing.

In the 1990s, various commentators have urged alternatives to the reasonable person standard, especially in the area of hostile work environment sexual harassment and when battered women who kill claim self-defense. In addition to the reasonable woman, proposed standards have included the rational woman, the respectful person, the reasonable victim, the reasonable person of the same gender, and the reasonable person with all the essential attributes of the target. A few commentators have argued for a purely subjective standard that judges the perpetrator's conduct according to whether or not the target believes it wrongful. A leading commentator, Kathryn Abrams, recently urged a return to a traditional reasonable person standard. In her 1998 article, "The New Jurisprudence of Sexual Harassment," Abrams, one of the first scholars to endorse a reasonable woman standard for assessing hostile work environment sexual harassment, shifts her support to the reasonable person standard. However, she defines the traditional term in a nontraditional way that requires appliers of the standard to understand the workplace changes that feminists seek:

> The term 'reasonable [person]' should be understood to characterize a person with a solid base of political knowledge regarding sexual harassment [including] understanding the workplace and elsewhere [and] understanding the ways in which a sex and gender hierarchy impinges on nonconforming men and women.

Abrams's proposal, like those of many others, improves on the present reasonable person standard. Some do a better job than others in avoiding traditional female stereotypes and in dealing with the problem of essentialism that any abstract standard creates. However, unlike our proposal, none recommend that the alternative standard be applied to a broad range of gendered injuries. And none recommends that the standard explicitly refer to women yet apply regardless of the gender, sexual orientation, or race of the parties. These features of our standard and our extensive elaboration of what we mean by "reasonable woman" make our proposal unique.

What we propose isn't unrealistic; some courts have already adopted a reasonable woman standard that is quite compatible with our proposed standard. During the 1990s a number of appellate courts have expressly adopted the perspective of the reasonable woman on one legal issue: what constitutes hostile environment sexual harassment under Title VII of the Civil Rights Act or analogous state statutes. Still other appellate courts, including, arguably, the United States Supreme Court, have adopted the substance of a woman-based standard, if not the terminology, when addressing hostile environment sexual harassment.

What these courts have done is revolutionary because they have *expressly* held the *male* actor to a standard of conduct determined by whether a reasonable woman would view his conduct as creating a hostile environment. Applying the reasonable woman standard to male conduct is a radical act. Throughout history, dating as far back as ancient Greece, women were viewed as innately having less capacity for reason. As Anita Bernstein notes:

> On this subject, great minds thought alike. According to Aristotle, "the deliberative faculty in the soul is not present at all in a slave; in a female it is present but ineffective; in a child present but undeveloped." And for Aristotle there could be no good life without reason: thus a woman's life is always slavish, never fully human. Kant wrote that women were not "capable of principles" and that their "philosophy is not to reason, but to sense." For Hegel, women could not "attain to the ideal" of rational thought: "The difference between men and women is like that between animals and plants." Rousseau denounced women as incapable of thought and unsuited to education; his "highest accolade" for a woman was "Oh lovely ignorant fair!" Schopenhauer described women as "in every respect backward, lacking in reason and reflection."

Fewer than twenty-five years ago, the reasonable woman was still an oxymoron: the only people the law could envision as reasonable actors were men.

Applying the reasonable woman standard to men accused of creating hostile work environments turns the tables so that men must conform their behavior to a woman-based standard, rather than women having to endure sexually abusive behavior that satisfies male expectations and perpetuates the existing power dichotomy. In openly recognizing differences between men's and women's perspectives of and relation to the workplace, and in giving the woman's perspective priority over the man's, these courts dramatically depart from the traditional judicial posture of "neutrality" and acknowledge that law contains male biases. This form of the reasonable woman standard offers a way for men—and women—to take women seriously as autonomous persons and to stop the unfairness to women inherent in sexual coercion and intimate violence. If the courts were to extend this standard to other gendered harms, the "we" in "We the people" would begin to meaningfully include women.

The Reasonable Woman Applied

The current structure of the law of harassment, rape, stalking, and domestic homicide in most jurisdictions allocates evidentiary burdens in a way that assumes a male perpetrator's conduct has been reasonable and asks if the victim behaved reasonably from *his* perspective. That is, the purportedly objective standard in fact reflects how men would view the male perpetrator's conduct and that of his victim. As a corollary, when women are the perpetrators, their behavior is judged according to how a man would have behaved in and viewed that situation. Our method changes the questions, asking whether a reasonable woman would have acted as the perpetrator acted, as well as whether a reasonable woman would have responded with behavior similar to the target's.

When a reasonable person standard is used to assess sexual or violent conduct, present social and legal norms make this standard male. What is "reasonable" is determined based on behavior that for many men is understandable and justifiable "under the circumstances." A reasonable woman standard removes the legal seal of approval from conduct based on belief structures that include acceptance of interpersonal violence as a means of getting one's way, the desire to dominate and control women, high authoritarianism, and difficulty empathizing. Psychology professor John Pryor has extensively studied the differences in the belief systems of men who harass and men who don't. He found that men with a high likelihood to harass sexually "tend to (a) hold adversarial sexual beliefs, (b) find it difficult to assume others' perspectives, (c) endorse traditional male stereotypes, (d) be high in authoritarianism, and (e) report a higher likelihood to rape." Most men do not fit this pattern, but most people who do are men. Law condones these beliefs by viewing them as falling within the range of what is reasonable for men, which deeply affects how women are treated. Pornography and sexist treatment in the workplace, not taking no for an answer, killing your wife if she tries to leave you, are all more justifiable when such values are deemed reasonable.

Adopting a woman's perspective would affect men's behavior. For example, studies show that men with value systems predisposing them to sexually harass are far less likely to do so when workplace social norms treat such conduct as wrong and unacceptable. If the employer disapproves of sexual conduct or degrading treatment that most women find unreasonable, most men predisposed to harass will exercise self-control. However, if such men know that this behavior is condoned or ignored, they are more likely to engage in conduct that women experience as sexual harassment. A reasonable woman standard would move the baseline for legally acceptable conduct. For example, a reasonable woman would be more likely to experience pornography and degrading treatment in the workplace as sexual harassment and consider no to mean no when sex is involved. She would also likely view killing a domestic partner who leaves or gets involved with someone else as murder and killing one's batterer out of fear of severe injury or death as self-defense.

A woman-based standard should apply in assessing the reasonableness of behavior in all areas in which women are disproportionately victimized and the experiences and perspectives of men and women differ. That is, the law should focus on the perpetrator's behavior and measure it by whether a reasonable woman would have behaved similarly in the circumstances. When the circumstances considered include the victim's conduct, the prevalent approach searches for female "provocation," implying that the victim got what she deserved. Instead, when the victim's behavior is relevant, the decision maker should consider whether such behavior would have induced a reasonable woman to respond as the perpetrator did, thereby short-circuiting archaic, patriarchal assumptions about both men and women.

Simply naming the standard "the reasonable woman," particularly when applying it to the conduct of men, tells judges and juries to look from a different perspective and perhaps to question their assumptions. But renaming is not enough. If the fundamental bias against women remains unexamined, the reasonable woman standard entails risks. The reasonable woman can become another reasonable man in disguise, as has happened too often in the rape and even in the sexual harassment context, and thereby represent another means of perpetuating the gendered status quo.

In this book, within the framework of particular legal cases and doctrine, we define generally who the reasonable woman is and who she is not. In practice, many cases will require carefully worded jury instructions and expert testimony to explain the different paradigm of what is reasonable. By an explicit change in the legal standard, testimony concerning patterns of violence, aggression, fear, and so forth will become relevant and admissible. Ideally, statutes and jury instructions will incorporate some minimal definition or description of the reasonable woman. All of these means will be needed to carefully delineate the reasonable woman standard so as to avoid portraying women as passive and delicate victims in need of male protection. Such delineation may also diminish the blaming of women who do not fit overt and covert gender stereotypes and who are frequently judged as provoking "whores," disobedient rebels, or failed men.

The standard we envision cannot be described simply by some prototype analogous to the "man who mows the lawn in his shirtsleeves" of the reasonable man/person standard, who epitomizes white, middle-class, male values. The reasonable woman standard should not become, as Anita Bernstein says, a "white, heterosexual, upper-income, something of a moderate or liberal feminist, untroubled by intense religious feeling, and a little prissier than the reasonable person in reacting to office shenanigans." Instead the reasonable woman represents values that transcend a particular class or race—and, we hope, may some day even transcend gender. It makes the law acknowledge that people should be treated with respect for their bodily integrity, agency, and autonomy in both the private and public spheres, where at present women are not so treated.

PART II

Sexual Harassment in the Workplace

Now that a few women have the tools to address the legal system on its own terms, the law can begin to address women's experience on women's own terms.   —Catharine MacKinnon, *Sexual Harassment of Working Women*

Reprinted by permission from Copley News Service and Steve Kelley

3

Men, Women, and Sex at Work

Is there such a thing, in life or in law, as reasonable people, or
only men and women, with all their differences?

—Susan Estrich, "Rape"

The concept of a nongendered reasonable person is sometimes a *non sequitur*. The reasonable person assessing sex at work is a
prime example. Psychology professors Barbara Gutek and Maureen
O'Connor note that the prevalent view that men and women perceive
sex in the workplace differently has "a basis in both common sense and
empirical fact." These gendered perceptions have real consequences.
Social science research, such as that conducted by Weiner and his colleagues, confirms what common sense tell us: sexual conduct in the
workplace that many men view as harmless and enjoyable, is experienced by many women as harmful and degrading. Because of this dis-
crepancy, it is simply unrealistic to believe that a truly genderless standard can be used for determining whether conduct is sufficiently egregious to justify liability. In practice, when asked to assess the conduct
of an actor accused of creating a hostile sexual environment, the decision maker will either explicitly (reasonable man or reasonable
woman) or implicitly (reasonable person) adopt a gendered perspective.

The 1991 Senate confirmation hearings for Supreme Court nominee
Clarence Thomas highlighted the different perspectives of men and
women. The hearings presented the fundamental problem of how to
convince decision makers (ninety-eight male and two female senators)
that conduct which many women view as sexual harassment merits serious consequences for the harasser. In the case of Clarence Thomas,
the stakes were extremely high: life tenure on the most powerful court
in the country. Not only sex but also race and politics shaped the

perspectives brought to the hearings. Nevertheless, the conduct that Anita Hill described exemplifies the fault line between men's and women's perspectives about what constitutes a hostile work environment. The hearings galvanized women around the issue of sexual harassment and gave new meaning to the phrase "they just don't get it."

Anita Hill testified before the all-male Senate Judiciary Committee, describing what happened to her while directly supervised by Clarence Thomas:

> After approximately three months of working [at the Department of Education], he asked me to go out socially with him. What happened next and telling the world about it are the two most difficult . . . experiences of my life. . . . I declined the invitation to go out socially with him, and explained to him that I thought it would jeopardize . . . a very good working relationship. I had a normal social life with other men outside of the office. . . . He pressed me to justify my reasons for saying "no" to him. . . .
>
> My working relationship became even more strained when Judge Thomas began to use work situations to discuss sex. On these occasions, he would call me into his office for reports. . . . After a brief discussion of work, he would turn the conversation to a discussion of sexual matters. His conversations were very vivid.
>
> On several occasions Thomas told me graphically of his own sexual prowess. Because I was extremely uncomfortable talking about sex with him at all, and particularly in such a graphic way, I told him that I did not want to talk about these subjects. I would also try to change the subject. . . . My efforts . . . were rarely successful.

Many of the senators hearing Hill's testimony believed that the conduct she described was not and should not be actionable as sexual harassment or discrimination, even if she was telling the truth. Nor did they think it should interfere with Thomas's confirmation. Senator John B. Breaux said, "I think the charges are *not of a sufficient nature* to either not support [Thomas] or delay the vote" (emphasis added). As Senator Paul Simon put it: "Many men were stunned to learn what women regard as sexual harassment. 'He didn't even touch her!' one of my Senate colleagues commented . . . when the issue first arose." Some of these reasonable men did not believe a reasonable *person* would have found that Thomas's conduct created a hostile work environment. After all, it wouldn't have felt like sexual harassment to *them.*

Polls indicated that at first, male or female, black or white, a majority of Americans didn't believe Anita Hill's version of "he said/she said." This is not surprising; as Catharine MacKinnon in *Feminism Unmodified* points out, most people find it difficult to believe women's "accounts of sexual use and abuse by men," particularly by powerful men. Interestingly, a year after Thomas was confirmed as a member of the Supreme Court, polls showed that public perceptions had changed dramatically: more people believed Hill than Thomas. Setting aside the issue of credibility, if Anita Hill had brought a timely sexual harassment action against Clarence Thomas, and if she had been thought credible at the time, would *any* standard of care have assured that his conduct would be judged sufficiently severe and pervasive to constitute illegal sexual harassment? Only under a standard that explicitly considered female perspectives would Thomas's conduct likely be viewed as sufficiently egregious to merit liability. Applying a reasonable woman standard, by requiring decision makers to consider how pressuring a subordinate for dates and subjecting her to graphic sexual stories is disrespectful and intimidating, enables them to comprehend the harm in such conduct.

The Evolution of Hostile Environment Sexual Harassment

Sexual harassment's recent appearance and rapid development as a legal claim is more her-story than history. Men have sexually harassed women for thousands of years, but the conduct wasn't given a name until 1975, when a group of feminists in Ithaca, New York held a meeting called "Speak-Out on Sexual Harassment." It took years of concerted effort by feminist lawyers and clients to establish a legal identity and remedy for such conduct. The breakthrough came in 1976, when the federal circuit for the District of Columbia heard two cases about retaliation against a female employee for refusing her supervisor's sexual advances. The court held in both cases that this was actionable sex discrimination under Title VII of the Civil Rights Act. Before these two pathbreaking decisions, punishing women workers who rejected sexual advances did not constitute employment discrimination on the basis of sex.

In 1979, Catharine MacKinnon published her influential book *Sexual Harassment of Working Women*, in which she defined sexual harassment as "the unwanted imposition of sexual requirements in the context of a relationship of unequal power." In MacKinnon's view, the power disparities between employer and employee and men and women lie at the core of sexual harassment. Her book treats sexual harassment as sex discrimination and outlines two basic forms: *quid pro quo* and hostile work environment. In the twenty years since MacKinnon's book was published, courts around the world, including the U.S. Supreme Court, have adopted her views and categories concerning sexual harassment.

The courts first recognized *quid pro quo* sexual harassment, which involves sexual coercion related to the terms or conditions of employment: offering rewards for granting sexual favors or threatening punishment for refusal. In the breakthrough cases, the plaintiffs lost jobs or other tangible job benefits when they refused to submit to their supervisors' sexual advances. After the first cases a consensus gradually arose, finding that *quid pro quo* harassment is unreasonable, harmful, and discriminatory. Thus, in most *quid pro quo* cases unreasonableness and injury are easily established, no matter which standard of care or whose point of view is adopted. In 1998 the U.S. Supreme Court decided *Burlington Industries, Inc. v. Ellerth*, holding that because tangible economic harm is involved, employer liability for *quid pro quo* sexual harassment is vicarious and strict—if the plaintiff proves *quid pro quo* sexual harassment, the employer is liable.

Courts took longer to recognize the more controversial hostile environment sexual harassment as a form of discrimination. Hostile environment sexual harassment is sex-based conduct that interferes with a person's job performance, even if it has no tangible or economic job consequences, and even if the interference is unintentional. Supreme Court Justice Ruth Bader Ginsberg in *Harris v. Forklift Systems, Inc.* has described this form of harassment simply as "discriminatory conduct [that makes] it more difficult to do the job." It may involve purely sexual conduct (e.g., groping breasts or pressuring for dates) or purely sexist/antiwoman conduct (e.g., saying, "You're a woman, what do you know") but often involves both. As the reaction to Anita Hill's allegations demonstrated, there is little consensus about what constitutes hostile environment sexual harassment. Therefore, unlike *quid pro quo* cases, perspective often controls the outcome.

Hostile environment sexual harassment did not emerge as a recognized claim until the early 1980s. Its status remained uncertain until 1986, when the Supreme Court's first sexual harassment case, *Meritor*

Savings Bank v. Vinson, recognized hostile work environment as a form of sex discrimination. The Court noted that unwelcome sexualization of the work environment, as long as it was "sufficiently severe or pervasive 'to alter the conditions of [the victim's] employment and create an abusive working environment,' is actionable sex discrimination" under Title VII. Furthermore, the Court noted that if the conduct has that effect, liability can be found even if the actor did not intend to sexually harass the victim.

The harassing conduct alleged in *Meritor*, which included multiple instances of rape, was clearly intentional and egregious. Once the Court recognized hostile work environment as a legal claim, the *Meritor* conduct created an obviously abusive work environment—under any standard. Consequently, the Court did not address whose perspective or what standard determines whether someone has "creat[ed] an intimidating, hostile, or offensive working environment," or even what kind of injury must be proved.

However, most hostile work environment claims are not as clear-cut as *Meritor*. Usually, alleged harassers assert that they did not intend to sexually harass the target; plaintiffs respond that the behavior had the *effect* of creating a hostile environment, regardless of *intent*. In these cases, the standard of care applied often determines the outcome. The issue of whether the conduct was "sufficiently severe or pervasive" to make it unreasonable requires a normative assessment of severity and pervasiveness about which men and women may, and often do, differ.

The Supreme Court has continued to play a crucial role in the development of hostile environment sexual harassment. In 1993 the Court decided *Harris v. Forklift Systems, Inc.*, which focused on what kind of harm must be shown. *Harris* is important in part because most of the abusive conduct at issue was *sexist*, not sexual. Much of the harassment women experience is not sexual as such but it is sex-based, which has tended to get lost in the common perception of what "sexual harassment" means. A better term for the discriminatory conduct would be *sex-based harassment*, as Professor Vicki Schultz sets out in her article "Reconceptualizing Sexual Harassment." However, the Supreme Court continues to use the term *sexual harassment,* so we do too.

Justice Sandra Day O'Connor's opinion for the unanimous Court in *Harris* declared: "So long as the environment *would reasonably be perceived, and is perceived*, as hostile or abusive, ... there is no need for it also to be psychologically injurious" (emphasis added). By making clear that neither tangible nor psychological harm was required, the *Harris* Court made the reasonableness of the conduct the critical issue. However, the Court was silent about whether reasonableness can be explicitly gendered.

The Court issued another unanimous decision, *Oncale v. Sundowner Offshore Services, Inc.,* in 1998, which appeared to endorse a standard of care that assesses the alleged harasser's conduct from the perspective of the injured party. Justice Antonin Scalia, writing for the Court, held that male-on-male heterosexual sexual harassment creates a viable claim under Title VII if the plaintiff proves that the harassment occurred because of his sex. He noted that "the objective severity of harassment should be judged from the perspective of a reasonable person in the plaintiff's position, considering 'all the circumstances.'"

If the phrase "in the plaintiff's position" includes gender as part of his or her position, or if gender is intended to be included by "all the circumstances," then Justice Scalia's standard might substantively equate to a reasonable man standard when the injured party is male and a reasonable woman standard when the injured party is female. This interpretation is especially plausible in light of his emphasis on the "because of such individual's . . . sex" requirement in Title VII, and his additional statement that all sexual harassment cases require "careful consideration of the social context in which the particular behavior . . . is experienced by its target."

That the Court might find a woman-based standard appropriate when the target in a hostile environment sexual harassment suit is female represents tremendous progress. However, we believe the law must go further to achieve equality and justice for all. As we elaborate in chapter 5, the reasonable woman standard should apply in all cases of hostile environment sexual harassment, regardless of the gender of either party.

Why Courts Should Adopt the Reasonable Woman Standard

Applying a reasonable woman standard in hostile environment sexual harassment cases alters expectations of both legal and employment decision makers about sexual and sexist conduct in the workplace. The more male dominated the workplace, the more expectations change.

Through the reasonable woman standard, our legal system can better achieve its important goals, including reducing the harm people inflict on others, compensating those harmed, and achieving substantive equality for all Americans. For claims of sexual harassment, the reasonable woman standard is a better vehicle than other standards for achieving these goals.

Working women are sexually harassed far more often than working men, and men are far more likely to sexually harass other workers. In part this can be attributed to the tendency of men to view a wider range of women's workplace behavior as sexual and welcoming, and therefore to assume they have permission to respond sexually. As psychology professor Barbara Gutek notes in *Sex and the Workplace,* "men [are] more likely than women to label any given behavior as sexual. Thus a normal business lunch seems to be labeled a 'date' by some men just because the luncheon partner is a woman."

Another reason women are sexually harassed at work more often than men is that traditional views of masculinity encourage dominating conduct—the exercise of power over someone else—and men often use sex as a means of asserting dominance. This explains why, if there are no women in the workplace, other men may be sexualized—treated like women—despite all the parties asserting heterosexuality. As Catharine MacKinnon argued in a "friend of the court" (amicus) brief in *Oncale,* the 1998 Supreme Court case concerning a man who had been sexually assaulted by his all-male coworkers: "Oncale's attackers were asserting male dominance through imposing sex on a man with less power. Men who are sexually assaulted are . . . feminized: made to serve the function and play the role customarily assigned to women as men's social inferiors."

In addition, men may sexually harass women more often because women's typically subordinate positions in the workplace tend to sexualize them. According to the *Oxford Dictionary of Quotations,* Henry Kissinger said that "power is the great aphrodisiac." For some male supervisors, having power over a female employee *makes* her sexy. A 1995 study by John Bargh and colleagues entitled "Attractiveness of the Underling" indicated that for men whose values make them likely to sexually harass women, having power over a woman enhances the sexual attraction. The aphrodisiacal quality of power also affects these men's perception: they interpret women subordinates' neutral or merely friendly actions as flirtatious or seductive.

The sexual thrill of domination, rather than romantic feelings, frequently motivates a sexual harasser to abuse his power. As a rule, men possess social, organizational, and physical power over women. Thus, when people abuse power through sex, the person abused is usually a woman. For men, being supervised by a woman is a rare experience, while for women it is the norm to be supervised by a man. Even in such traditional "women's" work as primary and middle-school teaching, principals and superintendents are usually men. In traditional "men's" work, such as construction or engineering, supervisors are almost certainly male and often are openly contemptuous of women workers.

Vicki Schultz, in her article "Reconceptualizing Sexual Harassment," provides another important reason why women are so frequently harassed in the workplace. In arguing that hostile environment should be viewed from a "competence-centered" paradigm, she asserts that harassment of women workers is not about sexuality as much as it is about "reclaim[ing] favored lines of work and work competence as masculine-identified turf—in the face of a threat posed by the presence of women (or lesser men) who seek to claim these prerogatives as their own." Schultz notes that the stakes are high for men:

> Motivated by both material considerations and equally powerful psychological ones, harassment provides a means for men to mark their jobs a male territory and to discourage any women who seek to enter. By keeping women in their place in the workplace, men secure superior status in the home, in the polity, and in the larger culture as well.

Women also suffer greater injury: they much more frequently lose their jobs or suffer other tangible work detriment as a result of sexual harassment. Studies of sexual harassment of men show that some sexual conduct that women find harmful men view as perhaps annoying but not upsetting. Expert witness Susan Fiske testified in *Robinson v. Jacksonville Shipyards* that "when sex comes into the workplace, women are profoundly affected . . . in their ability to do their jobs." By contrast, Fiske notes that the effect of sexualization of the workplace is "vanishingly small" for men. According to Barbara Gutek in *Sex and the Workplace,* the men she surveyed reported "significantly more sexual touching than women" and were more likely "to view such encounters positively, to see them as fun and mutually entered." Men apparently suffer no work-related consequences of sexual behavior at work, although they report more sexual behavior both directed at them specifically and in the workplace atmosphere generally. Even sexual conduct that does not meet the existing standards for sexual harassment lowers women's job satisfaction, while it has little or no negative effect on men.

One reason for the gendered reactions to and experiences with sex in the workplace may be that women have more to fear from sex. In our society, women are usually the targets of sexual violence. Except in all-male environments—where some men are "treated like women"—it is women who are raped and sexually assaulted. Because sex can be dangerous for women, when a workplace becomes sexualized, women are more likely to feel discomfort, fear, humiliation, or anger.

Women also prefer to keep sex out of the workplace more than men do because, when sex and work are combined, women are the ones objectified. Sex-role spillover partly explains this: societal gender expectations that sexualize and objectify women and assume men are asexual subjects carry over into the workplace from the broader culture. In "Understanding Sexual Harassment at Work," Gutek found that when men view women as sex objects rather than as serious workers, it undermines the women's credibility and job satisfaction. For example, in an article by Marian Swerdlow, a woman rapid-transit system worker described her arrival in the male-dominated workplace and how she quickly became aware of what it meant to be a woman in that environment. Shortly after her arrival, she realized that "a woman in the crewroom" had heretofore meant "something utterly forbidden, but more than that, something sexual. . . . a woman's presence in the workplace had already been defined as having, above all, a sexual connotation." As the woman transit worker put it:

> A new woman was immediately viewed sexually. The first information men sought about a new woman was her marital status, usually under the flimsy cover, "What does your husband think of you taking the job?" Our looks were the talk of the crewrooms. We were propositioned . . . endlessly.

This common experience of working women highlights the need to impose a woman-based standard on workplace sexual behavior in order to foster equality. Sexual harassment makes women appear and feel unequal. As Kathryn Abrams notes in her article "Gender Discrimination and the Transformation of Workplace Norms," sexualized behavior in the workplace creates both directly and by implication a radical inequality:

> A woman struggling to establish credibility in a setting in which she may not be, or may not feel, welcome, can be swept off balance by a reminder that she can be raped, fondled, or subjected to repeated sexual demands. . . . Sexual inquiries, jokes, remarks, or innuendoes sometimes can raise the spectre of coercion, but they more predictably have the effect of reminding a woman that she is viewed as an object of sexual derision rather than a credible co-worker. . . . Treatment that sexualizes women workers prevents them from feeling, and prevents others from perceiving them, as equals in the workplace.

Sexual harassment in the workplace keeps women "in their place"—which is why sexual harassment is sex-based discrimination. Women are often economically vulnerable. U.S. Department of Labor statistics show that women are disproportionately represented among the working poor in our society. Women's economic vulnerability makes it harder to resist sexual harassment. Many women cannot afford to risk losing their jobs or job benefits by complaining about, or even resisting, harassment. Unless employers know that courts will impose liability for sexual conduct that women find unreasonable, and therefore have incentive to prevent it, working-class women will have to endure not only low pay and low status but also sexual harassment.

Even in professions that are not female dominated, women are often paid less than similarly situated men. In part this can be attributed to the additional burden sexual harassment imposes on women. Sexual harassment diminishes a woman's professional credibility. Women may miss more days of work or have greater difficulty doing their jobs because they are being harassed. This often results in poor job evaluations that negatively affect compensation and advancement. Leaving a job because of sexual harassment may make it harder for a woman to get an equivalent job, particularly if she filed a claim of sexual harassment—regardless of the legal outcome. And many women simply rule out working in certain male-dominated workplaces because sexist behavior and sexual hostility from supervisors and coworkers is virtually inevitable.

People in charge set the tone of the workplace, including the level of sexualization that is tolerated. Supervisors tend to accept what seems "reasonable" to them. This may include harassment that comes solely

ments about women generally," and that he occasionally directed such comments at Rabidue. They acknowledged that Rabidue's employer was aware of Henry's antiwoman behavior. As to how the employer dealt with Henry, they simply said that the employer "had been unsuccessful in curbing his offensive personality traits during the time encompassed by this controversy."

The judges characterized Rabidue and other female employees as being "annoyed" by Henry's vulgarity. The majority's choice of the word *annoyed* here is critical. It enabled them to conclude that Henry's "obscenities, although annoying, were *not so startling* as to have affected seriously the psyches of the plaintiff or other female employees" (emphasis added). It exemplifies the reaction that, according to studies such as those described in Barbara Gutek's book *Sex and the Workplace,* men have to such conduct. As far as the majority was concerned, unless Henry's conduct caused his female coworkers to suffer severe psychological trauma, it wasn't something the law should remedy. By describing the conduct as merely annoying, the majority trivialized the women employees' response and framed Henry's behavior as within the bounds of acceptable workplace behavior. Even if the women did suffer serious psychic harm, they wouldn't be believed because, for men (including the trial and appellate judges), such conduct was at most annoying.

The majority then went on to point out that while "other male employees from time to time displayed pictures of nude or scantily clad women" in areas where plaintiff and other women worked, "the sexually oriented poster displays had *de minimis* effect on the plaintiff's work environment when considered in the context of a society that condones and publicly features and commercially exploits open displays of written and pictorial erotica at the newsstands, on prime-time television, at the cinema, and in other public places." In short, because women are pervasively portrayed as sex objects in American society, male workers' use of words and display of pictures that objectify and demean women do not harm their female coworkers. The majority's commentary on social mores implies that women like Rabidue are being intolerant when they object to language and pictorial displays that society, by consensus, condones.

The majority's decision that Osceola was not a hostile environment for women took into account "the lexicon of obscenity that pervaded the environment of the workplace both before and after the plaintiff's introduction into the environs, coupled with the reasonable expectation of the plaintiff upon voluntarily entering that environment." For the majority, the perspective of the men who first were there determined what was reasonable under the circumstances. The men who engaged in the challenged conduct set the standards for tolerable behavior. Rabidue and the other women employees, by choosing to work in this male-dominated environment, in essence consented to the anti-woman language and pictures. From the majority's male perspective, Rabidue and the other women workers had assumed the risk of being offended—it was *their* problem, not that of society, the employer, or the other employees. For the women workers at Osceola, the message was clear: adapt or quit.

The appellate majority quoted with approval the trial judge's statement that "indeed, it cannot seriously be disputed that in some work environments, humor and language are rough hewn and vulgar. Sexual jokes, sexual conversations and girlie magazines may abound." The majority then expressly endorsed the male-dominated status quo by saying that federal sexual harassment law was "not meant to—*or can*—change" sexualized workplaces (emphasis added). Further, sexual harassment law was not "designed to bring about a magical transformation in the social mores of American workers." For the majority, the role of law as an agent of change is extremely limited, and imposing liability would be unfair and unlikely to affect either workplace atmospheres or the values of "American workers." The meaning of this "neutral" term is clear: American workers are stereotypically masculine men who hold values allowing them to talk crudely about women and look at degrading pornography whenever they want to, including at work.

After endorsing male values as the appropriate workplace norms, the court further bolstered its finding of no sexual harassment by focusing Rabidue's problematic personality. Instead of getting along with everyone as a good female employee should, Rabidue looked for trouble. The majority described her as "capable, independent, ambitious, aggressive, intractable, and opinionated" and as "an abrasive, rude, antagonistic, extremely willful, uncooperative, and irascible personality." Thus, it was Rabidue, not the environment, that was hostile. Rabidue's personality somehow made her complaints less serious and less genuine. In contrast, Henry's "offensive personality traits" were tolerated as understandably masculine aspects of this "rough-hewn" workplace.

In reaching their decision that Osceola's workplace was not a hostile work environment for women, the majority purported to examine the workplace from "the perspective of a reasonable person's reaction to a similar environment under essentially like or similar circumstances." The majority's use of the genderless "reasonable person" standard masked the male bias that permeated their evaluation of the conduct in this workplace. For the majority, a reasonable person is someone who makes crude sexual comments about women and displays pornography at his workstation. Or, more charitably, a reasonable person is someone who is, at most, merely annoyed by crude sexual comments and pornography in the workplace.

The majority stated further that "in the absence of conduct which would interfere with [a] hypothetical reasonable individual's work performance and affect seriously the psychological well-being of that reasonable person under like circumstances, a plaintiff may not prevail on asserted charges . . . regardless of whether the plaintiff was actually offended by the defendant's conduct." Almost certainly, the reasonable person these male judges hypothesized was a male person. From such a perspective, it is understandable that they found the environment not hostile. When Henry's comments and the pornographic pictures are considered from a *male* reasonable person's perspective, it is unlikely that this person's work performance would suffer or that he would experience any, much less serious, psychological harm. Consequently, the majority asserted that even if the crude sexual conduct deeply disturbed Rabidue—as it would many *women*—it was not sexual harassment because, for these male judges, any reasonable person would consider it acceptable workplace behavior.

The Dissent's Story

Unlike the two appellate judges who wrote the majority opinion, Judge Damon Keith concluded that Vivienne Rabidue was sexually harassed. In reaching this conclusion, he was the first appellate judge to assert openly that in sexual harassment cases, the conduct at issue should be evaluated from the perspective of a reasonable woman. As he noted at one point, "the relevant inquiry at hand is what the reasonable woman would find offensive, not society, which at one point also condoned slavery." Looking at the workplace from the perspective of Rabidue and other women workers, Judge Keith's dissenting opinion tells a far different story from the one set out in the majority opinion.

Only in Judge Keith's opinion do we discover what, exactly, Henry said that "annoyed" the female employees. According to Judge Keith, Henry "regularly spewed anti-female obscenity" and "routinely referred to women as 'whores,' 'cunt,' 'pussy' and 'tits.'" Addressing Rabidue specifically, Henry called her "fat ass" and said, "All that bitch needs is a good lay." Judge Keith also pointed out that Rabidue, the only woman in a supervisory position, was the most active in trying to get management to do something about Henry. She arranged at least one meeting of women employees to talk about his behavior and filed numerous complaints on behalf of herself and other women employees. Judge Keith noted that the other women employees feared losing their jobs if they complained directly. Rabidue did complain, on her own and on the other women's behalf, and she lost her job.

Judge Keith also elaborated how Osceola's management dealt with Henry's antiwoman sentiments, which company vice president Charles Muetzel noted "greatly disturbed" employees. Apparently the company considered Henry to be indispensable—unlike Rabidue—so management neither reprimanded nor fired him. Instead, Henry's supervisor testified that he gave Henry "a little fatherly advice" about Henry's "prospects" if he could only try to be "an executive type person." Not surprisingly, these gentle suggestions had no effect.

Judge Keith's description of the pictures male workers displayed in the common work areas makes it clear that they were not erotic art. Rather, they intentionally demeaned women and blatantly depicted them as sex objects. In one poster—on the wall for eight years—a man stood straddled over a naked woman who had a golf ball between her breasts, shouting, "Fore!" as he swung a golf club. In addition to pictures, the women workers faced such words of wisdom as a desk plaque declaring, "Even male chauvinist pigs need love."

Unlike the majority, Judge Keith empathized with Rabidue. By doing this, he focused on what should matter in a sexual harassment suit: her male coworkers' conduct, not Rabidue's personality. He described the different treatment she was subjected to because of her gender, a subject the majority opinion omitted. Not all this behavior was sexual; much of it instead was antifemale discrimination. Rabidue was intentionally excluded from management-team perks and activities. For example: "Plaintiff testified that unlike male salaried employees, she did

from coworkers. When a male employer or supervisor engages in harassment himself or turns a blind eye on peer harassment, women workers don't thrive professionally—they experience their difference from men as inequality. Unless norms that are respectful of women are imposed from the outside, this male gaze will control.

To assure equal opportunity for professional growth and achievement, women's view on sex in the workplace—that there should be less of it—should be adopted for all workplaces. Men should be held to a woman-defined standard of behavior based on how a woman would treat a coworker. This does not mean that sex must be kept completely separate from work or make politely asking a coworker for a date (and respecting her response) unreasonable conduct. However, under the reasonable woman standard of care, behavior that many more men than women consider "reasonable," such as not taking no for an answer and gratuitous sexual comments or portrayals, would be sexual harassment. The credible threat of liability for allowing such conduct to continue would lead employers to require that their employees comply with the standards of a reasonable woman.

4

How and Why Different Perspectives Matter in Hostile Environment Sexual Harassment Cases

Why It Matters

Many sexual harassment cases arise in male-dominated workplaces such as heavy industry, law enforcement, gambling, and construction. In such settings women are clearly "the other." At best, women are ornamental, and at worst, they are intruders. Antiwoman sentiment is deeply embedded in the culture of these workplaces. In such environments derision and disbelief often greet a female employee's claim that she was sexually harassed. What she perceives as debilitating harassment her male coworkers and supervisors perceive as normal, acceptable behavior. Women who claim they are sexually harassed are seen as overly sensitive or vindictive—as troublemakers. Thus, the outcome of a sexual harassment case in such settings often depends on the point of view adopted in scrutinizing the conduct and conditions of employment. What appears unreasonable and therefore unlawfully discriminatory from a woman's perspective, based on women's experience, often looks harmless and lawful from a man's perspective.

Our first set of judicial opinions address hostile work environment sexual harassment in such male-dominated workplaces. They show why a reasonable woman standard is the right choice for determining if the environment was hostile. Examining legal decisions demonstrates that both the reasonable man and the reasonable person standard apply existing, male-defined and -delineated community norms, and that the reasonable woman standard more effectively remedies certain injuries and helps achieve equality in the workplace. By supporting the status quo, the reasonable person standard prevents substantive changes in how acceptable conduct is defined. The status quo still needs fundamental revision for women to be included as full members of the workforce and society in general. A deliberate rebalancing by applying the reasonable woman standard, which would reflect women's desire and right to be respected, can play an essential role in changing community norms to be inclusive of women's experience. By requiring men to change their workplace behavior toward women, the law can enable women to derive satisfaction from their jobs, rather than just to endure or escape.

The three cases in this chapter mark one extreme—the women who brought these claims dared to enter traditionally all-male jobs or reached positions of authority in male-dominated workplaces and were made to suffer for it. All three cases were brought against the women's employers as sex discrimination under Title VII of the Civil Rights Act. The cases were all tried before either a federal judge or magistrate without a jury because, before 1991, jury trials were not available for sex discrimination cases. In the first two cases, the women are harassed mainly by coworkers, and the employer's responsibility stems from ignoring or condoning the behavior. In the third case, the harasser is the employer himself, and therefore the sex discrimination and abuse of power is (or at least should be) obvious.

Love It or Leave It: Rabidue v. Osceola Refining Co.

Rabidue v. Osceola Refining Co., decided in 1986, is one of the earliest cases to discuss hostile work environment sexual harassment as a legal claim. The majority and dissenting appellate opinions in *Rabidue* illustrate how much difference the choice of perspective can make.

Rabidue involved a claim of hostile environment sexual harassment based on the widespread display of pornographic pictures in the workplace and a supervisory employee's use of crude, sexually explicit language. Three appellate judges reviewed the trial court's decision which had rejected the female employee's sexual harassment claim. Two of the three appellate judges issued the majority opinion that agreed with the trial judge. They declared that a genderless "reasonable person" would not find the conduct in this workplace to be hostile toward women.

The third appellate judge dissented from this decision. He expressly looked at the work conditions from the perspective of a person of a particular gender—a reasonable *woman*. Applying a reasonable woman standard to the language and conduct at issue, the dissenting judge concluded that the work environment was hostile and that therefore the employer should have been found liable for unlawful sexual harassment. The contrasting stories told in the majority and dissenting judicial opinions demonstrate how different perspectives can completely change the meaning of events. These stories reflect existing divisions in our society: those who believe men should define acceptable workplace conduct will agree with the majority; those who want women workers to set the standards for acceptable workplace conduct will side with the dissent.

The Majority's Story

Vivienne Rabidue was the only woman supervisor at Osceola Refining Company. She was originally hired in 1970, on an hourly basis, as an executive secretary whose duties included typing, reception, and bookkeeping. In 1973, Rabidue was promoted to administrative assistant and became a salaried employee with additional responsibilities. These included purchasing office supplies and dealing with customers. She later became the credit manager and office manager. When, in 1977, she was fired and replaced by a man, Rabidue sued her former employer and alleged sex discrimination, including sexual harassment. To prevail on her sexual harassment claim, Rabidue needed to prove that the work environment was hostile to women and that the employer was aware of this and failed to do enough to eliminate the problem.

According to the appellate majority, Rabidue's claim of sexual harassment primarily stemmed from "her unfortunate acrimonious working relationship with Douglas Henry." As the trial judge had noted previously, Henry was a "prominent character in the trial evidence." Henry was the supervisor of the company's keypunch and computer operators. He and Vivienne did not get along and were described as "constantly in a confrontation posture."

At a minimum, Henry was boorish. Even the majority appellate opinion described Henry as "an extremely vulgar and crude individual." The majority noted that he "customarily made obscene com-

introduction into the environs, coupled with the reasonable expectation of the plaintiff upon voluntarily entering that environment." For the majority, the perspective of the men who first were there determined what was reasonable under the circumstances. The men who engaged in the challenged conduct set the standards for tolerable behavior. Rabidue and the other women employees, by choosing to work in this male-dominated environment, in essence consented to the anti-woman language and pictures. From the majority's male perspective, Rabidue and the other women workers had assumed the risk of being offended—it was *their* problem, not that of society, the employer, or the other employees. For the women workers at Osceola, the message was clear: adapt or quit.

The appellate majority quoted with approval the trial judge's statement that "indeed, it cannot seriously be disputed that in some work environments, humor and language are rough hewn and vulgar. Sexual jokes, sexual conversations and girlie magazines may abound." The majority then expressly endorsed the male-dominated status quo by saying that federal sexual harassment law was "not meant to—or *can*—change" sexualized workplaces (emphasis added). Further, sexual harassment law was not "designed to bring about a magical transformation in the social mores of American workers." For the majority, the role of law as an agent of change is extremely limited, and imposing liability would be unfair and unlikely to affect either workplace atmospheres or the values of "American workers." The meaning of this "neutral" term is clear: American workers are stereotypically masculine men who hold values allowing them to talk crudely about women and look at degrading pornography whenever they want to, including at work.

After endorsing male values as the appropriate workplace norms, the court further bolstered its finding of no sexual harassment by focusing Rabidue's problematic personality. Instead of getting along with everyone as a good female employee should, Rabidue looked for trouble. The majority described her as "capable, independent, ambitious, aggressive, intractable, and opinionated" and as "an abrasive, rude, antagonistic, extremely willful, uncooperative, and irascible personality." Thus, it was Rabidue, not the environment, that was hostile. Rabidue's personality somehow made her complaints less serious and less genuine. In contrast, Henry's "offensive personality traits" were tolerated as understandably masculine aspects of this "rough-hewn" workplace.

ments about women generally," and that he occasionally directed such comments at Rabidue. They acknowledged that Rabidue's employer was aware of Henry's antiwoman behavior. As to how the employer dealt with Henry, they simply said that the employer "had been unsuccessful in curbing his offensive personality traits during the time encompassed by this controversy."

The judges characterized Rabidue and other female employees as being "annoyed" by Henry's vulgarity. The majority's choice of the word *annoyed* here is critical. It enabled them to conclude that Henry's "obscenities, although annoying, were *not so startling* as to have affected seriously the psyches of the plaintiff or other female employees" (emphasis added). It exemplifies the reaction that, according to studies such as those described in Barbara Gutek's book *Sex and the Workplace,* men have to such conduct. As far as the majority was concerned, unless Henry's conduct caused his female coworkers to suffer severe psychological trauma, it wasn't something the law should remedy. By describing the conduct as merely annoying, the majority trivialized the women employees' response and framed Henry's behavior as within the bounds of acceptable workplace behavior. Even if the women did suffer serious psychic harm, they wouldn't be believed because, for men (including the trial and appellate judges), such conduct was at most annoying.

The majority then went on to point out that while "other male employees from time to time displayed pictures of nude or scantily clad women" in areas where plaintiff and other women worked, "the sexually oriented poster displays had *de minimis* effect on the plaintiff's work environment when considered in the context of a society that condones and publicly features and commercially exploits open displays of written and pictorial erotica at the newsstands, on prime-time television, at the cinema, and in other public places." In short, because women are pervasively portrayed as sex objects in American society, male workers' use of words and display of pictures that objectify and demean women do not harm their female coworkers. The majority's commentary on social mores implies that women like Rabidue are being intolerant when they object to language and pictorial displays that society, by consensus, condones.

The majority's decision that Osceola was not a hostile environment for women took into account "the lexicon of obscenity that pervaded the environment of the workplace both before and after the plaintiff's

not receive free lunches, free gasoline, a telephone credit card or entertainment privileges." This discrimination served to emphasize that she was different from the rest of them—that she was less deserving. It also interfered with her ability to do her job.

Rabidue was not included in weekly management golf matches. From a male perspective, this exclusion can be seen as an innocent assumption that, as a woman, she wouldn't be interested in playing golf with the boys. From a female perspective, however, her exclusion meant that she was not part of the management team—she didn't belong, and she never would. Treating Rabidue differently from the rest of the supervisory employees was harmful sexism that contributed to making her workplace a hostile environment. Only Judge Keith, viewing the conduct from the reasonable woman's perspective, addressed this.

In addition, unlike all previous, male credit managers, Rabidue was not permitted to visit customers or take them to lunch. She was thus prevented from effectively doing her job. One reason the company gave was that she "might have car trouble on the road." Such a demeaning and patronizing reason gratuitously stereotyped Rabidue (and all women) as incompetent. The other reason given for treating her differently was that it would be unseemly for a woman manager to take a male customer to lunch. Impugning *her* morals in the midst of this highly sexually offensive atmosphere, her supervisor gave the following justification: "How would it look for me, a married man, to take you, a divorced woman, to the West Branch Country Club in such a small town?" However, no one explained why it was not similarly improper for male managers to entertain unmarried or divorced female clients. Then, adding insult to injury, Rabidue's supervisor commented to another employee: "Vivienne . . . is doing a good job as credit manager, but we really need a man on that job [because] she can't take customers out to lunch." That the majority did not find this to be harassment or discrimination of any kind again shows that they were looking at the situation from a male perspective.

Judge Keith pointed out that the majority's application of the reasonable *person* standard was actually a *male* standard. He said: "In my view, the reasonable person perspective fails to account for the wide divergence between most women's views of appropriate sexual conduct and those of men." Judge Keith then noted that "unless the outlook of the reasonable woman is adopted, the defendants *as well as the courts* are permitted to sustain ingrained notions of reasonable behavior fashioned by the offenders" (emphasis added).

In Judge Keith's view, without the reasonable woman standard, the law as judges apply it will not be expected to empathize with women workers, and the views and values of men will continue to hold sway. He also maintained that sexual harassment law can and should *change* work environments to make them more hospitable to women employees. He asserted that "no woman should be subjected to an environment where her sexual dignity and reasonable sensibilities are visually, verbally or physically assaulted as a matter of prevailing male prerogative."

Unlike the *Rabidue* majority, most courts and the Equal Employment Opportunity Commission (the federal agency charged with investigating and prosecuting sexual harassment claims) agree that sexual harassment law is intended to and should change the status quo to make workplaces more hospitable to women. Like Judge Keith, we maintain that in certain situations this can be done only if the perspectives of women are considered. Judge Keith is an African American, and his experiences as a black man in America may have made it easier for him to recognize discrimination—and that in certain situations the law needs to empathize with those who are viewed as the outsiders.

Looking from a reasonable woman worker's perspective at what Rabidue and her female coworkers had to endure, it is clear that the conduct at issue was harassment—it was not merely "annoying" and "startling." Judges who condone behavior like that in *Rabidue*, by looking at it from a male perspective, guarantee that women will continue to be treated with disrespect and contempt in certain workplaces. They ensure that sexual harassment law will not change either workplaces or the values of male workers.

Don't Try to Change Things: Robinson v. Jacksonville Shipyards, Inc.

Robinson v. Jacksonville Shipyards, Inc. exemplifies the wide differences in perspective that can exist in a sexually hostile environment. Decided five years after *Rabidue*, *Robinson* involved a totally male-dominated workplace where the perspectives of male and female workers could not have been more divergent. The very few women entering the skilled trades at defendant Jacksonville Shipyards, Inc. (JSI), faced an entrenched attitude that women did not belong at all, and certainly not on their own terms.

JSI operated shipyards, contracting with the federal government to repair naval vessels. Everyone at JSI agreed that it was, in the words of JSI's president, "more or less a man's world." When the women involved in this lawsuit sought to change this world, they encountered fierce resistance.

The only judicial voice in this case is that of the trial judge, Howell Melton, who clearly viewed the situation from the women's perspective. Applying a reasonable woman standard, Judge Melton found that the women's claims of hostile work environment sexual harassment were valid and deserved a remedy. Judges Keith and Melton's ability to empathize with women workers—to put themselves in the position of women workers through understanding and applying a reasonable woman standard—demonstrates that men can fathom such a female standard if they choose.

Although Judge Melton's decision was appealed, the parties settled when JSI closed its shipyards in 1994, so no further judicial opinions were written. The absence of a judicial voice expressing the male perspective in *Robinson* is unusual and may strike the reader as somehow unfair or even fundamentally wrong. Had a judicial voice affirming the female perspective been absent instead, this would not likely be viewed in the same way since, until very recently, judicial validation of this voice was an extremely rare occurrence. While women may consider the traditional exclusion of their perspective as frustrating and unjust, judges are still expected to express the dominant male perspective.

In countless cases, the woman's story is never told except through her rejected legal arguments and testimony. Recently, in a small number of cases such as *Rabidue*, a majority and a dissent will tell the men's and women's stories. In *Robinson*, the defendant's experts tell the men's story to Judge Melton, but he rejects this version. This unusual judicial stance and the discomfort one may feel by reading it demonstrate how totally our society accepts the male perspective and highlight how necessary it is to consciously adopt the perspective of the other half of our society. In the discussion that follows, we tell the male story through the defendant JSI's expert witnesses and male employees, as well as through arguments JSI made on appeal.

JSI employed very few skilled women craftsworkers between 1980 and 1991, the period covered by this suit. As Judge Melton notes, "JSI reported employing two women and 958 men as skilled workers in 1980, seven women and 1,010 men as skilled craftworkers in 1983." In 1986 only six women were working as skilled craftsworkers among 846 men; the women involved in this suit were three of the six. Their numeric isolation made them particularly vulnerable to harassment, and each of these women testified about incidents in which "she was the only woman in a crowd of men on occasions when each was sexually harassed." No woman ever held a supervisory position at JSI.

The hostile work environment claim centered on the pervasive display of pinups and calendars of naked and seminaked women. These pinups ranged from the mildly provocative to crude and obscenely degrading images of women. Such pinups and calendars had been displayed long before women entered this male work world. Although the gender battle that resulted in this case was fought mainly over these pinups, Judge Melton emphasized that he found JSI's work environment hostile to women based on the "totality of the circumstances." Those circumstances included sexual and sexist comments, unwelcome advances, and the male workers' targeting of the women who tried to change the "man's world" at JSI.

The Trial Judge's Story

Plaintiff Lois Robinson began working at JSI in 1977 as a third-class welder; eventually she was promoted and became a first-class welder. The case against JSI arose from Robinson's claim of sexual harassment and the failure of her attempts to resolve the situation in the workplace. Two other women skilled workers, Gail Banks and Leslie Albert, also testified about their experiences of JSI as a sexually hostile work environment. Both women had worked at JSI for a number of years. Each had encountered increasingly hostile behavior when she objected to the existing highly sexualized environment.

Judge Melton summarized the situation, saying: "Pictures of nude and partially nude women appear throughout the JSI workplace in the form of magazines, plaques on the wall, photographs torn from magazines and affixed to the wall or attached to calendars supplied by advertising tool supply companies." The judge noted that for many years vendors had provided such calendars to JSI, which then distributed the calendars to its employees, who were free to post them in the workplace. Supervisory employees "from the very top down" approved of the pictorial displays, and many had their own collections.

Not surprising, no similar pinups or calendars displayed nude men in provocative or demeaning poses. In his testimony, welding foreman Fred Turner noted that "it was accepted at the shipyards for vendors to supply calendars of nude women, but he had never known a vendor to distribute a calendar of nude men and, if one did so, he would think the 'son of a bitch' was 'queer.'" It was simply incomprehensible to many JSI workers and management that women workers would be interested in pictures of naked people, whether male or female, or that the sexualization and objectification of women (as opposed to similar treatment of men) could legitimately offend any workers at JSI, including the women.

In contrast to the shipyards' permissive policy toward posting pictures of naked women in the workplace, employees were prohibited from posting political or commercial materials and from bringing newspapers and magazines to the job site. Nonetheless, "male JSI employees read pornographic magazines in the workplace apparently without sanctions." Thus, both official and unofficial policies condoned workers displaying and reading sexually explicit material about women.

In Judge Melton's view, Robinson's testimony provided a "vivid description of a visual assault on the sensibilities of female workers at JSI that did not relent during working hours." He described numerous graphic images—some for the workers' general enjoyment, and others intentionally aimed at Robinson or other women workers.

These sexually explicit and degrading images included "a picture of a woman's pubic area with a meat spatula pressed on it, observed on a wall next to the sheetmetal shop"; "a picture of a nude Black woman, pubic area exposed to reveal her labia, seen in a public locker room"; "drawings and graffiti on the walls including a drawing depicting a frontal view of a nude female torso with the words 'USDA Choice' written on it . . . in an area where Robinson was assigned to work"; and "a dart board with a drawing of a woman's breast with her nipple as the bull's eye."

Robinson was the specific target of some of the material. For example, "a pornographic magazine [was] handed [to her] by a male coworker in front of other coworkers." In another incident, "a picture of a nude woman with long blonde hair wearing high heels and holding a whip, [was] waved around by a coworker . . . in an enclosed area where [she] and approximately six men were working"; Robinson had long blonde hair and worked with a welding tool called a whip. Another time someone placed "a picture of a nude woman . . . on the tool box where [she] returned her tools [which] depicted the woman's legs spread apart, knees bent up toward her chest, exposing her breasts and genitals." When she saw this, Robinson was visibly upset; several of her male coworkers laughed at her reaction.

The level of acrimony and harassing behavior escalated when Robinson complained about graphic pinups and a particular calendar. As a result of her complaints, the calendar was removed. Shortly afterward, the phrase "Men Only" was painted in six-inch-high letters on a door Robinson had to enter in order to do her work. Although the "Men Only" sign was soon painted over, the effort was half-hearted and the words remained readable.

When Robinson started complaining about the pornography, her coworkers reacted by repeatedly writing abusive language on the walls of her work areas. As soon as one "message" was painted over, another would appear. "Among the graffiti were the phrases 'lick me you whore dog bitch,' 'eat me' and 'pussy.'" Judge Melton pointed out that Robinson's complaints acted as a "catalyst for a new wave of harassing behavior directed against her and other women." According to both Gail Banks and Leslie Albert, the pictorial displays and comments became increasingly graphic. At one point, Banks asked Robinson to stop pursuing the complaints because her coworkers treated them as a joke, openly laughing at Robinson, and because they had begun to bring "'hard pornography' that they showed to female workers." All three women experienced an intensification of the harassment, making it more difficult for them to do their jobs.

Male workers also subjected the women workers at JSI to crude sexual comments and advances. Robinson was the target of coworker statements such as "The more you lick it, the harder it gets." In Robinson's presence a coworker told a joke about "boola-boola," which meant sodomitic rape; Robinson let it be known she was offended. Rather than apologizing, coworkers publicly teased her, nicknaming her Boola-Boola. Gail Banks described incidents in which coworkers said things such as "It's a cunt hair off" and asked, "Are you on the rag?" She also received repeated unwelcome sexual advances, including calls at her home. Banks testified that "she steered clear of men who worked where [pornographic] pictures were displayed because she came to expect more harassment from those men." Leslie Albert also described experiencing similar comments and behavior aimed at her.

Both Banks and Albert experienced unwanted sexual contact from coworkers in incidents that amounted to sexual assaults. When a coworker who had persistently propositioned Albert finally put his hands on her, she showed her displeasure "both verbally and physically." Another time, a coworker grabbed Bank's ankles, pulled her legs apart and stood between them. A foreman pinched her on the breasts. When Banks complained to her supervisor, he demonstrated his "sympathy" by placing "his arm around her shoulder and said, 'Well, don't worry about it. Let me blow in your ear and I'll take care of anything that comes up.'" In this hostile atmosphere, complaining to management provided no effective recourse—or worse, gender harassment—for women workers.

Not all the comments were sexual in nature—some were sexist or antiwoman. Women workers were frequently called "honey," "momma," "baby," "dear," "sugar," and "sugar-booger" instead of by their names. One coworker frequently reacted to being assigned to work with Robinson with remarks like "Women are only fit company for something that howls" and "There's nothing worse than having to work around women."

Judge Melton said that he took into account the various incidents, "including the sexual remarks, the sexual jokes, the sexually oriented pictures of women, and the nonsexual rejection of women by coworkers." Even without expressly considering the sexual assaults Banks and Albert had experienced, he concluded that a "reasonable woman would find the working environment at JSI was abusive." In reaching this conclusion, the judge relied on the evidence presented at trial, including the testimony of plaintiff's experts.

Both the plaintiff and the defendant presented experts who testified on the issue of whether a reasonable woman would have found that the conduct at JSI created a hostile work environment. Robinson's two experts were women; JSI's two experts were men. The experts' opinions about what would seriously offend a reasonable woman appeared to reflect their gender.

The Plaintiff's Experts

Robinson's first expert was psychology professor Susan Fiske, an expert in stereotyping. Professor Fiske's testimony addressed discrimination "defined by the treatment of a person differently and less favorably because of the category to which that person belongs." Here the stereotyping was along gender lines, which resulted in evaluations of a woman employee based on her femaleness. Thus, she "might be expected to be sexy, affectionate and attractive [and she might be] evaluated less favorably if she is seen as not conforming to that model without regard to her job performance." JSI witnesses illustrated this stereotyping when they disapproved of Robinson's demeanor because she was not affectionate and of Bank's "use of 'crude' language as inappropriate behavior for a 'lady.'" These reactions demonstrate that JSI women workers were in a double bind. If Robinson had been more affectionate, she would probably have been the recipient of unwelcome sexual advances; if Banks had spoken in a more "ladylike" fashion, she likely would also have been more seriously offended by the explicitly sexual pinups.

Professor Fiske also testified about male workers' inappropriate sexual expectations because of stereotyping. She "described the sex stereotyping at JSI as a situation of 'sex role spillover,' where the evaluation of women employees by their coworkers and supervisors takes place in terms of the sexuality of the women and their worth as sex objects rather than their merit as craftworkers." Commonly, "where sexualization of the workplace had occurred, the woman lodging the complaint would be the focus of attention, rather than the misconduct of which she complains. The woman would be perceived as the problem." Professor Fiske pointed out that "aspersions may be cast on the sexuality of the complaining employee regarding, for example, her sexual preference, background, experiences or traumas." In her opinion, the fact that negative rumors of this sort circulated about Robinson was consistent with common patterns in hostile workplace environments.

Professor Fiske also testified about the impact of the "ambiance" of JSI's work environment, saying that "studies show that tolerance of unprofessional conduct promotes the stereotyping of women in terms of their sex object status. For instance, when profanity is evident [as it was at JSI], women are three times more likely to be treated as sex objects than in a workplace where profanity is not tolerated." Pictorial displays of naked women create a similarly unprofessional ambiance that promotes inappropriate treatment of women workers.

Professor Fiske went on to describe the effects of unprofessional ambiance, harsher on women than on men: "'When sex comes into the workplace, women are profoundly affected . . . in their job performance and in their ability to do their jobs without being bothered by it.' . . . By contrast, the effect of the sexualization of the workplace is 'vanishingly small' for men." She continued by noting:

> Men and women respond to sex issues in the workplace to a degree that exceeds the normal differences in other perceptual reactions between them. . . . For example, research reveals a near flipflop of attitudes when both men and women were asked what their response would be to being sexually approached in the workplace. Approximately two-thirds of the men responded that they would be flattered; only fifteen percent would feel insulted. For the women the proportions are reversed.

Judge Melton found Fiske's testimony highly persuasive on the issue of how a reasonable woman would perceive the JSI workplace. He concluded that, based on her "theoretical framework . . . the presence of pictures of nude and partially nude women, sexual comments, sexual joking, and other behaviors previously described creates and contributes to a sexually hostile work environment."

The plaintiff's other expert witness was K. C. Wagner, a consultant on women workers and sexual harassment. Based on her experience counseling hundreds of nontraditional women workers who had experienced sexual harassment and training male workers to recognize and prevent sexual harassment, Wagner testified about women's coping strategies when they are sexually harassed. She described five strategies: "(1) denying the impact of the event . . . ; (2) avoiding the workplace or the harasser . . . ; (3) telling the harasser to stop; (4) engaging in joking or other banter in the language of the workplace in order to defuse the situation; and (5) threatening to make or actually making an informal or formal complaint." Wagner noted that filing a complaint was the least-used strategy because victims fear it will lead to escalation, retaliation, and embarrassment—all of which Robinson experienced when she complained.

Judge Melton explained that Wagner's description of various coping strategies demonstrated "why some women may not feel offended by some behaviors in the workplace that offend other women . . . and yet the work environment remains hostile to most women." That is, a common response is to deny the impact of sexual harassment, and many women cope by convincing themselves that the behavior doesn't bother them.

Like Professor Fiske, Wagner testified that "[m]en and women perceive the existence of sexual harassment differently." The testimony of plaintiff's two experts strongly supported finding that a "reasonable woman" would view JSI's work environment as hostile and constituting sexual harassment while a "reasonable man" might not. Their testimony starkly contrasts to that of JSI's two male experts. JSI's experts testified that both men and women are similarly unaffected by pinups and sexual language and therefore concluded that the environment at JSI was not hostile and did not constitute sexual harassment. This disparity of viewpoints highlights how even the reasonable *woman* can be warped into a male-biased standard (i.e., how men think a reasonable woman should act) and thus demonstrates the importance of consciously structuring the standard to make it truly woman-based.

The Defendant's Experts

Initially, JSI argued that the appropriate standard for determining whether a sexually hostile environment existed was the purportedly gender-neutral reasonable person, as applied in *Rabidue*. However, when Judge Melton rejected this standard, JSI through its experts attempted to show that, even under a reasonable woman standard, their workplace was not sexually hostile to women. Their testimony can be characterized as asserting that the "reasonable woman" reacts just like a "reasonable man," and that JSI's male workers and management were eminently reasonable men.

Psychology professor Donald Mosher, an expert on the psychological effects of sexual materials, gave his opinion about how such materials affected the reasonable woman. Regarding the provocative and often explicitly pornographic pinups and calendars present at JSI, Professor Mosher "expressed his expert opinion that those pictures do not create a serious or probable harm to the average woman." He stated further that when women workers reported that materials were "moderately disgusting and moderately offensive," this was not "a seriously negative response." By making this claim, Professor Mosher ignored the reality that such materials represent and facilitate an attitude in the workplace that demeans women and turns them into "the other." He also ignored the reality that "average" women did not work in such environments precisely because they are so hostile.

Professor Mosher also "testified that research suggests that pinups do not promote sexual aggression by men or induce calloused attitudes toward women." For Professor Mosher, as for the majority judges in *Rabidue*, a reasonable woman experiences workplace pornography as, at most, annoying. Any injury is minimal. Women like Robinson, Albert, and Banks were therefore unreasonable in claiming that the presence of such pictures constituted sexual harassment that hindered their ability to do their jobs.

The second defense expert, sociology professor Joseph Scott, echoed Mosher's views on how sexual materials affect men and women in the workplace. In his expert opinion, the average woman would not suffer substantial negative effects from exposure to pornography at work, nor would she find it offensive. While Professor Scott acknowledged that "women in the workforce would be slightly more offended by such materials than men," he did not consider this sufficient for a finding of hostile environment sexual harassment.

For the defendant's two experts, the reasonable woman would react similarly to the *Rabidue* court's reasonable person, who is really a reasonable man. She might be annoyed and even slightly offended, but essentially her reactions would mirror those of a reasonable man. According to these experts, the effect of pornography in the workplace is negligible—certainly, it is not sexual harassment.

On appeal, JSI argued that the trial court erred in applying a reasonable woman standard and that the case would have come out differently under a reasonable person standard, such as that applied by the *Rabidue* majority. The reasonable woman standard was described as an inappropriate form of protectionism for women; furthermore, JSI claimed such a standard would be impossible for men workers to figure out and therefore was unfair. In other words, fairness to sexist men justified unfairness to women because sexist men are untrainable and women workers are undeserving of protection.

In *Rabidue*, the majority characterized plaintiff Vivienne Rabidue as a troublemaker who was trying to change the way things had always been done. In its opinion, by choosing to work in a traditionally male environment, she assumed the risk. By adopting the male view of the plaintiff's claim, the *Rabidue* majority reached an outcome very different from that in *Robinson.*

In contrast, Judge Melton rejected the male perspective, despite the defendant's arguments concerning Robinson, which were strikingly similar to the *Rabidue* majority's assessment of Rabidue. In *Robinson,* however, JSI made an additional claim that treating the pictorial display of naked women and the sexual language as unlawful harassment violated JSI's and its male workers constitutional right to free expression under the First Amendment. While the debate over whether the right to be free from sex discrimination or the right to free expression should prevail in the workplace raises significant issues, it is beyond the scope of this chapter. (Those interested in the scope of the debate should look at the works of Catharine MacKinnon and Nadine Strassen, among others.) Nonetheless, pitting free speech against freedom from sexual harassment provides an interesting example of extremely divergent perspectives about which and whose rights matter. So far, even though the United States Supreme Court is highly protective of First Amendment rights, it has not indicated any concern for the free speech of sexual harassers.

In its arguments before the court, JSI asserted that much of the material and language that JSI's women workers found to be sexually harassing was not intentionally aimed at them until they complained about it and thus should not be actionable as sexual harassment. As they viewed it, JSI employees and management had posted explicitly sexual pictures "throughout the shipyards for at least nineteen years"—before any women were skilled craftsworkers at some of JSI's shipyards. Similarly, many JSI workers used crude, sexually explicit language whether women workers were present or not.

One of Robinson's supervisors explained to Judge Melton that "nautical people always had displayed pinups and other images of nude or partially nude women, like figureheads on boats, and that posting of such pictures was a 'natural thing' in a nautical workplace." He added that "there was nothing wrong with pinups in the shipyards, that he himself previously had posted such pictures . . . and that they certainly were not intended to intimidate, embarrass or cause concern to anyone." In the view of another supervisor, "shipyards were a man's world and . . . rules against vulgar and abusive language did not apply to the 'cussing' commonly heard there." However, there can be little doubt that some of the sexually explicit language directed at the women workers differed from ordinary cussing, even in a "man's world."

As the *Rabidue* case demonstrated, under a reasonable person standard the perspective of the men who have always been there is likely to be adopted over that of the women newcomers. Had he applied that standard, Judge Melton would most likely have sympathetically treated JSI's claims of tradition and lack of specific intent. A court applying a reasonable person standard would be expected to conclude that JSI's women craftsworkers assumed the risk of encountering sexually explicit pictures and words when they decided to take jobs in a traditionally male environment such as a shipyard. In this view, taking offense was the women's problem; they should just develop a thicker skin or find a different job.

In addition to claiming that women should adapt to the existing hostile workplace, JSI argued that the women workers were exposed to the same "offensive" materials outside the workplace. One supervisor "asserted that nudity on television was as bad as the pictures at JSI, and Robinson should look the other way just as she would turn off the television if she were offended." In general, JSI stated that because society as a whole, and women in particular, appeared to condone the public display of sexually explicit images, the workplace should not be held to a higher standard. In its argument to the appellate court, JSI noted that "in this society, advertisers often portray females as sexual objects in advertisements directed at women, and judicial notice should be taken that advertisers' extensive marketing studies establish that the reasonable consumer is not turned off by such messages." JSI expressly objected to Judge Melton's refusal to accept the argument that because popular women's magazines such as *Ms.*, *Glamour*, *Cosmopolitan*, and *Vanity Fair* commonly present sexually explicit articles and pictures, this constitutes evidence that women find such material acceptable. What JSI's objection fails to address is the critical difference in context between sex in women's magazines and sex in the workplace. Only if the women had been posting in the workplace pictures from women's magazines of provocatively posed naked men would JCI's objection have made any sense.

According to JSI, the women workers who claimed sexual harassment were extrasensitive, and the determination of whether a workplace is hostile to women should not be based on the "high morals" of such women. Taking offense at harmless terms such as *momma* and *dear* was evidence of this extrasensitivity. In particular, JSI argued that Robinson was extrasensitive about sexually offensive conduct, since she testified to only ten instances of sexually offensive conduct directed specifically at her during the eleven years she worked for JSI, none of which involved physical contact. In contrast, JSI pointed out that at least one woman worker was not offended by its work environment. Skilled craftsworker Barbara Dingle said pictorial displays of naked women did not offend her, and she suggested that Robinson "was spending too much time attending to the pictures and not enough time attending to her job." It was Dingle to whom the statement "Hey pussycat, come here and give me a whiff" had been directed. JSI used her lack of apparent concern as an example of how any *reasonable* woman would respond.

In its argument on appeal, JSI pointed out that Judge Melton "discounted evidence of the paucity of sexual harassment complaints at JSI and other females' engaging in sexual expression" because he erroneously relied on Robinson's expert K. C. Wagner, who attributed the lack of complaints to women's strategies for coping with sexual harassment. JSI argued that Wagner's coping-strategy theory was "based only on experience with those females who claimed to be victims of sexual harassment," and that the responses of such a group didn't represent what even the reasonable woman, much less the reasonable person, would consider to be appropriate behavior. In fact, Wagner's theory was based on her work with sexually harassed women, on her work with men in traditionally all-male environments, and on published research on this issue. Furthermore, although JSI was able to point to Dingle as a woman craftsworker who said her treatment in the workplace was not offensive, certainly a plausible explanation for her stated lack of concern is that this was how she coped with being asked: "Hey pussycat, come here and give me a whiff." She wanted to keep her high-paying job, and the best way she found to do it was to deny the negative effects of the hostile environment.

Robinson highlights how differently men and women in nontraditional workplaces may perceive their environment. For JSI's male workers, the environment was not objectively hostile; for JSI's female workers, it was. The sexually explicit language and pictures, sexual advances, and stubborn opposition to woman-friendly change clearly demonstrate the need for applying some form of woman-based standard of care for determining whether women workers are sexually harassed. If Judge Melton had applied the traditional reasonable person standard, the unjust status quo would have remained unchanged even though, objectively, JSI's women craftsworkers worked in a hostile environment.

Can't You Take a Joke? Harris v. Forklift Systems, Inc.

Harris v. Forklift Systems, Inc. is the second United States Supreme Court decision specifically addressing what constitutes hostile environment sexual harassment. Both male and female voices are represented in this case. The male voices deny the existence of sexual harassment; the female voices say that a hostile work environment did exist. The two male voices most frequently heard are that of the harasser, Charles Hardy, and that of the magistrate who conducted the original hearing. The magistrate's findings of fact and law were adopted verbatim by the trial court judge. The trial court's decision was then affirmed without a written opinion by three male judges from the Sixth Circuit Court of Appeals—the circuit that had previously decided *Rabidue*. Until the case reached the United States Supreme Court, the only female voice was that of the plaintiff, Teresa Harris. In the Supreme Court decision we hear the female voices of Justices Sandra Day O'Connor and Ruth Bader Ginsberg, who wrote the majority opinion and a concurring opinion, respectively.

The Supreme Court first recognized hostile environment sexual harassment in *Meritor Savings Bank v. Vinson,* which was decided in 1986, the same year as *Rabidue.* As the majority opinion in the 1993 *Harris* decision notes, *Meritor* involved "appalling conduct." According to the plaintiff in *Meritor,* her supervisor "made repeated demands upon her for sexual favors . . . ; she estimated that over . . . several years she had intercourse with him 40 or 50 times [and he] forcibly raped her on several occasions." The *Harris* majority points out that the behavior in *Meritor* was so egregious that it provided no meaningful guidance about what lesser forms of sexual or sexist conduct the Supreme Court would view as creating a hostile work environment. In the Court's view, the *Meritor* conduct clearly created a hostile environment under any objective standard—that of a reasonable man, reasonable person, or reasonable woman. In her opinion for the majority in *Harris,* Justice O'Connor noted that reference in *Meritor* "to environments 'so heavily polluted with discrimination as to destroy completely the emotional and psychological stability'" of workers of one gender presented only a particularly serious example of harassment; it did "not mark the boundary of what is actionable" sexual harassment. After the *Meritor* decision, different lower courts drew that boundary at different places, as demonstrated by the *Rabidue* and *Robinson* decisions. In *Harris*, the Supreme Court set out guidelines to define those boundaries more clearly and to clarify the kind of work environment a reasonable worker should be able to expect and, if necessary, demand.

The *Harris* Facts

As in *Rabidue* and *Robinson*, *Harris* involved a male-dominated workplace. Plaintiff Teresa Harris worked as the rental manager for leased equipment and coordinator of the sales department of defendant Forklift Systems, Inc., a heavy equipment rental company. Although the named defendant was the company, the person accused of creating the hostile work environment, Charles Hardy, was Forklift's president. Four of the five other managers—the sales, service, and parts managers and the comptroller—were men. The other woman manager was Hardy's daughter; as manager of the secretarial staff, she occupied a traditionally female role. Thus, Harris was the only woman in management who occupied a nontraditional position, and the only female manager not related to the boss.

Harris worked for Hardy from April 1985 until she quit in October 1987. She claimed that she was forced to quit because of the hostile environment Hardy's conduct had created. Much of Hardy's conduct was sexist and antiwoman rather than sexual. For example, he required Harris, alone among the managers, to bring coffee to management meetings. According to Harris's uncontradicted testimony at trial, Hardy repeatedly told her, in the presence of other Forklift employees, "You're a woman, what do you know?" and "We need a man as the rental manager." He and other male employees also told Harris: "You're a dumb-ass woman." Hardy's behavior toward Harris obviously reflected negatively on her role as supervisor, in the eyes of both her subordinates and the other managers. There was apparently no work-related basis for the sexist criticisms, since the magistrate found that Harris "was good at her job," and Hardy stated in his written argument to the United States Supreme Court that Harris "enjoyed a good working relationship" with him and her coworkers.

The sexual comments Hardy directed at Harris and other women ranged, in the magistrate's words, from the "inane and adolescent" to the "truly gross and offensive." In his defense, Hardy argued that these comments were both intended and taken as mere jokes. These "jokes" included telling Harris in front of other employees: "Let's go to the Holiday Inn to negotiate your raise." On a number of occasions Hardy told Harris she had a "racehorse ass," and once he told her that she couldn't wear a bikini "because your ass is so big, if you did there would be an eclipse and nobody could get any sun."

Hardy regularly made sexual comments about clothing that Harris and other women workers wore. Many other sexual comments expressly demeaned and sexualized the women employees; Hardy often told his female employees: "I have a quarter way down there. Would you get that out of my [front] pocket?" In addition to this request that his female employees sexually touch him, Hardy would throw objects on the ground in front of the women and ask them to pick the objects up, while he made comments about how they should dress to better expose their breasts.

Harris coped as best she could. As she put it, "I tried to let it roll off my back," but she found that her boss's conduct humiliated and deeply affected her:

> The comments about how I looked embarrassed me, but the comments about my ability to do my job and that I was stupid and I was dumb devastated me. I hated walking in there. . . . Everybody made fun of me because Charles Hardy did that. And I was supposed to laugh about it, and it wasn't funny. . . . I cried all the time. I was having shortness of breath. I wasn't sleeping at all. . . . I would get drunk every night so I would go to sleep so I could get up and go to work the next day, and I hated it. . . . I would sit in my office and I would shake. I hate it. I just hated it. . . . I went to see my doctor. He ran tests on me. . . . there was nothing physically wrong with me. He attributed it to all the anxiety and gave me tranquilizers and sleeping pills.

On August 18, 1987, Harris decided she couldn't stand the atmosphere at Forklift any longer and arranged a meeting with Charles Hardy. She secretly taped the conversation. During this meeting she told Hardy she would resign unless the abusive comments stopped.

Hardy admitted engaging in the behavior but said he was only "joking." He explained that such comments only reflected his effort to treat her "like one of the boys," and he expressed surprise that it bothered Harris. Interestingly, Hardy acknowledged that he would not like men to talk to his wife or his daughter (the clerical manager) as he spoke to Harris. He apologized and promised to stop the behavior. Relying on his assurances, Harris agreed not to resign.

However, he didn't stop. In the words of Justice Sandra Day O'Connor: "In early September, Hardy began anew: While Harris was arranging a deal with one of Forklift's customers, he asked her, again in front of other employees, 'What did you do, promise the guy some bugger Saturday night?'" Harris understood, and the magistrate found, that Hardy's "bugger" remark implied that Harris had promised to have sexual relations with the male customer in exchange for the business deal. This was the last straw; on October 1, Harris collected her paycheck and quit. Shortly thereafter she sued Forklift, claiming that Hardy's conduct created a sexually abusive work environment. Harris also claimed that she was "constructively" discharged, meaning that she was forced to quit because the working conditions were intolerable.

Harris's suit was assigned to a federal trial court judge, who appointed a magistrate to conduct the hearing and to issue an opinion, which the trial judge could either accept or reject. After listening to the testimony on both sides, the magistrate concluded that the atmosphere at Forklift did not amount to sexual harassment because, in his opinion, it neither caused Harris serious psychological harm nor made it impossible for her to do her job. In reaching this decision the magistrate applied a "reasonable woman" standard that was strikingly similar to the one described by the defendant's expert witnesses in *Robinson*. Such a refusal to take seriously a woman's perspective highlights the importance of insisting that a reasonable woman standard explicitly reflect the expectations of *women who would seek respect* in the workplace, rather than the expectations of men claiming to apply a woman's standard.

Disturbingly, the male trial and appellate court judges found the magistrate's conclusion to be correct. The trial judge considered the magistrate's opinion so uncontroversial and routine that he did not even publish it. This opinion was thus made inaccessible to the public and to those lawyers who do not subscribe to expensive computer data collections such as Lexis and Westlaw. Furthermore, both the trial court judge and the three-member panel of the court of appeals deemed it unnecessary to provide any commentary of their own. Only the United States Supreme Court found this case to be important and worthy of substantive review.

The court that found this case worthy of a written opinion had two women on it. This is likely not mere coincidence. In marked contrast to the lower courts' decisions, the Supreme Court found this an easy case in favor of the plaintiff. Tersely reversing the lower courts' decisions, the Supreme Court held that the lower courts clearly erred. The Court's nine members demonstrated unusual unanimity in their view that the magistrate, trial court, and Sixth Circuit Court of Appeals were all wrong in finding that Teresa Harris was not sexually harassed while working at Forklift.

Why did all the judicial actors prior to the Supreme Court get this case wrong? The most likely answer is that, regardless of the standard they said they had applied, they looked at the workplace environment at Forklift from the male perspective. And from a man's perspective, what happened to Harris was just not that bad—it was just part of a joking work environment.

Charles Hardy's Story

We hear Charles Hardy's view of what happened at Forklift through the appellate brief that argued his side to the United States Supreme Court. He claimed that Harris quit not because she felt sexually harassed but because a business deal between Hardy and Harris's husband soured. Furthermore, while admitting he said and did the things Harris alleged, Hardy asserted that he was merely joking, and that she and all his other women employees viewed him as a harmless kidder. In his view, since Harris talked and acted like "one of the boys," she couldn't have experienced his words and conduct as sexual harassment. Finally, he asserted that even under the reasonable woman standard, his conduct objectively did not create a hostile work environment.

Hardy's appellate brief stated that Harris and her husband, Larry, "enjoyed a social relationship with Hardy and his wife" while Harris worked for him, and that Harris's husband had a business relationship with Hardy. As the magistrate noted, six days *after* Harris quit, Hardy canceled his account with her husband's company, and the only evidence of a deteriorating business relationship between Hardy and Harris's husband occurred after Harris quit and filed a sexual harassment complaint. Yet, as the magistrate notes, "Defendant's theory is that plaintiff walked off the job on October 1, 1987, because defendant had terminated its business relationship with plaintiff's husband." One might have expected the magistrate to notice the sequential problem with Hardy's theory; however, instead he found Hardy's theory to be plausible and took it into consideration in deciding that Harris was not sexually harassed.

Hardy also asserted that everyone knew he was only joking when he made sexist and sexual comments to his women workers. In a two-pronged attack, he argued that Harris in particular was unharassable because she had evidenced consent to this kind of joking, and that none of the other women who worked at Forklift was bothered by his sexist statements and sexual innuendos. (He even implied that they enjoyed this kind of banter.) Thus, even if it would have offered a reasonable woman, Hardy's conduct didn't offend Forklift's women workers.

Focusing on Harris's unharassable character, one of Hardy's lawyers described her to a reporter as "'a four-time married white female' who had voluntarily joined the after-hour 'bull sessions' with fellow workers and had 'swapped' dirty jokes and 'utilized language, herself, that sank below the generally accepted norm.'" In his Supreme Court brief, Hardy asserted that Harris "fit into the atmosphere at the Company." The brief stated further that "she was the only woman who participated in regular, voluntary after-work gatherings in the office, and at these gatherings she drank beer, joked and used coarse language in the presence of Mr. Hardy and other [male] co-workers." In other words, by trying to be one of the boys, she gave Hardy permission to focus in on her female sexuality and denigrate her because she was a woman. The leap in logic here seems pretty obvious, but it escaped the magistrate: he found Harris's occasional use of coarse language to be evidence that, at most, she was merely annoyed by sexist and sexual comments about herself and other women workers.

All the other women workers—except for Hardy's daughter—were not management employees. These women were at a tremendous power disadvantage in relation to Charles Hardy, who was their boss and president of the company. Nevertheless, because none of these women complained, and because Harris was unable to get any of them to testify that Hardy's behavior offended her too, he argued: "None of the other female employees at Forklift found [his] behavior to be offensive or felt that there was a hostile work environment at Forklift." At least some of these women may not have wanted to speak out because they feared that, at a minimum, they would be viewed as troublemakers, as Harris was, and more likely, that they would lose their jobs. Furthermore, if Harris, a manager and social friend of Hardy, could not change his behavior, why should a secretary believe her complaints would have any effect or be worth pursuing at all? Yet the fact that none of these women testified that she felt sexually harassed seriously influenced the magistrate's view of Hardy's conduct.

Finally, Hardy argued in his appellate brief that neither a reasonable person nor a reasonable woman would have found the working conditions at Forklift to be abusive. Hardy claimed that, even if the *Rabidue* requirement that there be "serious psychological injury" was erroneous and therefore not relevant to whether Harris was sexually harassed, his behavior was annoying—maybe even offensive—but not severe enough to negatively affect Harris's work conditions. While Hardy's brief accurately quoted the Supreme Court's *Meritor* definition of hostile environment sexual harassment as conduct that is "sufficiently severe or pervasive to alter the conditions of [the victim's] employment and create an abusive working environment," he then argued that work conditions are altered only when "an employee must endure a 'gauntlet of sexual abuse' to be a member of the workforce." This is clearly a male test for when sexist and sexual conduct and comments alter the work conditions. It is therefore not surprising, although it is disappointing, that none of the four male judges who reviewed this case prior to its reaching the Supreme Court found this test for sexual harassment problematic.

The Magistrate's Story

The magistrate played a critical role in *Harris*. He did what the trial judge, sitting without a jury, would ordinarily do: listen to the witnesses and decide which evidence was admissible, whose evidence was believable, what law was applicable to the facts as he determined them, and, finally, whether Charles Hardy unlawfully sexually harassed Teresa Harris. Considering how much power was delegated to the magistrate, it is disturbing that he is so contemptuous of all the women who worked at Forklift. The magistrate believed these women enjoyed working for a man whose conduct was unquestionably both sexist and sexually offensive. The magistrate found that Forklift's women workers thought their boss's crude remarks about them were funny, and that thanks to Hardy's sense of humor, Forklift was a fun place to work. And even though the evidence presented to the magistrate clearly proved that Hardy was a perjurer who forged evidence "to manufacture a justification for [Harris's] termination," the magistrate sympathized with Hardy for being blindsided by her unfounded claim of sexual harassment.

In his findings of fact, the magistrate listed the specific instances of Hardy's sexist and sexual language that have been quoted earlier in this section. He also stated that Harris "was the object of a continuing pattern of sex-based derogatory conduct from Hardy" and described the incidents as "harassment" and Hardy as "the harasser." Later, however, he noted that "several clerical employees formerly employed at Forklift testified that Hardy's frequent jokes and sexual comments were just part of the joking work environment at Forklift." He then highlighted the views of a former receptionist at Forklift who "aptly expressed her feelings about comments Hardy may have made about her body. [She] jauntily testified, 'lots of people make comments about my breasts.'" It is revealing that the magistrate chose this woman's testimony as representative of the views and values of the women at Forklift, as she certainly comes across as a woman with less than a reasonable expectation of respect in the workplace. Yet the magistrate implied, by quoting her "jaunty" comment, that all the women employees at Forklift were just like her—including (at least until August 18, 1987) Teresa Harris.

The magistrate acknowledged in his conclusions of law that Hardy "is a vulgar man [who] demeans the female employees at his workplace." Yet he concluded that Forklift was not a hostile work environment and that Harris was not sexually harassed. Much of his justification for these legal conclusions seems to stem from his contempt for the women who worked at Forklift and from his mistrust of Harris. Even though the magistrate knew Hardy had attempted to defraud the court by forging evidence, he said, regarding Hardy and Harris, "Assignment of credibility was difficult in this case."

The magistrate appears to believe that women who swear and drink beer are simply unharassable. The fact that Harris drank beer with the guys seems especially significant to him—he mentions it twice in his opinion. Does this stand out because nice girls don't drink beer with the boys, and women who do drink beer are asking to be treated badly? For the magistrate, Harris's coarse language made her even more unharassable—apparently, women who swear do not mind, and perhaps even enjoy, being insulted and demeaned.

The magistrate also failed to understand how women react when they are harassed. Just because Harris laughed at Hardy's "jokes" and "appeared . . . to fit in quite well with the work environment" does not mean she wasn't feeling sexually harassed. K. C. Wagner, the plaintiff's expert witness in *Robinson*, listed one of five coping strategies women use when they are sexually harassed as "engaging in joking or other banter in the language of the workplace in order to defuse the situation." Harris had a well-paying job that she liked—if she wanted and needed the job, she was well advised to "fit in."

A particularly troublesome aspect of Harris's testimony for the magistrate was her focus on Hardy's comment to her in front of employees and a Nissan factory representative: "Let's go to the Holiday Inn to negotiate your raise." The magistrate commented on this statement twice. First, he said that Harris "knew this was meant as a joke, and treated it as a joke at the time. This comment must be viewed in context of the fact that the company often conducted management meetings at a nearby Holiday Inn." Why does this context matter? If the comment was meant as a joke, it seems highly likely that what made it funny was the implication that Harris and Hardy would negotiate the raise in bed—it would not have been funny if all it meant was that they would negotiate the raise in a meeting room. To joke in front of employees and business associates that you and your female manager sleep together does not merely show Hardy as "a man with a bad sense of humor"; it shows he was a man who did not respect women and enjoyed publicly humiliating them.

In his conclusions of law, the magistrate returned to Hardy's relationship to his female workers when he said that Hardy "is a vulgar man [who] demeans the female employees at his work place." But he excused this behavior because "many clerical employees tolerate his behavior and, in fact, view it as the norm and as joking." The magistrate failed to recognize that tolerating demeaning behavior because it's the norm and is the boss's version of humor doesn't mean that the women at Forklift liked it or took no notice of it. They very likely believed they had no choice but to accept the boss as he was. The magistrate explained their acceptance by concluding that the "clerical workers . . . were conditioned to accept denigrating treatment" and therefore were not being sexually harassed. Basically, the magistrate believed that when chronic sexually hostile conduct "conditions" the victims, the harasser is immunized from any claim of harassment.

Furthermore, from the magistrate's perspective, no matter how crude and harmful the sexual and sexist remarks were, unless Hardy realized they were offensive to Harris, she was not sexually harassed. And because they were "jokes" and Harris realized they were jokes, Hardy couldn't have known she was offended, and she couldn't *be* offended. Yet Hardy's knowledge is irrelevant under Title VII—if his behavior created a hostile environment, it was sexual harassment. Jokes can be harmful, and the law of sexual harassment focuses on the effect of conduct rather than on the knowledge of the actor. The magistrate should have recognized the humiliating and harmful effect jokes about female employees' bodies or about whom they slept with would have. Imagine, instead, that Hardy had employed African Americans and had told them jokes that made fun of their race, or that he'd said: "You're a colored man, what do you know?" or "You're just a dumbass black."

The magistrate noted that the critical legal issue here was "whether Hardy's continuous inappropriate sexual comments rose to the level of creating a hostile environment." He concluded that while "this is a close case . . . Charles Hardy's comments cannot be characterized as much more than annoying and insensitive." At one point the magistrate indicated that the sexually abusive language and conduct may have been especially problematic for Harris when he said: "I appreciate that plaintiff, as a management employee, was more sensitive to these comments than clerical employees." However, balanced against Harris's "going along" with the "jokes" and her "coarse language," this sensitivity didn't carry much weight in the magistrate's decision.

While the magistrate himself, and in his opinion, Forklift's clerical staff, viewed Hardy's sexist and sexual comments as merely "annoying," he acknowledged that both Harris and a reasonable woman would find them to be more hurtful. He noted: "I believe that some of Hardy's inappropriate sexual comments . . . offended plaintiff, and would offend the reasonable woman." However, being "offended" is not enough—the behavior must rise "to the level of interfering with that [reasonable woman manager's] work performance." The magistrate simply didn't believe Harris's testimony that it caused her great distress and interfered with her work performance, so he found that Hardy's comments and conduct did not "alter the conditions of employment and create an abusive working environment."

Because the magistrate was applying the law of sexual harassment as interpreted by the Sixth Circuit Court of Appeals, which had decided *Rabidue*, he found it "helpful to compare the instant case to *Rabidue*." In doing so, he concluded "that the degree of sexual hostility that existed in Teresa Harris's work environment was comparable to that in *Rabidue*. In both cases, the perpetrator of the offensive conduct was chiefly one person. He was vulgar and crude, but the sexual conduct was not in the form of sexual propositions or physical touching. It is true that Ms. Harris's nemesis was her supervisor and the owner of the company, whereas Ms. Rabidue's was merely a co-worker. However, Ms. Rabidue was able to show that the offensive conduct was severe enough to annoy her female co-workers, which Ms. Harris has been unable to show." The magistrate failed to recognize the ways in which power affects how people feel and behave. Thus, he did not see the connection between Harris's inability to get other women to admit being offended and the fact that the harasser was the boss. It is much more intimidating, abusive, and silencing when the boss—the person who hired you and can fire you at will—is the harasser.

The magistrate concluded that, despite irrefutable proof that Harris was going to resign on August 18 because of Hardy's previous behavior, that Hardy persuaded her to stay by promising to stop, and that he soon said something "truly gross" to Harris, it was not foreseeable that a reasonable woman manager would then resign. Clearly, the magistrate's "reasonable woman manager" does not expect to be respected in the workplace. Instead, this reasonable woman manager is, in reality, a guy who can take a joke or a woman who has been conditioned to tolerate demeaning sexual comments from her boss.

As in the *Rabidue* opinion, the magistrate's voice is that of a man who sees nothing wrong with a status quo that allows male workers and bosses to demean women workers sexually, because for him this behavior is not unreasonable. If the magistrate's voice had been countered by the trial court judge or at least by one of the three appeals court judges, we might have some reason to believe that women workers in America are making progress. But sadly, none of these men had any problems with the tone or the content of the magistrate's opinion, and they therefore affirmed it without changing a word. If the United States Supreme Court had not chosen to review and reverse this case, the conduct at Forklift would have been given a judicial stamp of approval.

The Supreme Court Opinions

The Supreme Court is asked to consider thousands of cases each year and agrees to review only approximately one hundred cases that it considers to be the most important. Only the extraordinary case is accepted for Supreme Court review. *Harris v. Forklift Systems, Inc.* was such a case, even though—or perhaps, because—none of the lower courts had viewed it as anything but routine and unimportant. When the Supreme Court stated that it was going to consider *Harris*, it was a case that lawyers, the press, and the public knew nothing about because no judicial opinions had been published.

The Supreme Court usually hears oral argument in cases in the fall and publishes its decisions in June of the next year. Acting with rare speed and urgency, the Court heard oral arguments in *Harris* on October 13, 1993, and, to everyone's surprise, published a terse and cogent decision in Harris's favor on November 9, 1993—a mere twenty-seven days later.

The length of the opinion also surprised everyone. Supreme Court decisions are frequently extremely long and complicated, often running to forty pages, with complex patterns of concurring and dissenting opinions. In *Harris*, the Court was unanimous in the result, and totaled less than four pages, with two concurring opinions. The present Supreme Court is known to be politically divided on many issues, and dissenting opinions are extremely common. Yet none of the seven male and two female justices disagreed with the outcome in this case. While Justices Antonin Scalia and Ruth Bader Ginsberg wrote concurring opinions, neither criticized the reasons that the majority opinion gave for deciding in favor of Teresa Harris. Even Justice Scalia, who is notorious for finding fault with the judicial reasoning of his fellow justices, stated: "I know of no alternative to the course the Court today has taken."

That the Supreme Court found *Harris* to be important, and that they found the five men who reviewed it in the lower courts to have been wrong, is, we believe, directly attributable to the presence of two women on the Supreme Court. Both women's voices were heard: Sandra Day O'Connor wrote the majority opinion, and Ruth Bader Ginsberg wrote a short but important concurrence. Both women jurists comprehended the effect certain workplace behavior would have on women workers and were therefore able to assist their brethren in understanding Harris's predicament.

Justice O'Connor's opinion is short and to the point. She began: "In this case we consider the definition of a discriminatory 'abusive work environment' . . . under Title VII of the Civil Rights Act of 1964." Justice O'Connor set out what she viewed as the critical fact in this case: "The Magistrate found that, throughout Harris' time at Forklift, Hardy often insulted her because of her gender and often made her the target of unwanted sexual innuendoes." Justice O'Connor then described the various things Hardy said and did. She noted that when Harris complained, Hardy apologized but soon began anew, and then Harris quit and "sued Forklift, claiming that Hardy's conduct had created an abusive work environment for her because of her gender."

Justice O'Connor next described how the trial judge accepted the magistrate's finding that Hardy's conduct "did not create an abusive environment." She quoted from that portion of the magistrate's opinion where he says:

> A reasonable woman manager under like circumstances would have been offended by Hardy, but his conduct would not have risen to the level of interfering with that person's work performance. Neither do I believe that [Harris] was subjectively so offended that she suffered injury. . . . Although Hardy may at times have genuinely offended [Harris], I do not believe that he created a working environment so poisoned as to be intimidating or abusive."

Justice O'Connor then stated that the Supreme Court accepted this case in order to decide "whether conduct, to be actionable as 'abusive work environment' harassment . . . must 'seriously affect [an employee's] psychological well-being' or lead the plaintiff to 'suffer injury.'" She concluded, on behalf of the Court, that neither of these criteria is required for sexual harassment to occur. Justice O'Connor explained that women don't have to suffer nervous breakdowns before they can be found to have been sexually harassed. Instead, a workplace that "does not seriously affect employees' psychological well-being" is abusive when it "detract[s] from employees' job performance, discourage[s] employees from remaining on the job, or keep[s] them from advancing in their careers." Her test is simply whether the work environment "would reasonably be perceived, and is perceived, as hostile or abusive." Unlike the five men who reviewed this case previously, the Supreme Court believed that a reasonable person in Harris's position would have viewed Hardy's words and conduct as not merely annoying or offensive but abusive and therefore sexual harassment. Furthermore, the Court didn't even refer to the magistrate's concern about ulterior motives for Harris quitting and his belief that the other women at Forklift viewed Hardy as just a joker.

Even though the Supreme Court never expressly addressed whose perspective they adopted in reviewing what happened at Forklift, it is obvious that Justice O'Connor's majority opinion looked at what happened to Harris with a different perspective from that of the men who had found no sexual harassment. Her opinion required that reasonableness be viewed from the perspective of someone who expects to be respected in the workplace. The majority opinion thus tells employers that American women workers who are subjected to sexual and sexist verbal abuse have a valid claim of sexual harassment. This extremely important and empowering message is all the more so because the words are spoken by Sandra Day O'Connor, the first woman to sit on the United States Supreme Court. She and Ruth Bader Ginsberg are the most powerful women in the American legal system, and in *Harris* they inform American employers that the status quo is no longer acceptable.

Ruth Bader Ginsberg's concurring opinion set out a simple and straightforward test for hostile work environment sexual harassment. For her, "it suffices to prove that a reasonable person subjected to the discriminatory conduct would find, as [Harris] did, that the harassment so altered the working conditions as to 'make it more difficult to do the job.'" In this sentence, Justice Ginsberg tells us that Hardy's conduct made Harris's job more difficult, that she was reasonable in her reactions, and that by making Harris's job more difficult, Hardy sexually harassed her. Suddenly the tables are turned —the perspective that matters is no longer that of male harassers but of women workers.

Harris v. Forklift Systems was a huge victory for America's working women. It sent a loud message to all employers that sexist gibes and one-sided sexual joking will no longer be viewed as merely annoying.

Instead, such conduct will be treated as a reasonable woman who expects to be respected in the workplace would view it: as unlawful sexual harassment. If this means that women workers are to be viewed as workers first and women second, then perhaps we have come a long way after all.

5

Gender, Race, Sexual Orientation, and the Reasonable Woman

As the cases in the previous chapter demonstrate, the reasonable *person* standard represents a *male* perspective. When applied in hostile work environment sexual harassment cases, it disadvantages women and perpetuates sex discrimination and inequality in the workplace. Accepting this claim of injustice, an important question remains: Is the reasonable woman, as we define it, the appropriate standard for gendered injuries, regardless of the gender, sexual orientation, or race of the parties involved? In most cases our answer is yes. In this chapter we discuss why the reasonable woman standard is the best solution in almost all instances where sexist or sexual harassment is involved. We also believe that the reasonable woman standard should apply in most cases of stalking, domestic homicide, and rape, for analogous reasons.

When men or women sexually harass others, they take on a stereotypically masculine role that derives pleasure and self-regard from dominating others. It doesn't matter who—that is, which sex—takes on this role, even though it has been starkly gendered in our culture. Taking on or endorsing the "female" or the "male" role when those roles remain characterized by subordination and dominance, respectively, simply perpetuates gender inequality and legal bias. We therefore argue that the reasonable woman standard should apply regardless of the gender of either the perpetrator or the target, so that the basic paradigm can change—so that masculine and feminine stereotypes can be broken down. As discussed below, we also believe that in most situations the reasonable woman standard should apply regardless of the race or sexual orientation of either the perpetrator or the target, because when the harm is sexual or sexist, it is this aspect of an individual's personhood that is at issue.

The most effective way to apply our standard is to ask the decision makers how a reasonable woman would view the perpetrator's and the target's behavior. In particular, they should assess whether the perpetrator behaved as a reasonable woman would have in similar circumstances. When the parties involved do not fit the traditional male-on-female mold, decision makers should be instructed to transpose the facts into male-on-female and then apply the reasonable woman standard to those facts. In this way, decision makers will be asked to think in terms of how a reasonable woman would act and should be treated in a situation like the one they are addressing.

This standard of behavior has the potential to transform the workplace. The reasonable woman standard respects other workers' bodily integrity, agency, and personal autonomy and expects the same in return. Applying the reasonable woman standard to all workers raises the standard of acceptable workplace behavior and improves working conditions for everyone. Conveying the political message inherent in combining the terms *reasonable* and *woman*—that women *are* reasonable and their values should be *everyone's* values when it comes to workplace gendered conduct—is essential at this stage.

Law can change behavior. And numerous studies of intergroup processes demonstrate the maxim that attitudes follow behavior. For example, Charles Moskos and John Sibley Butler studied how forced changes in behavior in the military changed racial attitudes. Demanding that everyone act like reasonable women when it comes to sex and sexism in the workplace appropriately assumes that men can learn to take responsibility for their treatment of others and to behave more respectfully. For many men, this change in behavior will also lead to a change in attitude. We want the phrase "reasonable woman" to resonate with decision makers, employees, employers, and the public in general, so that gender will matter by making a positive difference in the lives of women workers and, eventually, all workers.

Female-on-Male Sexual Harassment

Applying the reasonable woman standard when a woman sexually harasses a man treats his injury more seriously and respectfully than under a reasonable person/man standard. People assume, with some justification, that men usually welcome sexual conduct. Studies such as those examined by Barbara Gutek in *Sex and the Workplace* and by John Pryor, Janet Giedd, and Karen Williams in "A Social Psychological Model for Predicting Sexual Harassment" show that sex in the workplace has fewer negative effects on men than on women. Thus, applying a male or "neutral" standard to a female perpetrator excuses conduct that would be unacceptable if the roles were reversed. However, not all men welcome sexual or sexist behavior in the workplace, especially when the source is a supervisor, male or female. A valid sexual harassment claim should exist if a man felt a woman sexually harassed him and if a reasonable woman would find the conduct to be sexual harassment. Decision makers should be asked to determine how a reasonable woman would behave by reversing the roles and asking how a reasonable woman would assess the perpetrator's conduct if a man were treating a woman in this way.

A recent decision illustrates the risk of using a "neutral" standard. In *Williams v. Runyon,* the plaintiff Richard Williams, a married man, alleged that his female supervisor, Clora Grant, sexually harassed him for about two years. According to Williams, this is what happened:

> Grant, the afternoon supervisor, came near Williams two or three times a day. She did this as Williams sorted the mail in his cubicle. . . . Each time Grant came near Williams, she would stand close enough that Williams could feel her breath on his face. Grant also stood close enough that her hips and thighs would touch Williams' body. The uninvited touching of hips and thighs occurred several times over a period of time. . . .
>
> Grant also touched Williams on several occasions. On one occasion, Grant reached into Williams' shirt pocket and pinched his nipple while purportedly looking for cigarettes. On another occasion, Grant reached into the front pocket of Williams' pants. Williams repeatedly spurned Grant's advances.

Williams complained to other supervisors, but they ignored his complaints and made no attempt to remedy the situation. He ultimately sued, alleging sexual harassment.

The trial court found that Williams was not sexually harassed because "a reasonable person may find the actions of Grant unpleasant, but such a reasonable person would not perceive the actions as 'sufficiently severe or pervasive as to alter the conditions of employment and create an abusive work environment.'" Further, "Grant's conduct was simply not so severe or pervasive as to render Williams's work environment 'hostile.'"

If the roles and genders had been reversed, Grant's conduct would most likely have been viewed as severe enough to alter Williams's conditions of employment. Imagine a court saying that a male supervisor pinching a female worker's nipple and reaching into her front pocket is not sexual harassment! The genders of the parties should not determine the outcome. Under a reasonable woman standard, Grant's conduct would be judged sufficiently severe because it sexualizes the supervisor-subordinate relationship and intrudes on Williams's bodily integrity. A reasonable woman would neither behave like Grant nor find the conduct Williams experienced merely "unpleasant."

To view a woman's sexual conduct toward a man as less abusive than analogous sexual conduct by a man toward a woman fails to achieve gender equality and respect for the autonomy and bodily integrity of all workers. Holding harassers of men to a lower standard of workplace behavior excuses women who behave like some men regarding sex in the workplace and fails to recognize that some men experience harassment in the way that most women do. It therefore encourages negative gender stereotypes about both men and women by sending the message that women who act like insensitive men about sex can get away with it, and that regardless of context, men always find sexual conduct and gendered treatment acceptable. Under this version of masculinity, acting like a man means imposing one's sexual will and dominance and responding like a man means always welcoming workplace sex. The reasonable woman standard attempts to dismantle both these stereotypes.

Male-on-Male "Macho" Sexual Harassment

Often, when men are sexually harassed, other men are the perpetrators. A study by Craig Waldo, Jennifer Berdahl, and Louise Fitzgerald indicates that men are at least as likely to be harassed by other men as they are by women. However, male-on-male harassment often differs from male-on-female or female-on-male harassment. Intergender harassment may be sexual or sexist or both, but it typically does not focus on the targets' masculinity or femininity. In contrast, male-on-male harassment frequently involves attacks—often quite violent and abusive—on a man's "masculinity" by purportedly heterosexual male coworkers. This kind of harassment highlights the demeaning aspect of being treated like a woman when it comes to sex. It includes picking on "feminine" men and treating less dominant males in all-male environments as surrogate women. Not surprising, research such as that conducted by Craig Waldo and his colleagues indicates that the harassment men consider most offensive is this enforcement of stereotypical heterosexual male gender roles.

When men sexually harass men, what standard should apply? Consider the approach in the 1998 U.S. Supreme Court decision *Oncale v. Sundowner Offshore Services, Inc.* While working on a male-only oil rig, Oncale was subjected to extremely physical and intrusive sexual conduct, including physical assaults and threats of rape, by other workers, all of whom were identified as heterosexual. Justice Scalia described the conduct only generally, "in the interest of brevity and dignity," noting that "Oncale was forcibly subjected to sex-related, humiliating actions against him by Lyons, Pippen and Johnson in the presence of the rest of the crew. Pippen and Lyons also physically assaulted Oncale in a sexual manner, and Lyons threatened him with rape."

After making clear that Title VII covers same-sex harassment, the Court examined the alleged conduct "from the perspective of a reasonable person in plaintiff's position, considering 'all the circumstances.'" It seems likely that this "reasonable person" would be gendered male: the perpetrator's conduct would be viewed from the perspective of a reasonable (and, implicitly, heterosexual) man who was being subjected to male sexual aggression.

Male-on-male sexual harassment cases involve patterns of sexualized dominance similar to those seen in male-on-female sexual harassment. In a sense, the male targets are being gendered female and therefore treated as lesser. It is the rare context (outside male prisons) in which men are treated like women. When men experience aggressive sexual harassment, from men or from women, they learn how bad it feels to be treated like a woman.

In *Oncale*, once the Supreme Court had declared that the plaintiff could pursue his claim, application of either a reasonable man/person or a reasonable woman standard would likely result in a finding of sexual harassment because the conduct was so egregious. However, many cases of male-on-male harassment involve less extreme conduct, including "bagging" (grabbing another man's genitals) or repeatedly asking for oral sex. Under the reasonable man standard, such treatment might be viewed as mere "horseplay" or as "guys being guys" even if the man in question felt sexually harassed and even if analogous conduct would constitute sexual harassment of a woman. An Iowa district court judge's statement that "the only thing sexual about 'bagging' is that the aggressor aims his non-sexual aggression at genitals" exemplifies this skewed attitude.

A 1997 federal appellate court case, *Johnson v. Hondo, Inc.*, highlights how applying a reasonable woman standard might affect the outcome in certain male-on-male cases. Craig Johnson had been working at Hondo, Inc., for fifteen years as a "night loader," operating a forklift to move heavy boxes, when Ollie Hicks was also hired as a night loader. They worked together in an all-male environment. According to Johnson, Hicks's sexually harassing conduct included

> repeatedly telling the plaintiff, "I'm going to make you suck my dick,"
> "come down to the carwash and suck my dick," and the like. Often this
> conduct was accompanied by Hicks touching himself as if masturbating
> through his clothes and by his coming up to within inches of the plain-
> tiff's face. Hicks often also intimidated, demeaned and humiliated the
> plaintiff because of his gender by saying that he [Hicks] would have
> "that red-headed bitch (referring to the plaintiff's fiance, who often
> picked him up after work or brought him his lunch) suck my dick" and
> similar and worse remarks.

When Johnson reported Hicks's sexual harassment to his supervisors, they ignored his complaints and ridiculed him for making them. Johnson subsequently reacted to Hicks by using coarse language, including homosexual epithets:

> I said, "I'm getting sick and tired of your shit." Probably called him a
> punk or fag, or something. "you're the one who likes to suck dicks you
> son of a"—SOB, probably, or something on that order. And I just told
> him to stop fucking with me or harassing me.

One night, Johnson saw Hicks look at him threateningly and heard him say to another employee: "I think I'm going to get my dick sucked tonight." Johnson then challenged Hicks, saying he was sick of being treated this way. Hicks replied that they should go off premises to deal with it. Johnson argued that they should "talk about it now" but eventually agreed to meet outside during break. Once outside, Johnson demanded: "I want this stopped now." Hicks's response was to take a jack stand out of his car and brandish it at Johnson, who got a baseball bat from his car. They fought. Hicks was hospitalized, and both men were fired for violating company rules against fighting. In a criminal battery prosecution, the jury found Johnson acted in self-defense.

In Johnson's sexual harassment suit against his employer, the appellate court affirmed the trial court's decision to dismiss the case because no one could reasonably believe that Hicks's conduct was sexually directed at Johnson on the basis of his gender. The appellate court concluded that, despite the obvious sexual nature of the language,

> there is no connection whatsoever with the sexual acts to which they make reference—even when they are accompanied, as they sometimes were here, with a crotch-grabbing gesture. . . . No reasonable factfinder could conclude that Hicks directed his vulgar remarks at Johnson because of his gender.

This conclusion strains reason and common sense. Hicks sexually taunted, threatened, and humiliated Johnson, apparently with the goal of asserting dominance over him in their work relationship. Sexual conduct to achieve dominance is a classic example of sexual harassment. If Johnson had been a woman, the court would almost certainly have found a causal relationship between Hicks's words and her gender. So why is heterosexual male-on-male conduct different? Why does the target's gender define the injury?

To reach this decision, the *Johnson* court had to distinguish *Doe v. City of Belleville, Illinois,* an earlier case by the same federal court of appeals. *Doe* allowed a claim of male-on-male sexual harassment to go forward. In *Doe,* a sixteen-year-old, H, who wore an earring, was grabbed by his testicles, repeatedly taunted about his gender, and sexually threatened by his male coworkers. The court held that H could bring a sexual harassment claim, refusing to treat this case differently from more typical claims of sexual harassment simply because all the parties were purportedly heterosexual males. The court noted that "so long as the environment itself is hostile to the plaintiff because of [his] sex, why the harassment was perpetrated (sexual interest? misogyny? personal vendetta? misguided humor? boredom?) is beside the point." Instead, the court considered how the conduct would have been viewed if the plaintiff were female, noting:

> If H were a woman, no court would have any difficulty construing such abusive conduct as sexual harassment. . . . If H were a woman, there would be no agonizing over whether the harassment that [he has] described could be understood as sex discrimination. The happen-

stance that he is instead a male should not make for an entirely different analysis.

The *Doe* court's analysis is analogous to applying the reasonable woman standard to the defendants' conduct. In essence, the court concluded that if a reasonable woman would experience the conduct as harassment, then a male plaintiff may also claim harassment. Thus the court acknowledged that, as a society, we have different expectations for men than we do for women when it comes to sex, and that the expectations we have for women should apply universally. However, the court continued by noting that this did not mean that the target's experience would be the same if he had been a woman. The court explained:

> When a male employee's testicles are grabbed, his torment might be comparable, but the point is that he experiences that harassment as a man, not just as a worker, and she as a woman. In each case, the victim's gender not only supplies the lexicon of the harassment, it affects how he or she will experience that harassment; and in anything short of a truly unisex society, men's and women's experiences will be different.

The court's claim that men and women experience similar kinds of sexual harassment (e.g., someone saying "I'm going to make you suck my dick" differently is troubling. It reveals a huge zone of unexamined societal and legal assumptions about gender roles. Whether the target is male or female, the purpose of such a statement is to dominate, demean, and humiliate the "other." While one might say that for a man it goes further by challenging his masculinity, thereby "feminizing" him, we maintain that this kind of conduct, when addressed to a woman, feminizes her as well. It challenges her "masculine" side, which our culture defines as powerful, strong, intelligent, capable, and dominant, just as it challenges his. Applying the reasonable woman standard regardless of the parties' genders is intended to root out destructive gendered distinctions that link masculinity with dominance and femininity with submission.

The *Doe* decision seems to make the outcome in *Johnson* indefensible. Even the *Johnson* court acknowledged that its conclusion is "in some tension with the analysis in *Doe*." Nevertheless, the court insisted that, unlike the conduct in *Doe*, Hicks's comments and conduct "were nothing other than vulgar provocations having no causal relationship to Johnson's gender as male." While it is accurate to say that

Hicks's behavior probably was not based on sexual interest, neither was the defendants' behavior in *Doe*—nor, for that matter, Hardy's behavior in *Harris*. As the Supreme Court made clear in *Oncale*, "harassing conduct need not be motivated by sexual desire to support an inference of discrimination on the basis of sex." Furthermore, if the *Johnson* court had, like the *Doe* court, asked how the case would have been decided if Johnson were female, almost certainly the court would have acknowledged that Hicks's conduct constituted sexual harassment.

Applying the reasonable woman standard to male-on-male cases would force employers to respond to men's complaints in order to avoid liability. Thus, when Johnson complained, his supervisor would have taken the complaint seriously. Had that happened, the situation might have been resolved without violence. The fact that so many of the vicious male-on-male harassment cases arise in all-male environments is strong evidence that such workplaces would be unendurably sexually hostile for women. If the reasonable woman defined Johnson's workplace, even women might be willing to work there.

Gay Men and Lesbians and Sexual Harassment

Applying the reasonable woman standard to people who are not heterosexual raises a tangle of controversial issues. The basic structure of sexual harassment law presupposes heterosexuality, just as, until recently, it has viewed only male-on-female harassment as "real" harassment. In contrast, because we want all sexual and sexist harassment to be taken seriously, we believe that in most cases sexual orientation should not enter into the calculus. The two-step process we apply in cases involving both male and female harassment of males assures this: (1) transpose the facts into male-on-female, and then (2) hold the alleged harasser to the reasonable woman standard. The details of reported sexual harassment cases involving homosexuals reveal gender-based hostile environments. Transposing the facts and applying the reasonable woman standard should therefore divert the focus of decision makers from the sexual orientation of the parties and make them focus instead on the issue of gender discrimination.

Many Americans have strong prejudices against homosexuals. Such bias has no legitimate place in determining whether someone has experienced a hostile work environment. Regardless of the gender or sexual orientation of the parties, sexual or sexist behavior can create discriminatorily hostile working environments. However, when the perpetrator or target of sexual harassment is purportedly homosexual and when both parties are of the same sex, the traditional reasonable person standard, with its male heterosexual normative basis, increases the risk that homophobia will enter into the determination of whether a hostile environment exists. As one commentator, Gary Spitko, said: "To help eliminate the heterosexual bias inherent in the *Harris* standard, it would be far more useful to instruct the finder of fact to evaluate the actions of the gay same-sex sexual harassment defendant in the hypothetical context of a mixed-sex interaction." If the perpetrator is viewed as homosexual, the decision maker may find a hostile environment because of conscious or unconscious prejudices. If the target is homosexual, the decision maker may minimize the seriousness of the perpetrator's conduct for similar reasons. Asking the decision maker to consider how the case would come out if the perpetrator were male and the target female reduces these risks. Applying the reasonable woman standard, with its emphasis on bodily integrity, respect, and self-determination, further counters real or perceived prejudice against gays and lesbians.

In a number of decided cases, the alleged perpetrators are either admittedly or implicitly homosexual. These cases typically involve a supervisor harassing a subordinate through conduct that, if a heterosexual man engaged in analogous conduct toward a woman, would constitute hostile environment sexual harassment—under either a reasonable person or reasonable woman standard. For example, in *McCoy v. Macon Water Authority*, in which the trial court denied the employer's motion for summary judgment, Robert McCoy alleged that his supervisor Charles Birkencamper

> repeatedly and directly asked him about the size of his penis; indirectly inquired about the size of his penis by asking the size of his girlfriend's vagina; commented on his body; suggested that he take up bodybuilding or become a wrestler; speculated about his sexual performance; invited him to go to car shows out of town and share a hotel room; and discussed intimate relations [Birkencamper engaged in] with male friend.

Most of this conduct is either directly transposable or closely analogous to male-on-female harassment. For example, how would a woman subordinate view her male supervisor "repeatedly and directly" asking her about the size of her vagina and the size of her boyfriend's penis, inviting her to share a hotel room, or describing his sexual relations? Under most reasonableness standards, such conduct would be "sufficiently severe or pervasive 'to alter the conditions of [the target's] employment and create an abusive working environment'" and, as Justice Ginsberg put it in *Harris*, make "it more difficult to do the job." Although in many cases applying either the reasonable person or the reasonable woman standard would lead to the same outcome, applying the reasonable woman standard increases the probability of decision makers focusing solely on gender discrimination, without factoring in the perpetrator's actual or purported homosexuality.

Similarly, when a woman alleges that her female supervisor is sexually harassing her, the risk of homophobia affecting the evaluation of the conduct could be ameliorated by considering whether, under a reasonable woman standard, a woman would have viewed analogous conduct from a male supervisor as creating a hostile environment. For example, in the 1995 case of *Myers v. City of El Paso*, Veronica Myers alleged that her supervisor Reyna Sanchez subjected her to a sexually hostile work environment. Sanchez repeatedly commented on Myers's breasts, buttocks, hair, and clothing and touched her in ways that Myers found offensive. For example, one time Sanchez placed her hands on Myers's hips, turned her, and then opened Myers's blazer, saying she wanted to "see what you have underneath." Another time, while Myers was on the phone and unable to respond, Sanchez deliberately slid a pen down Myers's blouse.

If Sanchez had been a male supervisor, the conduct alleged by Myers would very likely, under any reasonableness standard, constitute sexual harassment. But because both Myers and Sanchez were women, the court dismissed the case. The harm to Myers and to other women in similar circumstances does not disappear when the harasser is another woman: the gender of the parties should not determine the outcome. Transposing the genders of the parties and applying the reasonable woman standard makes it more likely that demeaning sexualized or sexist workplace behavior will be actionable, while lessening the risk that decision makers will factor prejudicially in the parties' sexual orientation.

In many cases involving male same-sex harassment, it is unclear whether the perpetrator's conduct was based on homosexual attraction or enforcement of the heterosexual stereotypes of masculinity discussed in the previous section. These cases illustrate the necessity for looking beyond sexual attraction as a basis for sexual harassment. Conduct might be sexual, sex-based enforcement of gender norms, or both. Compare *Rushing v. United Airlines* to *Johnson*, discussed earlier. In both *Johnson* and *Rushing*, the claim of hostile environment centered on one man's repeated demand of another man to "suck my dick." However, plaintiff Leon Rushing made further allegations, indicating that sexual attraction was the motivation behind use of this phrase. Rushing recounted that when his supervisor, Guy Montes, was driving him from one part of the work area to another, Montes asked him to perform oral sex. When Rushing refused, Montes said: "Let me suck yours then." Rushing again refused. Montes then pointed to another male worker and said that the man had performed oral sex on him "real good," and asked Rushing: "Why don't you do me now?" Rushing repeated his refusal, interrupted Montes's attempt to touch him, and asked to be let out of the van.

Montes, while admitting that he often used the phrase "suck my dick," denied that his use of the phrase was based on sexual attraction and further denied that the incident described above ever occurred. As further evidence of his lack of sexual intent, Montes asserted that both he and Rushing were heterosexual and married.

As the Supreme Court noted in *Oncale*, whether the conduct was based on sexual attraction or not is irrelevant. Therefore, the sexual orientation of the parties involved should also be irrelevant. The only issue should be whether a reasonable woman would have found analogous conduct to be sexual or sex-based harassment, had the perpetrator been male and the target been female. Under this test, the parties' sexual orientation is of no consequence.

The same approach should be used in same-sex cases when either both parties or the target is admittedly or purportedly homosexual. *Roe v. K-Mart* provides an example of sexual harassment of one gay man by another gay man. As the court describes the claim, "Roe, a male homosexual, alleges that he was discharged from his employment with [K-Mart] because he refused his former male homosexual supervisor's sexual advances." Roe's allegations fit the classic mold for sexual harassment: a supervisor making unwanted advances to a subordinate and retaliating when those advances are rejected. Transposing the genders and applying the reasonable woman standard minimizes the risk that homophobia will affect the outcome in such a case.

Although no officially reported cases have involved a self-identified gay or lesbian target alleging sexual or gender-based harassment by a self-identified heterosexual man or woman, such conduct certainly occurs. For good reason, the homosexual target rarely pursues this kind of legal claim. *Dillon v. Frank* illustrates the problems involved in bringing such a case. In *Dillon* a postal worker suffered humiliation and physical injuries because his male coworkers believed he was gay. According to the court:

> Dillon was taunted, ostracized, and physically beaten by his co-workers because of their belief that he was a homosexual. . . . A fellow employee, Kenneth Barrett, began calling Dillon "fag," and saying that "Dillon sucks dicks." . . . This continued for five months, culminating in a physical assault by Barrett on Dillon in which Dillon suffered numerous injuries. The [employer] fired Barrett as a result. This did not end Dillon's travails. What had begun as a one-man band expanded into a full orchestral assault of verbal abuse. Other employees used similar epithets. Graffiti . . . appeared on conveyor belts and Dillon's loading trucks informing [others] that "Dillon sucks dicks" and "Dillon gives head." Dillon endured these circumstances for three years before he finally resigned . . . upon advice from his psychiatrist.

The *Dillon* court dismissed this case because it concluded that the conduct was discrimination based on sexual orientation rather than on gender and therefore not subject to legal protection. However, it is obvious that Ernest Dillon was discriminated against and attacked because he was a man—a certain kind of man that his coworkers reviled. It really didn't matter whether Dillon was actually gay or not. His fellow workers despised him for his failure to act like a stereotypical macho man.

Undoubtedly, gay men and lesbians are often subjected to discrimination, including harassment, because of their sexual orientation. However, under federal and most state antidiscrimination laws, people are not entitled to legal protection from discrimination on the basis of sexual orientation. In most states, a boss or coworker is allowed to severely harass another worker as long as the sole reason is described as the target's real or perceived sexual orientation as a homosexual. This failure to protect against sexual orientation discrimination evidences American society's deep homophobia.

One's sexual orientation should be protected under antidiscrimination laws such as Title VII. In fact, even though neither is expressly protected, sexual orientation, like gender, should be implicitly protected under the U.S. Constitution. But as long as it is not so protected, courts should at least be persuaded to address sexual orientation harassment as sexual or gender-based harassment using our reasonable woman standard. As was arguably the case in *Dillon*, often the harassment is not solely or even mainly because of the target's actual sexual orientation but because the target fails to behave like a "real" man or a "real" woman. Such harassment legitimately can be considered to be a form of gender-based harassment, because most homosexuals are discriminated against in part because they do not fit the stereotypical male or female role.

Even where a jurisdiction's law protects against discrimination based on sexual orientation as Oregon's does (according to a 1998 appellate court decision, *Tanner v. Oregon Health Sciences University,* interpreting the Oregon Constitution), a gay man or lesbian who suffers harassment will often experience sexual or gender-based harassment in addition to or instead of sexual orientation harassment. As discussed more fully in the next section, when this occurs the target should have the option of bringing separate claims for sexual harassment and sexual orientation harassment or solely for one or the other—or even, for example, sexual harassment as a lesbian, using a reasonable lesbian standard.

Strategically, considering American society's extreme homophobia, even in a jurisdiction such as Oregon a homosexual target may choose to focus solely on sexual or gender-based harassment using the reasonable woman standard. For example, if male workers subjected a female coworker to conduct analogous to that experienced by Dillon, application of the reasonable woman standard would result in a finding of hostile environment sexual harassment. By transposing the facts of *Dillon* to a male-on-female situation and using the reasonable woman standard as a minimum standard, unexamined gender and sexual orientation bias no longer controls the outcome. Instead, the decision makers are made to recognize the fundamental respect and dignity due to all persons—respect that precludes degrading sexual and sexist behavior—and to empathize more with the target.

The Reasonable Woman and Essentialism

The reasonable woman standard in sexual harassment cases has been criticized as essentialist for failing to acknowledge explicitly differences in experiences and perceptions among women based on their race, class, sexual orientation, and other attributes. Obviously such differences exist among women, and failure to consider these differences in certain situations can lead to injustice.

Many women, notably women of color, lesbians, and poor women, experience multiple consciousness and multiple oppressions. So do many men. Voicing the multiple-consciousness experience, poet Audre Lorde observed:

> As a Black lesbian feminist comfortable with the many different ingredients of my identity, and a woman committed to racial and sexual freedom from oppression, I find I am constantly being encouraged to pluck out some one aspect of myself and present this as the meaningful whole, eclipsing or denying the other parts of self.

However, Lorde also powerfully noted:

> Some problems we share as women, some we do not. You fear your children will grow up to join patriarchy and testify against you, we fear our children will be dragged from a car and shot down in the street, and you will turn your backs upon the reason they are dying.

Lorde's example illustrates that difference is relational and dependent on what issue is involved. Here, Lorde highlights the difference between black women's and white women's fears for their children. In this particular example, Lorde's experience as a lesbian compared to that of a heterosexual woman is not at issue. Highlighting the different experiences of African American women and white women doesn't *deny* the other parts of herself, because the harm described is essentially racial—black mothers, lesbian or heterosexual, share the fear Lorde describes, which differs from the fear that white lesbian or heterosexual mothers experience. In another context a lesbian's sexual orientation, regardless of her race, might be the basis for the injury. For example, when a state refuses to recognize a marriage between two women, race is not particularly relevant to the injury suffered. In fact, when it comes to same-sex marriage, gender is not particularly relevant either; both gay men's and lesbians' choice of marriage partners of the same sex is the aspect of their personhood that matters.

The facet of a person's identity brought to the forefront varies by context. Focusing on gender through the reasonable woman standard in sexual harassment cases usually does not ask women to deny the other important aspects of themselves. The color of a woman's skin or her sexual orientation or her social status may affect *how* or even *why* she is sexualized, but often her femaleness provides the primary basis for the harmful conduct and the method of subordination.

Martha Minow, in her book *Making All the Difference*, highlights the relational nature of difference. Any one of us, standing alone, is not intrinsically different. Only when compared to someone who represents a societal norm do we become different and, all too often, lesser; the particular difference depends on the particular comparison. For example, Patricia Williams and Zora Neale Hurston have both recalled the moment when they *became* "colored." In "How It Feels to Be Colored Me," Hurston described her experience of leaving home to go to school: "I left Eatonville, the town of the oleanders, as Zora. When I disembarked from the river-boat at Jacksonville, she was no more. It seemed that I had suffered a sea change. I was not Zora of Orange County anymore, I was now a little colored girl." Similarly, Patricia Williams wrote in *The Alchemy of Race and Rights*:

> I remember with great clarity the moment I discovered that I was "colored." I was three and already knew that I was a "Negro"; my parents had told me to be proud of that. But "colored" was something else; it was the totemic evil I had heard my little white friend talking about for several weeks before I finally realized that I was one of *them*. I still remember the crash of that devastating moment of union, union of my joyful body and the terrible power of that devouring symbol of negritude.

Neither Williams nor Hurston was "colored" until someone defined them as colored. Once compared to the unstated norm of whiteness, they were found to be different, to be wanting, to be colored. Similarly, women typically do not experience themselves as sex objects until men make sexuality an issue in inappropriate situations. The intrusion of sex and sexism into the work relationship often changes how a woman perceives herself and is perceived by others, so that she is made to be different, to be inferior, to be female. When this happens, the woman's subordination derives primarily from her gender—not her color, sexual orientation, or class.

Working women share the problem of sexual harassment. The harm a working woman suffers when she is sexually harassed or subjected to sexist behavior primarily involves her gender. In this area, women's commonality vastly exceeds their differences. Women are objectified and sexualized in the workplace *because* they are women, whether they are black or white, heterosexual or lesbian, rich or middle-class or poor. In fact, most of the women who brought the pathbreaking sexual harassment cases were African American, including Michelle Vinson, in whose case the U.S. Supreme Court first recognized hostile environment sexual harassment.

Some courts and commentators would routinely incorporate factors in addition to gender, such as race and sexual orientation, into the sexual harassment determination. The Equal Employment Opportunity Commission's (EEOC's) draft guidelines on harassment which, because of the controversy they engendered, were never promulgated, provided that the "'reasonable person' standard includes consideration of the perspective of persons of the alleged victim's race, color, religion, gender, national origin, age, or disability." Thus, if a black woman claimed hostile environment sexual harassment, it is not clear under the EEOC standard that gender would be the only characteristic considered, even if the claim were solely for sexual harassment. The EEOC's standard might be "a reasonable person who is female" or "a reasonable person who is black and female." In fact, the standard could end up considering numerous aspects of the person's identity even though they were, at most, marginally relevant to the issue of sexual harassment. Thus, for one case, the standard would be "a reasonable person who is black, female, protestant, heterosexual, and middle-class"; for another the standard would be "a reasonable person who is latino, male, agnostic, gay, and poor."

A few courts have espoused such multifaceted standards in sexual harassment cases. For example, the 1994 Ninth Circuit Court of Appeals decision *Nichols v. Frank* noted "a reasonable person is not defined solely by his or her sex. Other immutable traits possessed by the person bringing the charge, including but not limited to race, age, physical or mental disability, and sexual orientation, may in particular cases be relevant to the inquiry as well."

In response to the *Nichols* language, a 1998 case, *Kortan v. State of California*, applied a "reasonable caucasian woman" standard where the target of sexual harassment was a white woman. The *Kortan* approach is problematic where the harassment is not aimed at multiple aspects of the target's personhood. Shifting the focus from women's commonality and toward differences among women will, at a minimum, distract the decision makers. A multifaceted standard creates risks of stereotyping different groups of women based on extraneous factors. It misses the basic point of our proposed reasonable woman standard: a singular, more respectful standard should define the appropriate behavior of the *perpetrator* when the conduct is sexist or sexual and is therefore focused on the target's gender. In such cases, neither the perpetrator's nor the target's race, sexual orientation, or class should be relevant. For example, in the Supreme Court decision *Harris v. Forklift*, that Teresa Harris was white and heterosexual is not relevant to whether her boss sexually harassed her. Asking the decision makers to decide whether her boss's statements, such as "You're a dumb-ass woman" and "You're a woman, what do you know?" along with suggesting that they "go to the Holiday Inn to negotiate" her raise, would have been viewed as severe or pervasive by a reasonable white heterosexual woman suggests that the test for whether sexual harassment is serious enough to be actionable depends on what kind of woman is involved.

In particular, by expressly focusing on the target's race in sexual harassment cases, race-specific standards increase the risk of perpetuating racial stereotypes about women of color. For example, consider what Clarence Thomas allegedly did to Anita Hill, or what the African American defendant in *Meritor* did to Michelle Vinson. Both of these black women very likely had experienced racism in the past. But this time they were injured because they were female. Perhaps race was a factor in *why* they were treated that way; however, the conduct and language involved were directed at their gender, and focusing on race might actually increase dependence on racialized gender stereotypes.

When a woman of color's claim is clearly one of sexual harassment instead of racial harassment, as in Anita Hill's case, racial stereotyping occurs even when race isn't highlighted. As Emma Coleman Jordan points out, Hill's critics combined the myths and stereotypes about women (translate: white women) as hysterical liars who falsely accuse men of sexual abuse with those about black women's sexuality:

> Because . . . Hill is a black woman, she was portrayed not only as delusional, but also as Sapphire: the black, gonad-grinding woman "out of control." The Sapphire image with all of its connotations of black male emasculation resonated within the black community. Hill's status as a black woman multiplied the possible lines of attack by making available additional stereotypes that could be used against her.

Kimberlé Crenshaw argued similarly in "Race, Gender, and Sexual Harassment" that Anita Hill was perceived in a particular stereotypical way because she was a black woman. She incisively criticizes commentators such as sociologist Orlando Patterson, who denied Hill's injury by characterizing Clarence Thomas's behavior as "downhome style courting" that Hill should have found normal and flattering within her and Thomas's culture as African Americans.

The combined racial and sexual stereotyping experienced by women of color makes insertion of race into the reasonable woman standard risky. Inserting sexual orientation or class creates similar risks. When a target is not white, middle-class, and heterosexual, decision makers are likely to harbor negative stereotypes about the *kind* of woman she is. Thus, highlighting a woman's race, class, or sexual orientation as well as her gender increases the risk of stereotypes, such as "hot" Chicana, "submissive" Asian, "loose" African American, "macho" lesbian, "trashy" lower-class white (consider how the media has portrayed Paula Jones), overwhelming the facts. And of course, highlighting a white middle-class woman's race and gender plays into prejudices about such women being more deserving of protection. When the harm suffered is *sexual* or *sexist*, it is pragmatic to focus solely on that aspect of a person that is the fulcrum of her injury: gender. Similarly, when the harm suffered is racial harassment, it makes practical sense to focus solely on her race.

Still, there are times when a woman of color suffers both sexual harassment as a woman and racial harassment as a person of color. There are also times when a woman of color suffers sexual or sexist harassment *because* she is a woman of color. In her 1989 article about the intersection of race and sex, Crenshaw noted, regarding African American women:

> Black women sometimes experience discrimination in ways similar to white women's experiences. . . . Yet often they experience double-discrimination—the combined effects of practices which discriminate on the basis of race, and on the basis of sex. And sometimes, they experience discrimination as Black women—not the sum of race and sex discrimination, but as Black women.

For example, in *Brooms v. Regal Tube Co.*, an African American woman's supervisor showed her racist pornography involving bestiality and a pornographic photo depicting interracial sodomy. This supervisor told her that, as a black woman, she had been hired for the purposes indicated in the photo. In *Washington v. City of Cleveland*, a supervisor constantly sexually propositioned an African American woman employee, rubbed up against her, looked down her blouse, and made sexual comments. He also made various racial comments regarding black women and interracial relations, at one point stating, "Since you like white guys, why not try me out."

Concerns about the intersection of gender and racial harassment have great validity, as do concerns about the intersection of gender and sexual orientation and other important aspects of one's personhood, such as religion, class, disability, and age. In certain cases where, for example, racism and sexism or homophobia and sexism both clearly lie at the heart of the harassment, the target should have the choice of how she presents her claim. Thus, for example, the plaintiff in *Brooms* should be allowed to bring a claim solely for sexual harassment from a reasonable woman's perspective or for both racial harassment assessed from the reasonable African American perspective and sexual harassment assessed from the reasonable woman's perspective. Or, if she prefers, she should be allowed to bring a single claim for harassment assessed from the reasonable African American woman's perspective. In a 1998 article, Tam Tran sets out an appropriate method of determining which cases justify application of a combined test. She recommends that "the reasonable minority woman standard . . . [only] apply . . . if the plaintiff can put forth sufficient facts to satisfy a prima facie finding for both forms of discrimination." We would add that such a standard would apply only if the plaintiff chose to bring a combined claim.

The 1997 Second Circuit Court of Appeals decision *Torres v. Pisano* highlights the problem with mandating application of both a reasonable woman standard and a reasonable person of color standard in cases involving intersectionality. Jenice Torres worked at New York University's Dental Center from 1990 to 1994 as administrative secretary to Eugene Coe, the Dental Center's facilities manager. She was the only woman among approximately thirty employees. Torres experienced harassment because she was a Puerto Rican woman. However, she brought two claims, one for sexual harassment and another for racial harassment. As the court noted, her boss, Coe, "constantly harassed her on the basis of her sex and race." The court listed specific instances of harassment.

Coe: 1) "habitually referred to [Torres] as a 'dumb cunt' or 'dumb spic' in the office"; 2) made insulting remarks about the size of Torres' breasts and buttocks; 3) made sexual innuendoes towards Torres; 4) crudely indicated to other employees his desire to have sex with Torres; 5) frequently told Torres that she should stay home, go on welfare, and collect food stamps like the rest of the "spics"; 6) remarked to other people that when Torres called in sick she was "probably out sucking cocks to earn extra money"; 7) ridiculed Torres' pregnancy, calling her "beer belly" and suggesting she was not smart enough to use birth control; and 8) allowed friends of his who visited him at the office to tell people that Torres "gave a blowjob to every man who came into the office," and to throw money on the table and mockingly order Torres to strip.

Renowned scholar and former dean of Yale Law School Judge Guido Calabresi wrote the opinion for the unanimous court. Judge Calabresi acknowledged that Torres alleged both racial and sexual discrimination. Nevertheless, without explaining why, he treated it as a sexual harassment case, yet assessed some incidents under the reasonable woman standard and others under the reasonable Puerto Rican standard:

A reasonable woman would find her working conditions altered and abusive when her own supervisor repeatedly referred to her as a "dumb cunt," suggested that she was in the habit of performing oral sex for money, ridiculed her pregnancy, commented on her anatomy and his desire to have sex with her, and allowed friends of his who visited him at the office to make crude sexual remarks about her. Likewise, a reasonable Puerto Rican would find a workplace in which her boss repeatedly called her a "dumb spic" and told her that she should stay home, go on welfare, and collect food stamps like the rest of the "spics" to be hostile. Torres has therefore established a strong prima facie case of sexual harassment.

It is commendable that Judge Calabresi acknowledged both the racism and the sexism in this case. However, though probably mandated in the second circuit, Torres may believe that Judge Calabresi's application of two standards, one addressing her sex and the other addressing her race, inadequately assessed her injury as a Puerto Rican woman. Torres might have found Marcia Gillespie's words in *Ms.* magazine reflected her feelings after the court separated out sexual/sexist and racist behavior: "I cannot separate my race from my sex, cannot separate racism from sexism. . . . So don't ask me to choose, I cannot; I am myself, I am not you. Nor will I let you choose for me. And I will not let you pretend that racism and sexism are not inseparable issues."

It is unclear whether Torres had an option of bringing this case as one claim involving harassment of a Puerto Rican woman. Under existing law, her attorneys may have rightly believed that such a claim would be rejected. However, given the option, she might have preferred that the harassment be assessed by a reasonable Puerto Rican woman standard, or she might have preferred that the incidents be assessed by separated standards, as Judge Calabresi did. But she and other women of color should have that choice.

Other courts have separated racial and sexual harassment when a woman of color was the plaintiff. For example, the 1996 federal district court decision *Harley v. McCoach* involved a motion to dismiss Lisa Harley's claims of sexual and racial harassment. Harley, who is black, was one of two women among thirty-five people working in a warehouse. Most of the alleged conduct was sexually offensive—it included workers simulating sexual conduct, telling sexually oriented jokes, and making open displays of sexually oriented magazines. One coworker, Jamie Mazzacano, subjected Harley to unwanted attention and followed her around "like a puppy dog." Other workers placed a sticker on her truck reading "Jamie's main squeeze." Another worker thrust his pelvis and crotch against her backside. A rumor circulated that Harley and a white male employee were having an extramarital affair.

A limited number of incidents involved her race. Harley received an e-mail message addressing her as "Brown Sugar" and was told by one employee that her supervisor had referred to her as a "nigger." When teasing her about the rumored extramarital affair, other workers referred to her as the Whitney Houston character in *The Bodyguard*, a film depicting an interracial love affair.

Like Torres, Harley framed her suit as involving both sexual and racial harassment. The court separated out the incidents and found that she had made a claim for sexual harassment under a reasonable woman standard but had failed to state a claim for racial harassment. As a result, when this case went to trial she was likely allowed to present only evidence of purely gender-based harassment. For example, the use of the name Brown Sugar may have been deemed irrelevant to her sexual harassment claim, since the court viewed it as racial rather than sexual or sexist, when in fact it was both. If Harley had been allowed to bring the claim under a reasonable black woman standard of care, she might have been able to present evidence of all the incidents—whether sexual, racial or both. However, if she had chosen this combined standard, she might have run a risk that some jurors would use racist stereotypes about black women in assessing her claim, which, for the most part, involved sexual or sexist behavior. Again, that should be her choice.

In contrast to the previous two cases, one federal circuit requires that claims involving both racism and sexism be determined under a reasonable woman of color standard of care. The 1996 trial court decision *Anthony v. County of Sacramento* is illustrative. Plaintiff Linda Anthony worked as a deputy sheriff for the defendant county. Anthony alleged numerous instances of harassment. She was called a "black bitch" and frequently overheard other officers refer to black inmates as "tree-swinging," "niggers," and "nappy heads." An empty bottle of over-the-counter medicine for relief of PMS symptoms was left anonymously in Anthony's mailbox. She also received a flyer in her mailbox that said: "Warning, I can go from 0 to Bitch in 1.1 seconds!" Anonymous graffiti at work criticized the "Nigger Deputy Sheriff's Association," commenting: "A mind is a terrible thing to waste. It's too bad niggers didn't get one."

Anthony sued for racial and sexual harassment. In selecting the applicable standard, the court said: "The Ninth Circuit now recognizes combined race and sex discrimination claims." The sufficiency of Anthony's allegations was therefore assessed by "whether a reasonable African-American woman would have considered the conduct sufficiently severe and pervasive to alter the conditions of employment, and create an abusive work environment." The court noted that "where a woman of color alleges that she has been subject to discrimination on the combined bases of her race and gender, it is error for the court to analyze sex and race separately." Thus, in the Ninth Circuit, women of color who allege both racial and sexual harassment must combine the claims.

When the harassment involves both sexual or sexist and racist behavior, a woman of color should have the choice among focusing only on her gender, only on her race, on both her gender and her race in separate claims, or on both in one claim. Lesbians, gay men, and other minorities should also be given the choice of which standard to apply when the harassment involves both gender and another important facet of their personhood. And in the rare case where a man of color is being both sexually and racially harassed, he, too, should have a choice of standards. However, in most cases involving sexual or sexist harassment, regardless of the race, sexual orientation, or other attributes of the person involved, the focus of the conduct is mainly on the target's gender, with its purpose being domination based on gender stereotypes; in these cases, the reasonable woman standard should apply.

Sexual and sexist stereotypes abound about persons of any color or culture. Our purpose is to step away from invidious stereotypes and hold everyone to a minimum standard of respect for the personal, physical, and dignitary rights of others in the workplace. Creating different standards for people of different racial or cultural groups can be misinterpreted as meaning these groups deserve less respectful treatment. If the harassment includes significant injurious racial or other invidious content, the additional discriminatory aspect should be considered *if the target chooses* to have it considered. However, in most cases of sexist or sexual harassment, the reasonable woman should be the standard applied, entitling all persons to the same high standard of respect and dignity.

Questions and Complexities

This chapter teases out an apparent contradiction in our analysis and proposal. Throughout the book, we place great emphasis on the experience of being female. Yet we argue that our standard should apply in male-on-male, female-on-female, and female-on-male contexts, because the harm is analogous; we also argue that courts should usually apply our reasonable woman standard regardless of the race of either the perpetrator or the target. This highlights the inherent tension between our emphasizing women's oppression, thus seeking to make the world a better place for women, and our emphasis on all forms of human oppression, thus seeking to make the world a better place for everyone. We want both, and we believe that changing the fundamental paradigm of gendered subordination will ultimately change the workplace positively for everyone. The particular gender, sexual orientation, or racial label applied to someone should not determine how he or she is treated. Everyone should be treated like a woman who expects her dignity, bodily integrity, and right to self-determination to be respected.

We have demonstrated that the existing reasonable person standard is, in fact, a male standard. The other alternative to our reasonable woman standard is a standard that considers all the various factors that determine personhood. The possible combinations of genders, sexual orientations, races, religions, and cultural groups is mind-boggling. If all the many aspects of a person's social identity were considered in assessing harassment claims where sexualization or sexism were the core harms involved, standards would virtually disappear in the subjective nature of the inquiry. Some commentators have argued for such a purely subjective, "how the target perceived the conduct" test. Under this test, as long as the person claiming injury testified, "I felt sexually harassed in my work environment," her claim would depend entirely on her own credibility; if the decision maker believed her, she would have a valid claim of sexual harassment.

Some favor such a subjective test because it avoids the risk of essentialism. That is, the perceptions of the person claiming injury are not measured against a universalizing "woman" or "person" standard that is likely to reflect white, heterosexual, middle-class values. Her perceptions aren't even measured against a woman of color standard, which would still imply that all women of the plaintiff's race have similar experiences and perceptions. Thus, in theory, each plaintiff would be judged on her individual merits, rather than being held to a standard that may not adequately represent her experiences and perceptions. However, the subjective test provides no guarantee that decision makers will judge women (or men) solely on their individual merits. Ironically, eliminating the "essentialism" of a reasonable woman standard increases the probability of decision makers applying personal standards that include unexamined biases and assumptions about the values and experiences of women, particularly women of color, lesbians, and working-class and poor women.

The purely subjective test poses other problems precisely *because* the inquiry focuses entirely on the individual woman claiming injury. Instead, the primary focus should be on the conduct of the alleged harasser and the employer. To change workplaces so that women, both as individuals and as a group, achieve meaningful equality requires that some universalized standard of behavior be imposed on all workers and employers. A subjective test fails to do this—male workers' conduct would not be held to any standard beyond that of the individual women with whom they work. In the legal arena, each case would be entirely fact and plaintiff specific, providing little guidance for subsequent cases. As a result, in contrast to our reasonable woman standard, which has substantive content that would provide guidance to employers, under a subjective test employers would have no meaningful legal guidelines about what sexual behavior is appropriate in the workplace.

Without standards, employers might be reluctant to have gender-integrated workplaces, fearing that any woman who overheard an off-color joke, who was touched in any way or asked out once by a male coworker, or who just didn't feel comfortable with how someone looked at her could recover for sexual harassment. Employers would also be likely to adopt policies discouraging or even prohibiting men and women traveling together or even dining out together on business. Such responses would inevitably reduce employment opportunities more for women than for men. In contrast, applying our reasonable woman standard to everyone would eliminate any reason for employers to prefer men or women, or people of any particular race over another. In fact, in male-only workplaces where men are harassed "like women" and no reasonable woman could thrive, applying our reasonable woman standard to the harassment of men by men would most likely make the workplace one that even women could tolerate.

The subjective test has other drawbacks. Focusing solely on the person claiming injury increases the risk that some women will be viewed as unharassable; because of what she wears, what she talks about, or whom she socializes with, a woman may not be believed when she claims injury. Also, a purely subjective standard lacks the necessary linguistic resonance needed to change the legal paradigm. Like the word *rights*, the word *reasonableness* lends legitimacy to legal claims. A reasonableness test that is applied to everyone regardless of gender, race, sexual orientation, or class acknowledges that society as a whole views certain behavior as unacceptable and that penalizing such behavior appears just. In short, the rhetoric of reasonableness involves a mythology too influential to be abandoned.

We recognize that the rationales supporting our reasonable woman standard become more tenuous outside "simple" male-on-female sexual or sexist harassment. Nevertheless, except in situations involving intersectionality, uniform application of our reasonable woman standard to all forms of sexual harassment provides the best, albeit imperfect, means of eliminating debilitating gender stereotypes and creating an equality that respects and values, rather than punishes, difference.

6

The Reasonable Woman after *Harris v. Forklift Systems*

After *Harris*, courts still disagree about whether to apply the reasonable woman or the reasonable person standard to the hostile work environment determination. We believe that shifting the boundary between acceptable and unacceptable workplace behavior by applying the reasonable woman standard will help accomplish the goal of equality in the workplace. This standard, fleshed out to require respectful treatment consistent with equality, will affect the outcome in cases on the margin and encourage employers to create workplace norms that foster treating women as workers rather than as sex objects or intruders.

The post-*Harris* cases in this chapter illustrate how the reasonable woman standard might make a difference in close cases—cases in which a jury could plausibly decide in favor of either party. Three of the cases arose in the Seventh Circuit, well known for its smart but conservative judges. The fourth case, which arose in the Fourth Circuit, starkly demonstrates why harassment law must address anti-woman conduct even when that conduct is not explicitly sexual.

Most harassers choose to harass. The following cases show that harassers can and do change when faced with serious consequences. In every case where a superior told the alleged harasser to stop or be penalized, he stopped. And in every case where the harasser was the boss, he stopped when warned about the liability risks. If continuing—or starting—to harass will cost them professionally or economically, harassers change their behavior. They *can* behave like reasonable women—they simply choose not to unless the cost becomes too high.

Once a Model, Always a Model: Dellert v. Total Vision, Inc.

Dellert v. Total Vision, Inc. was decided in 1995. The trial judge refused to allow the case to be tried because she concluded that, based on the essential facts, no reasonable person could find that the challenged conduct created a hostile work environment. In this case, the only voice is that of the judge who dismissed the case. She uses a paper record based on pleadings and supporting documents to present the facts in a way that justifies the outcome she reaches. When there are ambiguities, we are left to conjecture. A trial would have fleshed these ambiguities out and required the decision makers to observe and listen to witnesses subjected to cross-examination.

The plaintiff should be denied her day in court only when the outcome is clear. Had the judge applied a reasonable woman standard that requires a woman to be treated with respect in the workplace, a jury probably would have been allowed to decide whether plaintiff was sexually harassed. Instead, the judge held that under the reasonable person standard, the alleged harasser's conduct was so clearly legally permissible that a jury must not be allowed to decide otherwise.

The plaintiff, Jill Dellert, was hired for an entry-level optician position at Total Vision, Inc. (TVI). All the other employees mentioned in the judge's opinion were men. The alleged perpetrator, Tony Mackin, like the defendant in *Harris*, was the company president. However, because Mackin lived in California and the store where Dellert worked was in Chicago, he played no part in hiring Dellert. Before being hired by TVI, Dellert worked as a model of sportswear, casual wear, and business attire. The judge deemed it necessary to mention in her written opinion that Dellert had, on one occasion, modeled lingerie for Sears and included in her modeling portfolio some photos of herself "in a conservative swimsuit." The opinion is silent as to whether anyone at TVI ever saw this portfolio, during the hiring process or later.

While Dellert worked at TVI, Mackin visited the Chicago store four or five times. He also phoned the store regularly for both business and "chitchat." Soon after Dellert began working, Mackin visited and, on meeting her, commented on her previous work as a model and on the fact that she was engaged. His remarks did not offend Dellert, but she thought they were unnecessary.

Two weeks after Dellert started her job, Mackin visited again. While looking at a new shipment of eyeglasses, Mackin asked Dellert to try on a pair. When she did, he commented that they would look much better on her if she wasn't wearing a skirt. A male employee was present in the store when this incident occurred, but the court is silent as to whether he heard this comment. Obviously, whether the comment was overheard or at least whether Dellert thought it had been overheard is important in assessing its impact.

During the same visit, Mackin brought in a photo that he said he was considering using for an eyewear ad. The photo depicted a female model lying on her stomach with her back completely naked and most of her buttocks showing, with glass frames balanced on her back. Mackin showed this photo to all the employees, including Dellert and her male supervisor. Mackin then commented to Dellert's supervisor in front of Dellert: "This is why I can't have Dellert model for us. If she were in this position, I would have to jump her."

Later that day, Dellert and Mackin had a conversation about different kinds of film processes that could be used for ads. Dellert offered to show Mackin how various types of film looked by showing him black-and-white photos, color photos, and laser prints from her modeling portfolio. Within earshot of her male supervisor and male coworker, Mackin responded: "Do you have any pictures of you in sexy lingerie or bikinis? If not, I don't want to see it." Thus, Dellert's boss totally disregarded her as having anything useful to offer as an employee and instead treated her ideas as jokes and her as a sexual object.

Shortly thereafter Dellert complained to her supervisor. The supervisor did not inform Mackin. Instead, he told Dellert that Mackin "was a little rough around the edges and that she should not let him affect her." In other words, the company response to Dellert's complaints of unwelcome sexualized conduct was "get used to it."

Over the next two months, Mackin asked Dellert by phone on five to ten occasions if she was still engaged. During his visits, he also made a number of sexual comments about women's bodies. However, the judge noted that "the evidence does not indicate Ms. Dellert heard him make these comments." The judge noted further that Mackin "made one such statement in front of a female eyeglass representative." She added that Mackin also made crude remarks "about pretty women who were customers or passersby such as 'God, those are big' or 'God, those are great legs'" but noted that Dellert did not claim that she heard Mackin make these comments. Again, without a trial we cannot be sure how much Dellert heard, either directly or secondhand.

The next month, Dellert phoned Mackin to discuss a raise. Mackin said he needed to talk it over with his partners and get back to her. Dellert explained that she was going to be off work during the time he planned to call back, so Mackin asked for her home phone number and Dellert gave it to him. Mackin then asked her whom she lived with. When she explained that she lived with two female roommates, Mackin responded by saying "he would be right over." This was intended as a joke, since Mackin was in California. Still, Dellert viewed Mackin's inquiry as to whom she lived with and his response offensive. She therefore complained again to her supervisor, who this time spoke to Mackin. After learning of Dellert's objections to his conduct, Mackin stopped all his comments, including those about her marital status. Three months later Dellert resigned, telling her supervisor that "she could not work in a situation where she did not know where or when the sexual comments would recur."

In reviewing this evidence, the trial judge applied both the subjective and the objective prong of the Supreme Court's *Harris* test. Thus, she considered "the actual effect" of Mackin's conduct on Dellert "as well as the effect similar conduct would have on a reasonable person in Ms. Dellert's position." The "reasonable person in Dellert's position" test could have been interpreted explicitly to include Dellert's gender and the power differential between her and Mackin. However, it does not appear that the judge considered either of these factors. And while the judge found sufficient evidence for a jury to conclude that "the actual effect" on Dellert was that "she subjectively perceived her work environment to be hostile and abusive," she held that objectively no reasonable person could find that Mackin's conduct was "severe or pervasive enough to create an objectively hostile or abusive work environment."

The circumstances that the judge found relevant to the issue of whether "severe and pervasive" were limited. First, she concluded that Mackin's repeated queries about Dellert's engagement and the comments made outside Dellert's hearing could not be considered. Thus, the judge concluded that, from a reasonable person's perspective, these comments couldn't conceivably be factors in making Mackin's conduct "severe or pervasive."

The only conduct the judge considered occurred in four separate incidents: Mackin's comment that Dellert would look better "without wearing a skirt"; his comment that he "would have to jump her"; his not being interested in her portfolio if there were no bikini photos; and saying "I'll be right over." Of these four comments, the first two were deemed "objectively offensive in the context of the workplace." However, the judge found this conduct insufficient to create a hostile environment because the comments were "each made once, during a one- or two-day period early in Ms. Dellert's employment." The judge completely discounted the sexist comment about Dellert's modeling portfolio, made during the same visit. She noted that it was "undoubtedly embarrassing to her and . . . certainly rude [but] considering that her job did not in any way involve modeling or photography [it was not] sexual harassment." The judge's assessment of these incidents would likely be different under a reasonable woman standard, because the timing of the comments during the first two weeks of Dellert's job could be viewed as intending to put her in her place, both as a subordinate and, more important, as a woman.

Regarding Mackin's inquiry about whom Dellert lived with and his response when she told him, the judge noted that there was no valid "reason for Mr. Mackin to have asked her who she lived with but it is also clear that Mr. Mackin was not about to come right over and that Ms. Dellert knew that [because] [s]he called Mr. Mackin in California, where he lived." From the neutered perspective of a reasonable person, the questions about Dellert's marital status and whom she lived with were viewed as inoffensive. And since it was clearly intended as a joke, Mackin's statement that he'd be right over was harmless kidding.

If the judge had viewed these facts from the perspective of a reasonable woman who wishes to be treated with respect in the workplace—to be treated as a worker rather than as a sex object—it is likely these comments would have been seen as more offensive and discriminatory. They would more obviously be part of a pattern of lecherous presumptions about female subordinates. Had the judge believed that the perspective for measuring "severe or pervasive" conduct was that of a reasonable woman, she might have concluded there was sufficient evidence of a hostile environment to allow the jury to decide this case.

The United States Supreme Court's reasonableness test for assessing the alleged harasser's conduct in a hostile environment sexual harassment case is from the perspective of the person claiming discrimination. As stated in its 1998 *Oncale* decision, "The objective severity of harassment should be judged from the perspective of a reasonable person in the plaintiff's position, considering 'all the circumstances.'" The trial judge's application of the objective prong in *Dellert* does not sufficiently consider the gendered and degrading nature of the comments that Mackin made.

All Mackin's behavior that Dellert complains of was attributable to her gender. The four comments that the judge in *Dellert* considered had sexual connotations and were made because Dellert was a woman. Many of the incidents the judge failed to consider were also gender based. Even though not explicitly sexual, the constant questioning about Dellert's marital status was based on her gender: it is highly improbable that Mackin would have repeatedly asked a male employee if he was still engaged. At a minimum, his repeated inquiries were sexist. More likely, Mackin's continued focus on this aspect of Dellert's private life suggested sexual interest on his part. Thus, the evidence presented can be viewed as satisfying what Justices Ginsberg and Scalia have described as the critical test for finding sex discrimination based on a hostile environment: exposing Dellert to "disadvantageous terms or conditions of employment to which members of the other sex are not exposed."

In *Oncale,* the Court said "harassment cases . . . require . . . careful consideration of the social context in which particular behavior occurs and is experienced by its target." In assessing all of Mackin's comments and inquiries, it makes a huge difference that he was Dellert's boss. It is much more risky to tell your boss "Mind your own business" than to tell a coworker, especially when you are new on the job and in an entry-level position. Mackin's position as Dellert's boss—as the company president—made his comments that much more abusive. He abused his power by sexualizing his relationship with a newly hired female employee. A reasonable woman in Dellert's position would very likely have found his conduct humiliating and a form of taking advantage because it denied her identity as a worker.

In determining whether Dellert's workplace was a hostile work environment, the trial judge held that Mackin's antiwoman conduct outside Dellert's presence was not relevant. Under a reasonable woman standard, the fact that Mackin, as company president, set a tone that was contemptuous of women is pertinent to the issue of whether a hostile environment for women existed. The men who worked for Mackin heard him make sexist comments about women, including customers. At least one of these comments was made in front of a female eyeglass representative. Most likely this pattern of behavior affected what conduct toward women other male employees viewed as acceptable in the workplace. It is therefore probable, in such a small workplace, that such conduct tainted the environment for Dellert.

Dellert is a close case. On the one hand, even under a reasonable woman standard, it is conceivable that a jury might have found Mackin's conduct, while offensive and obnoxious, not sufficiently severe or pervasive to create a hostile working environment. On the other hand, a jury might have found the evidence sufficient for a reasonable woman to have viewed the workplace at TVI as hostile to women and therefore allowed Dellert to prevail. The judge's application of a reasonable person test in screening this case on a paper record and deciding it wouldn't go to a jury eliminated Dellert's opportunity to try to convince the jury, through her own testimony and that of her coworkers, that Mackin's conduct was sexual harassment. Considering how important the demeanor and credibility of witnesses are in cases such as this one, justice was not served by denying Dellert her day in court.

Smoke Gets in Your Eyes: Baskerville v. Culligan International Company

Baskerville v. Culligan International Company, decided shortly after *Dellert,* also arose in the Seventh Circuit. The one voice presented is that of an influential appellate judge, Chief Judge Richard Posner. The trial judge, in an unreported decision, conducted a jury trial. The jury found that the plaintiff was sexually harassed and awarded her $25,000. On appeal, Judge Posner's decision for a three-judge panel held that the trial judge erred by letting the jury decide the case because no reasonable person could have found the alleged harasser's conduct to have been severe or pervasive enough to constitute actionable sexual harassment.

Judge Posner described the events that resulted in this lawsuit as follows:

> Baskerville was hired on July 9, 1991, as a secretary in the marketing department of Culligan, a manufacturer of products for treating water. A month later she was assigned to work for Michael Hall, the newly hired Western Regional Manager. Baskerville testified . . . to the following acts

of sexual harassment of her by Hall between the date of his hire and February 1992, a period of seven months:

1. He would call her "pretty girl," as in "There's always a pretty girl giving me something to sign off on."

2. Once, when she was wearing a leather skirt, he made a grunting sound that sounded like "um, um, um" as she turned to leave his office.

3. Once when she commented on how hot his office was, he raised his eyebrows and said, "Not until you stepped your foot in here."

4. Once when the announcement "May I have your attention, please" was broadcast over the public-address system, Hall stopped at Baskerville's desk and said, "You know what that means, don't you? All pretty girls run around naked."

5. He once called Baskerville a "tilly," explaining that he uses the term for all women.

6. He once told her that his wife had told him he had "better clean up my act" and "better think of you as Ms. Anita Hill."

7. When asked by Baskerville why he had left the office Christmas Party early, Hall replied that there were so many pretty girls there that he "didn't want to lose control, so I thought I'd better leave."

8. Once when she complained that his office was "smokey" from cigarette smoke, Hall replied, "Oh, really? Were we dancing, like in a nightclub?"

9. When she asked him whether he had gotten his wife a Valentine's Day card, he responded that he had not but he should because it was lonely in his hotel room (his wife had not yet moved to Chicago) and all he had for company was his pillow. Then Hall looked ostentatiously at his hand. The gesture was intended to suggest masturbation.

Three months after she started working for Hall, Baskerville complained to his supervisor about three of the incidents. Hall's supervisor spoke to him about her concerns "apparently with some acerbity, because Hall reported to Baskerville that his supervisor had taken a big bite out of his behind." Nevertheless, the behavior continued until Baskerville complained again, three months later, this time to the company's resources department. When the company responded by again telling Hall to stop and also placing him on probation and holding up his salary increase for several months, "he got the point. He ceased the offensive behavior immediately, and there was no recurrence."

This is a problematic case, in part because the employer appeared to respond promptly to Hall's complaints. In fact, Judge Posner found that the trial court erred in finding the company liable for Hall's conduct "because the company took all reasonable steps to protect [Baskerville] from Hall." The appellate court could have limited its basis for reversing the trial court to the employer liability issue. Instead, Judge Posner also instructed the lower court, as well as judges and attorneys in future cases, about when conduct is actionable sexual harassment. He concluded that *Baskerville* was a case of mere juvenile boorishness. The line he drew is critical, not only with regard to when courts will find sexual harassment but also with regard to when employers will take employee complaints seriously. The employer in *Baskerville* had responded promptly and effectively to Baskerville's complaint, which is why reversing the trial court decision was appropriate here. Judge Posner's discussion of Hall's conduct as merely a silly boss's shenanigans will make it less likely that employers will take similar employee complaints seriously.

Unquestionably, it was a close case whether Hall's conduct was "severe or pervasive." The conduct was not extreme. Some of Hall's comments, such as the use of the word *tilly* and the reference to Anita Hill, appear to be relatively innocuous. Other comments, the "um, um, um" sound, and the masturbation gesture are more obviously sexual and problematic. However, at least under certain circumstances they would likely not be sufficiently severe or pervasive to create a hostile environment under either a reasonable person or a reasonable woman standard.

Hall's repeated use of "pretty girl" raises the issue of whether such a term, which is more sexist than sexual, should be viewed as abusive. Under our proposed reasonable woman standard, sexist conduct is to be scrutinized as closely as sexual conduct. The implication of Hall's use of "pretty girl" toward Baskerville, especially after he was told to stop, is that she's *just* a pretty girl—not a person, not even a woman, certainly not someone to be reckoned with. "Pretty girl" connotes someone who is valued as part of the scenery—as ornamental—and not for her skills or ability. It is clearly gendered. "Pretty girl" and "pretty boy" are both demeaning but have very different gendered connotations. Consider how unlikely it is that a boss would ever call one of his male subordinates "pretty boy." Consider how negatively, in our homophobic society, use of such a term toward a man would be viewed. It, too, should be viewed as abusive under the reasonable woman standard.

Judge Posner never says whether the standard applied is that of a reasonable person or a reasonable woman. However, his description of what he believes must be shown before an environment is sufficiently abusive or hostile to merit a legal finding of sexual harassment strongly suggests a lack of empathy for Baskerville and other working women:

> The concept of sexual harassment is designed to protect working women from the kind of male attention that can make the workplace hellish for women. . . . It is not designed to purge the workplace of vulgarity. . . . On one side lie sexual assaults; other physical contact, whether amorous or hostile, for which there is no consent express or implied; uninvited sexual solicitations; intimidating words or acts; obscene language or gestures; pornographic pictures. . . . On the other side lies the occasional vulgar banter, tinged with sexual innuendo, of coarse or boorish workers.

A reasonable woman who expects to be treated, as the Fifth Circuit Court of Appeals described in *Bennett v. Corroon & Black Corp.*, "with professional dignity and without the barrier of sexual differentiation and abuse" may find that Judge Posner's distinctions have validity where the alleged harasser is a peer rather than a supervisor. Depending on the context, if a coworker had said such things to Baskerville, they might amount to no more than offensive annoyances that would best be dealt with by her ignoring him, telling him stop, and then, if he didn't, reporting him. However, in this case, as in *Dellert* and *Harris*, the alleged harasser was plaintiff's supervisor, who had substantial power to affect her working conditions and terms of employment. Judge Posner does not pay sufficient attention to the difference in how words and gestures can affect an employee when the actor is the boss rather than a coworker.

In deciding that "no reasonable jury could find that Hall's remarks created a hostile working environment," Judge Posner said the following about Hall's conduct:

> He never touched the plaintiff. He did not invite her, explicitly or by implication, to have sex with him, or to go out on a date with him. He made no threats. He did not expose himself, or show her dirty pictures. He never said anything that could not be said on primetime television. . . . Some of his repartee, such as "Not until you stepped your foot in here," or, "Were we dancing, like in a nightclub?" has the sexual charge of an Abbott and Costello movie. The reference to masturbation completes the impression of a man whose sense of humor took final shape in adolescence.

Hall's conduct was more juvenile and boorish than predatory and assaultive. But that was also true of the conduct the Supreme Court found to be actionable in *Harris*. The critical issue is whether a supervisor who behaves this way toward his subordinate, particularly after he has been told to stop, sufficiently alters his employee's working conditions to create a hostile work environment. The answer to that question is likely to depend on whether the conduct is viewed from a reasonable person (translate: man) or a reasonable woman standard.

In a close case such as this one, not only the standard of care but the demeanor and credibility of the parties and of witnesses as they place the conduct in context may be decisive. After listening to the testimony the jury, viewing this case from a woman worker's perspective, might find Hall's comments to have been annoying but relatively inoffensive; or they might find, as they apparently did in this case, that Hall's comments amounted to abuse and actionable sex discrimination. As Judge Posner notes, there are "dangers . . . in trying to assess the impact of words without taking account of gestures, inflection, the physical propinquity of speaker and hearer, the presence or absence of other persons, and other aspects of context." Under a reasonable woman standard, this case might go either way. That decision was for the jury, not an appellate court, to make.

Dellert and *Baskerville* raise another concern. Does allowing a jury to find liability in such cases make women appear prudish and overly sensitive rather than reasonable and deserving of respect as equals? Judge Posner believes it does. He comments, in describing what he calls Hall's "shenanigans," that "it is no doubt distasteful to a sensitive woman to have such a silly man as one's boss, but only a woman of Victorian delicacy—a woman mysteriously aloof from contemporary American popular culture in all its sex-saturated vulgarity—would find Hall's patter substantially more distressing than the heat and cigarette smoke of which the plaintiff does not complain." Of course, we have no way of knowing if Baskerville also complained about the heat and smoke; and there may not have been any administrative or legal remedy for exposure to heat or cigarette smoke, unlike exposure to sexist language, so that complaining would have been fruitless.

The fact that women are treated badly outside the workplace should not be used to justify treating them badly in the workplace. It appears that Judge Posner, like the majority in *Rabidue*, believes a woman's work environment must be considered "in the context of a society that condones and publicly features and commercially exploits open displays of written and pictorial erotica in the newsstands, on prime-time television, at the cinema, and in other public places." But in the workplace, one cannot easily avert one's eyes or turn the channel. Workers are captive audiences. Without a sexual harassment remedy, they can either endure sexist and sexual conduct, even if it interferes with their work, or quit. Judge Posner's view perpetuates sexism and subordination of women at work and in society. In contrast, when coworkers and supervisors are required to treat women with respect, as true equals in the workplace, the atmosphere outside the workplace is likely to change for the better, too.

Other judges are concerned that the reasonable woman in particular encourages stereotypes of women as delicate, overly sensitive beings. Consider the following comments made by Judge Edith Jones in *DeAngelis v. El Paso Municipal Police Officers Ass'n* in 1995:

> A claim for a sexually hostile working environment is not a trivial matter. Its purpose is to level the playing field for women who work by preventing others from impairing their ability to compete on an equal basis with men. One must always bear this ultimate goal in mind.

So far so good. However, in critiquing a reasonable woman standard that she rejects as subjective, Judge Jones continues:

> In fact, a less onerous standard of liability would attempt to insulate women from everyday insults as if they remained models of Victorian reticence. A lesser standard of liability would mandate not equality but preference for women: it would create incentives for employers to bend over backwards in women's favor for fear of lawsuits. Now that most American women are working outside the home, in a broad range of occupations and with ever-increasing responsibility, it seems perverse to claim that they need the protection of a preferential standard. The careful heightened phrasing of a hostile environment claim, enforceable where working conditions have palpably deteriorated because of sexually hostile conduct, aims to enforce equality, not preference.

Judge Jones interprets equality in male terms—as long as women are treated the same as men, as one of the boys, they are men's equals. This kind of equality is not helpful to either men or women. Judge Jones might have a valid point if the "reasonable woman" standard were subjective and applicable only when women were the targets. However, it is neither. Our reasonable woman standard gives men the same "preferential" treatment as women. It does not look at the conduct at issue from the perspective of the individual plaintiff. Instead, regardless of the gender of either party, it steers the decision makers' focus away from the target and onto the alleged harasser. It asks the decision maker to determine how a reasonable woman in the alleged perpetrator's position would behave under the circumstances; how a reasonable woman who demands respect in the workplace would assess the alleged harasser's conduct; and how such a reasonable woman would have responded to the target's conduct. There is nothing Victorian or idiosyncratic about such a standard of care. It is intended to achieve the goals that Judge Jones seeks and is more likely to do so than the masculine reasonable person standard she endorses.

"My Girl": Eckroth v. Rockford Products Co.

Eckroth v. Rockford Products Co. is an unreported 1996 trial court decision that arose in the Seventh Circuit and for which *Baskerville* is precedent. Like *Baskerville*, it addresses two issues: Was the actor's conduct sufficiently severe or pervasive to create a hostile work environment? Did the employer act reasonably in dealing with the plaintiff's complaints? Here, the judge determined that the plaintiff provided sufficient evidence to allow a jury to find the environment sexually hostile; however, he still dismissed her case because he found that the employer had responded reasonably to her complaints. The conduct described in this case again raises the issue of where the boundary between offensive but nonactionable conduct and unlawful sexual harassment should lie. But unlike in the two previous cases, the judge in *Eckroth* expressly applies a reasonable woman standard. His application of a woman-based standard is arguably decisive to his finding that the conduct could reasonably be viewed as creating a hostile work environment.

Nancy Eckroth was employed as a drill operator by Rockford Products, Co., from July 1991 until September 1992. Eckroth accused her coworker and team leader Arthur Whitaker of harassing her. While the court notes that he did not supervise her or anyone else, his leadership role is likely to have given him some evaluative power over Eckroth. The trial judge described the conduct at issue as follows:

In July 1991, Whitaker kissed Eckroth on her cheek and told a temporary employee who was present, "this is my girl." In August 1991, Eckroth was bending over her machine, whereupon Whitaker commented that she should bend over a little further. In September 1991, while Eckroth had her leg raised while she was tying her shoe, Whitaker told her he could see up her shorts, although she knew [this was] impossible . . . because of the manner in which she was standing. In October 1991, Eckroth asked Whitaker for a 10-inch copper tube, whereupon Whitaker stated: "Sure you can handle 10 inches?" In November 1991, after Eckroth asked for some nuts and bolts, Whitaker responded: "I have got some nuts for you." Between December 1991 and February 1992, Whitaker made various comments to Eckroth about bending over her machine, his sex life and her sex life, although Eckroth does not remember any specifics or the dates upon which Whitaker made the comments. The frequency of these comments ranged from once or twice a week to once every two weeks. In May 1992, Whitaker again made comments about Eckroth bending over her machine and also stated to her that "once you go black you never go back." In July 1992, Whitaker made a sexual gesture towards Eckroth by putting a popsicle in his mouth with the comment "Remind you of anything?" Approximately a half-hour later, Whitaker commented that he could see Eckroth's nipples.

Soon after the July 1992 incidents, Eckroth reported Whitaker's conduct to her employer's director of operations and director of human resources. The same day both directors met with Whitaker about Eckroth's complaint. They told him that such behavior would not be tolerated and that he would be fired if it continued. Whitaker said he would stop and that he would apologize to Eckroth. Whitaker did apologize and made no further sexual comments to Eckroth. Whitaker was also denied a raise because of the behavior that Eckroth reported.

In reviewing Eckroth's sexual harassment claim against her employer based on Whitaker's conduct, the trial judge concluded that the company had acted reasonably and therefore dismissed her case. However, before reaching this conclusion, he discussed whether the conduct alleged was sufficiently severe or pervasive to justify allowing a jury to find sexual harassment. He found that Eckroth subjectively perceived the environment as hostile and then addressed whether Whitaker's conduct created an objectively hostile work environment. The judge quoted the "kind of male attentions than can make the workplace hellish for women" language from Judge Posner's *Baskerville* opinion. Based on that language, the judge noted that he "would have little difficulty in concluding that the various incidents, if considered separately, were not severe or pervasive enough to create an objectively hostile work environment."

But the trial judge did not consider the incidents separately. Instead, he asserted that a judge "must also consider the possible cumulative effect these incidents would have upon a *reasonable woman* in Eckroth's position." He then did just that, noting:

> The court is presented with eight distinct incidents and with some evidence (albeit slight) that Whitaker made frequent comments to Eckroth between December 1991 and February 1992 when she would bend over. Apart from the weekly or bi-monthly comments between December and February the exact nature of which is unclear, the different incidents occurred relatively infrequently, scattered approximately a month apart over a period of twelve months. . . . While the court regards this as a close issue . . . it is of the opinion that a reasonable jury could find the remarks as objectively creating a hostile work environment.

The alleged conduct in this case is more egregious than that in *Dellert* and *Baskerville*. In particular, Whitaker actually touched Eckroth, and his sexual comments were made fairly regularly. If Whitaker had been Eckroth's supervisor, these distinctions might explain the different legal conclusion in this case, even though one kiss on the cheek is relatively innocuous and most of the sexual comments were not described with any specificity. However, a critical difference here is that Whitaker was *not* Eckroth's supervisor. And although he probably had some power over her as team leader, the severity of the actor's conduct was not as exacerbated by abuse of power as it had been in the previous cases. A likely explanation for the finding that the conduct was sufficiently severe or pervasive is the court's application of the reasonable woman standard of care. A reasonable woman who wishes to be viewed and treated as an equal in the workplace would find such conduct from a coworker crossed the line, whereas a reasonable man/person might not.

Whoever Heard of a Woman Truck Driver? Munday v. Waste Mgmt. of North America

The final post-*Harris* case, *Munday*, highlights how the reasonable person standard both fails to consider antiwoman conduct as harassment when it is not explicitly sexual and fails adequately to recognize the gendered hostility women face when working in nontraditional jobs.

Munday involved a female truck driver in an otherwise all-male environment. Truck driving had been Dawn Munday's career all her working life. Before going to work for the defendant, Munday and her former husband had been independent truck drivers, operating their own rig; after leaving the defendant's employ, Munday continued to work as a truck driver.

None of the four judges who examined this case openly acknowledged Munday's isolated position or that she was doing stereotypically male work. Yet these clearly were major reasons that she was treated with hostility. All the other employees mentioned in this case were men, and according to Munday's attorney, during the four years at issue, except for a short time period, Munday was the only woman truck driver. Furthermore, during most of her employment there were no female dispatchers; the only other female employees were clerical workers, whose jobs fit traditional expectations for women's work.

When Robert Bohager, general manager of Waste Management of Maryland, Inc., hired Munday as a truck driver, he warned her "that her job duties would be tough ones." But Munday, as an experienced truck driver, had previously proved herself capable of handling such tough duties. However, from the beginning her gender was the basis for making her job more difficult. The trial court summarized Munday's testimony about her treatment as follows:

> First, John Utterback, a dispatcher . . . who kept the key to the women's bathroom, regularly denied Munday access to the bathroom, which was the only women's bathroom on the premises. Moreover, Utterback repeatedly made comments to her such as, "How bad do you have to go?", and "Can't you hold it in?". Second, she received less pay than her male co-workers. Third, when she asked to have extra work assigned to her, Fred Heider, her immediate supervisor, remarked that she had "one strike against her because she was a woman" and that she should not be in her job "taking food out of the mouths of men." Fourth, when she was assigned additional work, more often than not, her pay was not adjusted to compensate her for the added undertaking until she complained of the same. Fifth, her paperwork, including her route and schedule, was constantly placed in the "driver's lounge," which was in actuality the men's changing area and bathroom. Sixth, drivers and dispatchers made comments and jokes over the two-way radio installed in every truck, in-

cluding comments that Munday was "on the rag" and "under sexual pressure."

After nine months of working under these hostile conditions, Munday was fired for insubordination when she walked off the job because she was not provided with a truck in proper working order. She then filed a state sexual harassment claim. Other employees informed the Maryland Office of Human Rights investigator Robert Coggins that "Munday was constantly the subject of jokes and that her paperwork was often left in the men's changing area." This meant that, to do her job, Munday had to go into what served as the men's room for more than thirty male coworkers. In addition, Coggins concluded that Munday's immediate supervisor, Fred Heider, lied at the behest of his supervisors when he told Coggins he had been admonished for telling Munday that she had one strike against her and that by working as a truck driver she was taking food out of men's mouths. Even though Munday complained about these comments to her supervisors and was assured that Heider had been reprimanded, in fact Heider was not reprimanded for these clearly sexist comments. This lie was revealed when Heider told Coggins that he "was not willing falsely to testify under oath."

As a result of the Human Rights Office investigation, defendant Waste Management agreed to reinstate Munday, expunge her termination from her employment record, provide adequate restroom facilities, and not retaliate against her for having filed the sexual harassment claim. However, the trial court concluded that Munday's boss, Bohager, "determined that when Munday returned to work, [he] would, without getting himself into trouble, handle Munday in such a way that she would find work sufficiently unpleasant and would, given sufficient passage of time, herself determine not to continue her employment." To carry out this plan, Bohager held a meeting of approximately thirty to thirty-five male drivers prior to Munday's return and "told the assembled drivers to have as little to do with Munday as possible and not to socialize with her as they did with other drivers and had done with Munday prior to her discharge."

When Munday returned to work on July 8, 1991, she found the new women's bathroom was located in a trailer in an unsafe, dark area, lacked proper supplies, and was not hooked up to the water supply. Following orders, Munday's fellow drivers refused to talk to her even when she spoke directly to them. Eventually some of the drivers apologized to Munday for snubbing her and explained that they had been acting on orders from above. At least one employee also told Munday that Bohager had instructed them to report back to him anything Munday said. At trial Bohager denied this, but the trial court concluded that he was lying. On July 26, 1991, Munday's immediate supervisor, Heider, told Munday that Bohager had instructed the other drivers "not to talk to the bitch," and that Bohager had told him that he wanted to get rid of Munday before she could "retire the company." That same day Munday met with Bohager to discuss her concerns about the bathroom and about the other drivers' behavior toward her, both issues of discriminatory treatment. Bohager did not respond to these concerns, saying that he "didn't give a shit" about her problems. Instead he exploded at her, "yelling that he had heard a rumor that Munday had stated that she would be suing defendant again." He demanded "that she admit such an intention," which she denied. At trial Bohager testified that this was not what happened at the meeting, but the trial court, relying on the contrary testimony of Munday—which was corroborated by Operations Manager Chad Johnson, who also attended the meeting—concluded once again that Bohager was lying.

Based on her doctor's order, Munday took disability leave from August 1991 until March 1992. When she returned to work on March 23, 1992, the other drivers still refused to talk to her, and the driver who was designated to train her for a new route refused to help her. Thus, the one woman truck driver continued to be treated as a pariah. The method of ostracizing her was gendered. She learned that rumors had been spread among the other employees that she was a lesbian but also that she had sex on the premises with male coworkers. Munday missed more work, partly due to a work-related knee injury and partly because of what the trial court described as "so-called panic attacks while driving on her route." The inclusion of the adjective *so-called* indicates that the trial judge found her claim of illness to be either suspect or trivial. On October 26, 1992, while on disability leave from Waste Management, Munday began a new job with East Coast Sweeping.

The discriminating and harassing conduct Munday described can obviously be attributed to her gender. As Vicki Schultz noted in "Reconceptualizing Sexual Harassment," such "harassment serves a gender-guarding, competence-undermining function." It should also have been obvious to the judges that this sexist conduct was pervasive and that it met Justice Ginsberg's test in *Harris* of making it more difficult for Munday to do her job.

This case was tried by a judge without a jury. The trial judge found that Munday was "subjected to many inappropriate comments and actions concerning gender while she was employed by defendant" and was retaliated against and constructively discharged because she filed a sexual harassment claim. Nevertheless, he concluded that Munday did not experience a sufficiently hostile work environment to justify a legal finding of sexual harassment.

When the defendant employer appealed the trial judge's findings of retaliation and constructive discharge, the appellate court's two-judge majority purported to treat the plaintiff with special deference by referring to her throughout as "Miss Munday" while referring to her male supervisors and coworkers simply by their last names. This perversely archaic use of "Miss" was ironic, since at work Munday neither received nor expected the courtesy and deference that this title implies. And while the appellate court addressed her by this deferential title, the outcome of the appeal was anything but deferential.

The appellate court noted that prior to being fired and rehired, Munday "was subjected to a number of instances of sexual harassment." Nevertheless, it concluded that she suffered no gender-based discrimination and—reversing the trial court—that she was not constructively discharged. Thus, despite her boss Bohager's express intent to make her working conditions so unpleasant that Munday would resign, his method, an extreme form of shunning, was not so intolerable that it would have forced a "reasonable person" to resign. Since the court found she was not constructively discharged, it was also able to conclude that the legal requirement for retaliation—that "the terms, conditions, or benefits of her employment [be] adversely affected"— had not been met. The appellate court therefore found that Munday did not quit because her working conditions were objectively intolerable, despite her claim to the contrary. As a result, the appellate court denied Munday's gender-based claim entirely. Judge Heaney dissented, but even his opinion framed the hostility toward Munday in gender-neutral terms.

The reasonable person standard allowed all the judges to ignore the reason that Munday was treated differently from the rest of the workers. Even though it was obvious that she was viewed as an unwanted outsider—a woman who had no business in this male environment—the judges examined the conduct from the nongendered perspective. By not considering how a woman who wants to be treated with respect and as an equal would view Munday's work experience, they failed to recognize the magnitude and the gendered nature of the harm Munday suffered and how unwelcome she was made to feel.

In evaluating her sexual harassment claim, the trial judge looked at Munday's employment at Waste Management both before and after her termination and rehire. However, he decided that only the events occurring before she was fired could conceivably be viewed as gender-based harassment; the retaliatory conduct after she was rehired was seen as neither sexual harassment nor sex discrimination but simply as genderless animosity because she forced the company to rehire her.

The trial judge concluded that Munday "was subjected to many inappropriate comments and actions concerning gender [which] should, of course, not have taken place." Nevertheless, he determined that her cumulative negative experiences were not "sufficiently severe or pervasive 'to alter the conditions of [her] employment and create an abusive working environment.'" According to the judge, Munday's negative experiences stemmed from the "difficult and demanding" type of employment involved. As is typical in cases involving women in nontraditional workplaces, the judge also found Munday to be "a difficult and demanding employee." In other words, the judge blamed Munday at least in part for the treatment she received. He blamed much of her negative experience on her own "abrasive conduct and . . . tendency to blame her problems on others and to assume little responsibility for her own errors, as well as . . . her general dissatisfaction with her life." Thus, while the judge recognized that "the entire work atmosphere can only be described as a rather tough one," it was Munday's fault that she didn't fit in.

The judge said not a word about why it might have been particularly "tough" to be the only woman in a virtually all-male workplace. Instead, the court credited Bohager, whom it previously had found to have perjured himself on a number of occasions, with hiring Munday and thereby giving her a chance, implying that Munday blew her opportunity. Ignoring the reality that her fellow workers didn't view her as one of them, the judge blamed Munday for not being just one of the boys. This is sadly reminiscent of how Vivienne Rabidue was blamed when she complained about disparate treatment and a sexually harass-ing environment.

The trial judge also trivialized Munday's distress about the false sex-ual rumors about her. In response to Munday's assertion that rumors about her sexual activity continued to spread until her eventual resig-nation from employment, the court concluded that this wasn't enough to demonstrate pervasiveness: "Mere utterance of an epithet which en-genders offensive feeling in a female employee would not affect the conditions of employment to a sufficiently significant degree to violate Title VII." These rumors were not isolated, not "mere utterances." Rather, rumors about Munday's sexuality were part of her boss's coor-dinated effort to make her quit. As particularly offensive and personal attacks, this rumormongering most likely made a big difference in how Munday felt about her job and her fellow employees. Further, her gen-der made a difference in how she responded, because rumors about a woman having sexual relations with male employees have negative connotations, whereas a male coworker having such affairs confirms his masculinity. The implication of the rumors was that Munday was a slut, a man-hating lesbian, or both. The rumors portrayed her as de-viant—as even more of an outsider than she was by simply being a woman.

The court described the workplace atmosphere as a "tough" and "earthy" one "in which there were undoubtedly statements and ques-tions which would have grated upon a reasonable woman." Neverthe-less, Munday's claim that she experienced sexual harassment and sex discrimination was rejected—because *a reasonable person* would not have found the harassment to be severe or pervasive.

Munday's hostile treatment at work for the most part was not sex-ual, but it certainly was severely and pervasively antiwoman. And it continued throughout her four years of employment as a truck driver for Waste Management. It's difficult to grasp how the trial court could discount so many obviously gendered harassing incidents: the taunting refusal to let her use the women's bathroom and the subsequent provi-sion of a grossly inadequate women's bathroom; her supervisor's accu-sation that she was taking food from men's mouths; the forcing her, in order to do her job, to enter the men's changing and bathroom area—called the "driver's lounge" because a driver, by definition, was a man. These acts were all clearly gender-based harassment.

Furthermore, even if the retaliation against her when she returned was based partially on anger at her for bucking the system and forcing her boss to rehire her, the methods were gender based: the impact of shunning was more pronounced on her because she was then completely isolated as the only woman; and the rumors focused on her sexuality, as either slut or lesbian man hater.

If the standard applied had been that of a reasonable woman who expects to be treated with respect, as an equal, the outcome in this case would have been different. Looking at Munday's treatment through the lens of a reasonable woman, it becomes clear that the discrimination against her and the hostile environment were due to who she was—to her being a woman doing a man's job, who had the gall to demand equal treatment.

The court's adoption of the male-biased reasonable person standard also blinded the judges to the seriousness of the harm Munday suffered. At trial, Munday claimed she suffered severe emotional distress as a result of her mistreatment at work. Two psychologists testified at trial about the impact of the defendant's conduct on Munday. Dr. Lawrence Adler, who attended Munday for many months, testified on Munday's behalf, while Dr. John Lion, who met with her twice after being hired by the defendant for purposes of litigation, testified on the defendant's behalf. The defense introduced a laundry list of possible non-work-related causes of her psychological distress, including "her life long tensions with her mother, her mother's death from cancer during Munday's employment with defendant, her divorce at an earlier time, sexual advances made by an aged uncle, a break-up with a long-time boyfriend and her general dissatisfaction with life." These outside factors were irrelevant to the question of whether Munday was sexually harassed, especially since the United States Supreme Court in *Harris* expressly held that a claim of sexual harassment does not require proof of emotional injury. Nevertheless, these other explanations for any alleged emotional harm suffered clearly impressed the trial judge.

Dr. Adler diagnosed Munday as suffering from major mood swings and posttraumatic stress disorder during the time she worked for Waste Management and for a few weeks after she quit, resulting from how she was treated at work. In contrast, Dr. Lion testified for the defendant that Munday's work experiences at Waste Management only partly caused her stress, although he could not say how much of her stress was attributable to outside factors. The trial judge acknowledged that Dr. Adler had a much greater opportunity to observe and evaluate Munday; nevertheless, he adopted Dr. Lion's views of the causes and degree of Munday's emotional trauma. In the judge's opinion, Dr. Adler's assessment of the level of Munday's suffering was simply not credible. In other words, the court didn't believe that what happened to Munday at work was bad enough to cause the kind of emotional harm that she and her treating psychologist claimed.

The trial judge clearly viewed Munday through a male-biased lens— as a woman who couldn't make it on her own, who couldn't hack it in a man's world, who blamed her employer for all her problems, and who then tricked her own doctor into believing she was seriously harmed. The facts do not support this view, but applying a reasonable person standard instead of an explicitly gendered reasonable woman standard made it difficult to meaningfully consider the treatment Munday experienced. Because of the so-called neutral assessment, the court failed to acknowledge, or even to recognize, Munday's virtually complete isolation and "otherness" and how such extreme and deliberate shunning would affect a woman so isolated. The reasonable person against whom Munday, rather than her employer, was measured was a stereotypical macho guy who would have handled the hassles without complaint. But a macho guy would not have experienced what Munday did: he would never have been treated "like a woman," who is innately subordinate because of her gender. Thus, the court ignored Munday's experience and perspective as a woman.

Making a Difference

Our discussion of how the reasonable woman can make a difference in the context of sexual harassment illustrates the power of language and the importance of empathy. The short history of sexual harassment is a history of how the law can empower women. Sexual harassment redefined gender discrimination to include sexual and sexist conduct that makes it harder for women to do their jobs and thereby transformed many workplaces. But more is necessary to make women workers truly equal to their male peers, especially in male-dominated workplaces. The reasonable woman standard, with its demand that women workers be treated with respect and dignity, will assist judges and juries in taking law and society the next step down the road toward true equality.

PART III

Stalking

For if she begins to tell the truth, the figure in the looking-glass shrinks; his fitness for life is diminished. How is he to go on giving judgement, civilising natives, making laws, writing books, dressing up and speechifying at banquets, unless he can see himself at breakfast and at dinner at least twice the size he really is? . . . The looking-glass vision is of supreme importance because it charges the vitality. . . . Take it away and man may die, like the drug fiend deprived of his cocaine.

—Virginia Woolf, *A Room of One's Own*

7

Stalking and the Gendered Meaning of Reasonable Fear

Paul and Diane Orsello were married for over nine years, but were divorced in 1992. Diane Orsello received custody of their three children. [Paul] was granted visitation and the right to phone his children on certain days of the week. However, . . . he continued to contact his wife and children frequently via the phone and in writing. Often [he] suggested reconciliation, or at least social contact, with his former wife. While the tenor of these contacts was often affectionate, sometimes [Paul] was threatening or angry. On one occasion, [he] showed his ex-wife a gun, stating he hoped "it wouldn't go off," and later told her she could "burn in hell."

Diane Orsello sought and received a harassment restraining order in June 1992, prohibiting [Paul] from contact with his family in any manner other than that allowed by a previous court order. Repeated contacts with his family resulted in his conviction for violating the harassment order in 1993. His contact with his wife and children continued and, based on incidents occurring from June to October 1993, he was charged with stalking.

—*State v. Orsello* (1996)

The Minnesota Supreme Court reversed Paul Orsello's conviction for stalking, finding that the prosecution had not proved that he "intended to stalk his wife." (Note that the court refers to Diane as his wife, even though they were divorced.) The court's reasoning can be understood only in the context of the deep gender bias that still permeates stalking law. Because stalking is viewed through a male-focused lens, the court views the defendant's intentions in the best possible light. It therefore denied that Paul Orsello had the specific intent to stalk "his wife," even though he had repeatedly violated court protection orders and had repeatedly threatened her.

The Minnesota stalking statute required evidence that the defendant "(1) directly or indirectly manifested a purpose or intent to injure the person, property, or rights of another by the commission of an unlawful act; (2) stalked, followed, or pursued another. . . ." The defendant must also have intended to harass, to "engage in intentional conduct in a manner that would cause a reasonable person under the circumstances to feel oppressed, persecuted or intimidated and caused this reaction on the part of [the target]." This case demonstrates the problem with statutes that require proof that the defendant intended the victim to feel persecuted or intimidated, rather than simply that the defendant intended to engage in conduct that caused the target's reaction. It also shows the intrinsic bias that the reasonable woman standard could remedy. It's obvious from Paul Orsello's overt threats that he intended to intimidate and oppress his ex-wife. Nevertheless, the court did not see this.

Stalking involves a series of actions that, taken individually, might be legal and harmless and that cumulatively, in many circumstances, would not constitute stalking. For example, sending flowers, writing love notes, and waiting for someone outside her place of work are actions that, on their own, are not criminal. When the recipient welcomes the flowers and attention, it is romance. However, when these actions are unwelcome, when the person engaging in the conduct persists after being told to stop or accompanies the actions with threats, it is stalking. In short, stalking involves one person terrorizing another—most often, a man terrorizing a woman. Not infrequently, this happens after the woman breaks off even a brief relationship. For example:

> After dating Jack for several months, Anne ended the relationship. Jack reacted with anger and verbal abuse. He threatened to "make it so that Anne couldn't live in town any more and would have to deal with Jack the rest of her life, whether she married him or not." Jack also warned that while he might not do anything "you never know what my friends might do."
>
> Jack called Anne the next day and demanded that their relationship continue. When Anne refused, Jack renewed his prior threats, . . . and told her that he intended to force her to leave town because running into her would be too painful for him. Two weeks later he asked her to marry him which Anne refused. Jack then called Anne's friend and told her that

"if he could not have Anne then no one could." When Anne learned of this threat she called Jack and told him to leave her alone. Over the next four months Jack made as many as 200 harassing phone calls to Anne. He sent her cards, including one that said "I'm doing what I got to do for myself and you. Ignoring me won't make me go away. It's just gonna make me try harder. I'm entitled to one more chance with you, and you get one more chance to rectify a mistake. You're gonna have to deal with me one way or another." Around Halloween Jack carved a pumpkin, smashed it, and left it on Anne's porch with a note. . . .

Finally Anne sought and obtained a protective order against Jack that required him to stay away from her and stop the harassment. He left her alone. Two months later, as Anne was leaving the rink where she regularly ice skated, she saw Jack lacing up his skates. Seeing him there frightened her because he'd never shown interest in skating before. The next week Jack watched Anne for almost her entire 45 minute private skating lesson. He repeated this on three more occasions at which point Anne asked the police to arrest him for stalking her.

—*People v. Holt* (1995) (names changed)

In the spectrum of stalking terror, Jack's stalking of Anne was mild. She was also comparatively lucky: stalking most often occurs when and because a woman leaves a violent relationship and not infrequently culminates in the stalker seriously injuring or killing her. Nevertheless, it is only in the last few years that stalking has been codified and treated as a form of criminal activity.

Although each stalking case is different and incidents within the same case vary, over time a stalker's behavior typically becomes more and more threatening, serious, and violent. While the media generally publicize only celebrity stalking by obsessed fans, the vast majority of stalkers are personally acquainted with their targets. Stalkers have various motivations. Most commonly they are romantically obsessed would-be suitors or, like Jack, rejected lovers bent on revenge. The women they target may be strangers, acquaintances, former lovers, or ex-wives. And while no stalking case is typical, many stalkers have certain behaviors and traits in common with Jack: unwelcome persistence, possessiveness, and, in reaction to rejection, vengefulness. Like Jack, they are usually men—men who won't accept no for an answer, who feel entitled to continued possession of the woman. Most stalkers are highly self-referential and narcissistic, viewing their conduct entirely from a proprietary perspective. They view their targets as "their" women, and either refuse to consider or derive gratification from how their behavior disrupts the lives of others.

As with sexual harassment, until quite recently the law refused to recognize stalking as a specific legal harm. The California legislature made stalking a crime in 1990—the first state in the nation to do so. Until then, the law failed to provide any remedy for a harm that, according to Patricia Tjaden and colleagues, affects approximately 1.4 million people annually. The center's 1995–96 *National Violence Against Women Survey* of eight thousand men and eight thousand women found that 87 percent of all stalkers are male—94 percent of those who stalk women and 60 percent of those who stalk men. Furthermore, one in twelve women but only one in forty-five men surveyed reported being stalked at least once in her or his lifetime.

That the vast majority of stalkers are men and most targets are women explains why the law has ignored this harm. The male-defined legal system didn't acknowledge, or perhaps didn't even recognize, women's fear of stalking or that the danger and injury were serious enough to merit legal protection. Law identifies with men. The law's inaction on stalking exemplifies how the male-biased legal system values the male stalkers' freedom of action and speech over the female targets' security and emotional well-being. The stalkers' and their targets' behavior are both viewed from a male perspective. When a woman complains that a man injured her, especially a man she knows, the law too often assumes the woman must have asked for it, must have deserved it. Stalkers justify their behavior by blaming it on the target: she left him, she rejected him, she's seeing someone else—she's asserting her free agency when she really belongs to him. If it happened, then she caused it or she's lying and it didn't happen.

The male view of stalking is based on a perception that this kind of conduct rarely happens to men, and when it does, it's usually annoying, not terrifying. From the macho stereotype of what's reasonable, a man who is afraid when a woman calls, writes, watches, and pursues him is a sissy. And indeed, targets have less to fear from female stalkers. Almost all the many stalkers who are also batterers are male. Furthermore, it is male stalkers who kill, and it is women who end up dead. As commentator Jennifer Bradfield notes, California's 1990 enactment of the first stalking statute occurred in response to five stalking murders:

In 1989, actress Rebecca Schaeffer was murdered at her Los Angeles apartment by an obsessed fan who had stalked her for over two years. That same year, within a five-week period, four women from Orange County, California, all of whom had obtained restraining orders against their former boyfriends or spouses, were murdered by their stalkers.

Fatal Attraction (1987) is Hollywood misogyny, not real life. When men watched the film *Fatal Attraction,* they found the female stalker's behavior terrifying—when a female stalker was portrayed acting like a male stalker, men "got it." They understood that it isn't really "just annoying" to be stalked in the way men stalk women. The reasonable woman standard would require decision makers to "get it" in real life, which, based on statistics and popular media, they certainly do not.

A recent popular "romantic comedy," *There's Something about Mary* (1998), illustrates the male view of how stalking affects women. Stalker jokes and antics abound. As presented in this movie, stalking is funny, and appropriate stalking leads to romance with the woman stalked—even when she completely outclasses the stalker. Mary is an extremely pretty, single, professional woman living an ordinary life. The comedy revolves around the antics of the four men who are obsessed with her, none of whom she knows as more than an acquaintance. The "hero" is a man who has thought about no one but Mary since they went to the same high school. Thirteen years later, still obsessed, he hires a private investigator to locate Mary. After seeing her, the investigator also becomes besotted and decides to stalk Mary. As the movie develops, we learn about two more men who just can't stop stalking her. There's just something about Mary—not something wrong with these guys. They can't help it; she's responsible for what happens by just being who she is.

After the hero locates Mary, he travels thousands of miles and arranges to "accidentally" run into her. He picks up a traveling companion—a psychopathic murderer—who, by contrast, makes the hero and the rest of the stalkers look good. The stalkers watch and follow Mary constantly, listening in on her every word. The culminating scene involves three of the stalkers rescuing her from the most disturbed stalker—the one who was so scary and bizarre that Mary got a stalking protective order against him, moved to another state, and changed her last name. Not that any of this did any good—he still stalked her. Next to him, the others look pretty innocuous—they are the funny, harmless stalkers, the "normal" ones. After rescuing her, the three normal stalkers demand that Mary choose among them. Even when they give her the option of choosing the one man in her life who has not stalked her, she still chooses the movie's hero. At the end, we are left with the impression that Mary realizes that she loves this stalker—whom she knows only *because* he has been stalking her—instead of her sensitive, handsome, rich, famous, and nonstalking boyfriend, and that she and her stalker will live happily every after.

What makes this movie funny, in contrast to the reverse-gender terror of *Fatal Attraction*, is its portrayal of stalkers as just regular guys who go a little overboard. They are goofy. This movie tells us that stalking women is, for the most part, harmless—even the scariest stalker was just interested in Mary's shoes. And when a stalker physically invades your home and chases you around, it's only a little bit frightening. The rest of the time it's annoying at worst, while still being flattering and entertaining. But for real women stalked by real men, stalking is anything but flattering or fun. Real women want their stalkers to leave them alone and want the law to help make this happen.

Compare the ultimate response of the fictional Mary to that of Jane McAllister. Testifying at the Senate Judiciary Committee hearings anti-stalking legislation in 1992, Jane described how a chance meeting with a minor acquaintance turned into a nightmare. The man began to follow and call her repeatedly, often to tell Jane that he loved her and wanted to marry her. He wrote bizarre notes, came to her house, and offered her money. When she didn't respond to his "advances," his behavior became hostile and threatening. Once, while she was walking, he followed her in a truck, shouting obscenities at her; another time he said that when she died, he would dig up her body so he could have her. Needless to say, she didn't suddenly realize—as did the fictional Mary—that she was in love with her stalker. As she testified:

> I changed my routine, I lived in constant fear of an attack. . . . It was clear that this man, who was apparently crazy, was not going to let up and that the authorities were powerless to stop him. Though he was free to move about, I was living in a state of siege.
>
> The police were not insensitive, but they were stymied. The man violated almost every area of my life, but had broken no law. The police worked with me to prevent an assault, but, in the final analysis, said there was nothing they could do until an assault occurred.

Today there are stalking laws, which clearly benefit women more than they do men. However, without a reasonable woman standard, their application continues to be male biased, and therefore they remain an inadequate remedy. As in sexual harassment, we advocate applying the reasonable woman standard in stalking cases in order to raise the minimum standard of conduct the law demands of certain interpersonal behavior and to enable decision makers to understand why targets are terrified. As with the issue of what sexual or sexist conduct is sufficiently "severe or pervasive" to make it unlawful sexual harassment, the issue of what stalking conduct is sufficiently severe or pervasive to merit legal intervention will sometimes depend on whose perspective is adopted. Applying the reasonable woman standard in determining what conduct creates reasonable fear explicitly incorporates the perspective of women, the group most commonly stalked and the group with the most to fear when they are stalked. This gendered standard will help decision makers recognize that the "reasonable" fear of bodily injury that must be shown for a stalking remedy should be women's fear—not men's.

Further, as in the other legal contexts explored in this book, the stalkers themselves should be held to a reasonable woman standard of care. Most states require as a necessary element in the crime of stalking that the stalker pose a "credible threat" of harm. In those states that retain the credible threat requirement—which we believe they should reject entirely—it should be measured by a reasonable woman standard. In other words, the statutes should criminalize "credible threats" that a reasonable woman would, or should, know to cause fear. In that way, stalking would be defined by what would place a reasonable woman in fear of bodily harm and by what a reasonable woman would expect to induce such fear.

Stalking frequently accompanies or follows other gendered legal harms, most notably sexual harassment and domestic violence. The two chapters in this part bridge our detailed examination of hostile environment sexual harassment and domestic homicide. In this chapter, we examine and critique existing stalking laws. Chapter 8 considers cases involving both stalking and sexual harassment and stalking and domestic homicide. These cases illustrate how stalking fits into the spectrum of gendered violence against women.

Stalking Law

States now provide as many as four statutory remedies against stalkers: stalking protective orders, the crime of stalking, criminal prosecution for violation of stalking orders, and civil liability for stalking. All four remedies present a question of what is sufficiently fear-inducing conduct to merit legal action. At present, the explicit and the implicit standard for determining reasonable fear or apprehension of bodily injury is the reasonable person. Because stalking involves primarily men stalking women, and because male stalkers are more likely than female stalkers to seriously injure or kill their targets, the standard should be the reasonable woman. All stalkers' conduct should be measured by how a reasonable woman would behave and what she would expect to cause fear, and all targets' fear should be measured by the fear of a reasonable woman.

Stalking Remedies

By 1996, all fifty states had enacted stalking statutes, which generally define stalking as "willful, malicious, and repeated following and harassing of another person." The statutes vary in substance, but each contains a provision expressly making certain repetitive, fear-inducing behavior a crime. Some statutes also specifically provide for a stalking protective order, mandating that the stalker stay away from his target. Others require targets to rely on existing, nonspecific protective order provisions to restrain their stalkers. A few statutes also provide that the target can recover money damages from her stalker.

The stalking laws in most states involve three elements that must be proved beyond a reasonable doubt for conviction: a stalker must (1) engage in a course of conduct or pattern of behavior (2) that poses a threat or that would cause a reasonable person to feel afraid, (3) with intent to cause fear in the victim (specific intent) or intent to commit the act or acts that caused fear (general intent). The kind of intent the statute requires can affect the outcome in many stalking cases. Statutes requiring specific intent look at the subjective perspective of the person accused of stalking: What did he intend by his conduct? In contrast, general-intent statutes look at what the person accused of stalking actually did: What effect did his conduct have on the target, and how would it have affected a reasonable person?

Oregon's stalking statutes illustrate the distinction. Unlike many states, in addition to making stalking a crime, Oregon expressly provides for a stalking restraining order, civil liability, and criminal liability for violating a stalking order. Oregon's statute has specific-intent provisions for its criminal and general-intent requirements for its civil stalking statutes. As a result, women may be able to prove sufficient intent to obtain a stalking restraining order but not to convict for the crime of stalking. General-intent statutes better serve stalking targets because they focus on whether the conduct would induce fear rather than on whether the accused intended or knew that fear would result.

In Oregon, the crimes of stalking and violating a stalking order require that the prosecution prove "the person *knowingly alarms or coerces another person* . . . by engaging in repeated and unwanted contact with the other person" (emphasis added). In contrast, to obtain a stalking order or money damages against a stalker, the target must prove "the person *intentionally, knowingly or recklessly engages in repeated and unwanted contact with another person* . . . thereby alarming or coercing the other person" (emphasis added). The statutes define *alarm* to mean "to cause apprehension or fear resulting from the perception of danger." They define *coerce* to mean "to restrain, compel or dominate by force or threat." If there is force or a threat, specific intent should be easy to show; often, however, the victim suffers only alarm, and in some cases that makes it difficult to show specific rather than general intent.

Oregon's crime of stalking requires proof that the accused *knew* the target would experience fear, alarm, or coercion. Like statutes requiring that the stalker intend to cause such fear, alarm or coercion, it focuses on the stalker's actual perceptions or state of mind. Under these specific-intent statutes, which have been enacted in the majority of states, evidence must demonstrate that the accused wanted to coerce, alarm, or frighten the target or knew his conduct would have these effects. These standards do not accurately reflect the reality of this crime. Requiring proof of their intent to coerce or alarm immunizes many stalkers from legal responsibility, even when the targets genuinely and reasonably fear them.

The U.S. Department of Justice's highly regarded Project to Develop a Model Anti-Stalking Code for States notes: "A suspected stalker often suffers under a delusion that the victim is actually in love with him or that, if properly pursued, the victim will begin to love him." For some stalkers the goal is romance, not terror. Like many acquaintance rapists who think intercourse after a woman says no is just seduction, their amorous obsession and selfish desire blind them to their targets' actual and reasonable response to their unsolicited and unwelcome conduct. For such stalkers, their targets' negative reaction is a "normal" part of the seduction process. Another type of stalker, the former intimate who frequently is also a batterer, may also claim he doesn't have specific intent to cause fear. He would argue that he merely wants what's best for her—that she be reunited with him. For such a stalker, the target belongs with and to him, and he's simply trying to regain possession.

The intent requirement for Oregon's stalking order and stalking civil liability claims illustrates the general-intent alternative that about a quarter of the states have adopted. Instead of focusing on whether the alleged stalker intended to cause fear or knew his conduct would do so, such statutes simply require proof that he intended to engage or knew he was engaging in conduct that qualifies as stalking. In this way, general-intent statutes assure legal penalties will be imposed on love-obsessed stalkers who are too deluded to recognize, much less to intend, the terror they inflict. They also negate the claim of former intimates that in seeking to regain possession of women who have left them, they don't mean to frighten them. As long as such stalkers cause actual fear and that fear is reasonable, legal penalties apply.

Stalking statutes have been constitutionally challenged for being vague and for violating the free-speech rights of stalkers. People have even challenged stalking statutes with specific-intent provisions. Fortunately, most courts have upheld the constitutionality of both specific- and general-intent stalking statutes, usually because the statutes include an objective reasonableness standard along with required proof of the target's fear. As a 1999 Oregon Supreme Court decision, *State v. Rangel*, noted in holding that Oregon's crime of stalking did not violate a stalker's free-speech rights:

> The statute does not expressly require that the contact involving communication be established with proof of specific intent to carry out the threat or of any present ability to do so. However, we conclude that the requirements . . . of actual alarm and the subjective and objective reasonableness of the alarm in the circumstances have the same purpose and effect. . . . Those elements limit the reach of [the statute] to a threat that is so unambiguous, unequivocal, and specific to the addressee that

it convincingly expresses to the addressee the intention that it will be carried out.

We hope that courts will adopt this kind of reasoning, which punishes a stalker for how the target perceives his acts. As long as courts view conduct that creates both reasonable and actual fear to be sufficiently unambiguous and clear about what will and will not be considered criminal stalking, our proposal that the fear be that of an objectively reasonable woman should withstand scrutiny as well.

Reasonable Fear—A Woman's Perspective

Broadly stated, stalking is repetitive, unwelcome behavior focused on a particular person that interferes with that person's autonomy and peace of mind by causing fear of bodily harm. The conduct varies greatly, including physically following the target, writing letters or E-mail messages, sending unsolicited gifts, engaging in verbal confrontations, and, most commonly, telephoning. These behaviors in themselves can be harmless. However, when they are unsolicited, unwelcome, and occur repeatedly, they can become threatening and create terror. Stalkers intrude into a person's space and privacy. As the 1997 *Domestic Violence and Stalking Second Annual Report to Congress* notes, stalking "creates a psychological prison that deprives its victims of basic liberty of movement and security in their homes."

To obtain legal remedies, a stalking target must show that she is afraid for her safety and that her fear is reasonable. Measuring fear by the reasonable person standard assumes that, for stalking, reasonable fear is not gendered. However, based on the realities of men's and women's lives, reasonable women are likely to experience fear in situations where reasonable men would not. Therefore, for purposes of what constitutes reasonable fear from stalking behavior, the standard should be what would cause a reasonable woman to be afraid for her safety. All persons accused of stalking should be held to this reasonable woman standard: if their behavior would cause a reasonable woman to be afraid, legal liability should be imposed.

Such a standard would take into account the fact that, in our culture, men and women are not similarly situated when it comes to being able to defend and protect themselves from others. It also factors in, as the cases we examine demonstrate, that it is often reasonable for women to be afraid in situations where most men would be merely annoyed. Finally, it acknowledges that the vast majority of cases in which stalkers have seriously injured or killed their targets involve men stalking women.

Women are most often the targets of stalking. In thinking about why men stalk women, the sexual aspect of the behavior cannot be ignored. The stalker often either wants to form a romantic (translate: sexual) relationship with his target or has had such a relationship and is reacting to the target's ending it. The traditional roles of men and women when it comes to sexual intimacy are relevant here. Stereotypically, men pursue women; men seduce women; men initiate intimate relationships. Although these roles are socially constructed and are not in any way natural or inevitable, they are embedded in our culture. It is therefore not surprising that men more often than women take these roles to an extreme by engaging in stalking, and in particular, violent stalking. Therefore, for women, in contrast to men, stalking behavior often creates reasonable fear of sexual assault.

Stalkers are often male batterers. The 1995–96 *National Violence Against Women Survey* found that almost 60 percent of female victims were stalked by an intimate partner, and that 80 percent of those reported being physically assaulted by their stalker. It should be self-evident that a batterer who engages in stalking creates reasonable fear. In fact, adoption of a reasonable woman standard should mean that stalking behavior by a batterer presumptively satisfies a stalking statute's reasonable fear requirement.

Most stalkers are scary people who, according to psychiatrist J. Reid Meloy, "have prior criminal, psychiatric, and substance-abuse histories." Stalkers often are mentally unstable. The psychological profiles of different types of stalkers provide an additional reason for viewing the fear necessary for a stalking remedy from a woman's perspective. Dr. Michael Zona of the University of Southern California School of Medicine has identified three mental disorders in stalkers: erotomania, love obsession, and simple obsession. Erotomanic stalkers are often celebrity stalkers, who delusionally believe someone they don't even know is in love with them. Most erotomanic stalkers are women, and their targets are usually men. They are the least likely to commit violent acts against their targets.

In contrast, love obsessional and simple obsessional stalkers are usually men, and their targets are usually women. Love obsessional stalkers typically have not had a prior relationship with their targets and often suffer from mental disorders, such as schizophrenia or bipolar affective disorder. In such cases, the women are often repeatedly contacted by male acquaintances or even strangers who want to form a romantic relationship with them.

The most dangerous and most common mental disorder in stalkers is simple obsession. Such stalkers have had some kind of relationship with their targets. Their obsessions begin when they believe their targets have rejected them or mistreated them in some way. A 1998 study by Ronnie Harmon, Richard Rosner, and Howard Owens confirms that a prior intimate relationship, either sexual or familial, is one of the clearest indications that a stalker will be violent. This risk holds true regardless of whether the reason for stalking was sexual or persecution.

Women are justified in being more frightened than men by stalkers, based on the violent proclivities of stalkers who are more likely to stalk women. This makes it appropriate in stalking cases to assess the reasonableness of the fear from a woman's perspective. When a woman repeatedly follows, writes to, or phones a man for whom this conduct is unwelcome and unreciprocated, he will probably be annoyed and irritated. Different emotions are likely to be experienced when the roles are reversed. It is reasonable for a woman to be frightened when she experiences repeated and unwelcome visual, verbal, or written contact that indicates sexual interest or anger at rejection. Because, in the context of stalking, fear is gendered, stalking statutes need to explicitly take this into account.

Incorporating Women's Perspectives

Existing stalking statutes do not adequately account for the impact stalking conduct has on women. For example, Oregon's stalking statutes have two reasonable fear requirements when only one is necessary. The statutes that create the crime of stalking and provide for obtaining a stalking order and recovering money damages against a stalker all require proof that "it is *objectively reasonable* for a person in the victim's situation to have been alarmed or coerced by the contact; and [t]he repeated and unwanted contact causes the victim *reasonable apprehension* regarding . . . personal safety" (emphasis added).

These statutes require too much. Two amendments would greatly enhance the stalking statutes' effectiveness in protecting women from stalkers. First, when examining the conduct of the accused, "objectively reasonable" should be determined using a reasonable woman standard. One way to do this is to provide that "the victim's situation" includes the victim's gender. However, no one, male or female, should have to endure stalking conduct that would create fear or apprehension for a reasonable woman and does create actual fear for the person being stalked. Therefore, it would be better to require proof that "a reasonable woman in the victim's situation would have been alarmed or coerced by the contact."

The second amendment would focus on the actual harm to the target by eliminating the "reasonable apprehension" requirement and replacing it with a requirement that the victim subjectively experienced apprehension regarding personal safety. The "reasonable apprehension" language places an unnecessary burden on targets of stalking. It shifts the focus as to what is reasonable from the accused to the target. Once a target has established that, considering the accused's behavior, it was reasonable for anyone in her situation to be alarmed or coerced, it is unnecessary and unfair to make her also prove that her apprehension was reasonable. It implies that some targets' actual, subjective fear was not reasonable fear, even though it was reasonable to have such fear! Instead, a target should be required to prove that she in fact was apprehensive or fearful. Allowing legal sanctions when the accused's conduct caused fear or apprehension from both a reasonable woman's perspective and from the target's subjective perspective assures fair treatment of both the accused and the target.

Additionally, the intent of the stalker can be measured by a reasonable woman standard. For example, Washington's stalking statute requires that the stalker "knows, or reasonably should know, that the person being followed is afraid, intimidated, or harassed even if the stalker did not intend to place the person in fear or intimidate or harass the person." This standard is quite good. However, for the law to seriously address this highly gendered crime, a reasonable woman standard should determine the reasonableness of the stalker's behavior.

Incorporating the reasonable woman standard is easier for some statutes than others. In 1993, at Congress's direction, the National Institute of Justice drafted "The Model Antistalking Statute for the States." This statute criminalizes the conduct of anyone who:

(a) purposefully engages in a course of conduct directed at a specific person that would cause a *reasonable person* to fear bodily injury [and]

(b) has knowledge or should have knowledge that the specific person will be placed in *reasonable fear* of bodily injury [and]

(c) whose acts induce fear in the specific person of bodily injury. (Emphasis added)

Although this statute includes two reasonableness requirements, unlike the Oregon statute, both focus on the behavior of the person accused of stalking by examining his purposeful conduct and whether, even if he didn't intend to cause fear, he was negligent in not realizing that this conduct would cause fear. In order to better protect stalking targets, the "reasonable woman" standard should replace the nongendered "reasonable person." This simple change will require the decision maker to consider how the conduct involved would affect a woman.

One more change in the model statute is needed to make it reflect a reasonable woman standard. The drafters of the model statute note that their phrase "reasonable fear of bodily injury" does not necessarily include fear of sexual assault. In fact, they assume that sexual assault without additional physical harm, is not a "bodily injury." As the drafters explain: "It is likely that victims who fear that a defendant may sexually assault them most likely also fear that the defendant would physically injure them if they resisted." From a reasonable woman's perspective, if, by sexual assault, the drafters mean rape or attempted rape, this physical invasion *is* a bodily injury, even if no other physical injury is suffered or anticipated. To assure that decision makers recognize sexual assault as a bodily injury, it should be explicitly included in the statute.

Stalking statutes vary widely in the terms they use and the legal sanctions they impose. Incorporating a reasonable woman's fear into each state's statute will require carefully tailored changes that reflect a woman's perspective and a close examination of the statute's particular language. Once this is accomplished, it will no longer be possible to argue that actionable stalking must, in the words of the 1995 decision *Bouters v. State,* "induce fear in the mind of a reasonable man."

8

The Continuum of Stalking, Sexual Harassment, and Domestic Homicide

The primary focus in the discussion of stalking and sexual harassment is on two cases that use a reasonable woman standard to assess sexual harassment claims, *Ellison v. Brady* and *Fuller v. City of Oakland*. Both cases also involve stalking. By applying stalking laws to the *Ellison* and *Fuller* facts, we demonstrate how the reasonable woman would work in the stalking contexts, and why that standard is also needed to remedy this gendered harm.

On the more violent end of the stalking spectrum, someone ends up dead—most often a female target. In this chapter, we briefly examine cases of severe stalking in which the target was ultimately killed, and one case in which the stalker was killed. Many of the cases discussed in Part IV, "Domestic Homicide," also involve mild to severe stalking preceding the homicide. The sheer number of stalking murders is overwhelming; we touch on some of the most recent cases as reported in major newspapers to provide a glimpse of the magnitude of the problem. These cases demonstrate that stalking laws continue to be grossly inadequate, and that the law continues to underestimate the dangerousness of stalking behavior. While the reasonable woman standard would by no means be a panacea, it could increase reporting, convictions, and penalties, thereby at least reducing the number of women killed by their stalkers.

Stalking and Sexual Harassment

Examining the facts of actual cases highlights the need for a reasonable woman standard. Two important sexual harassment decisions, *Ellison v. Brady* and *Fuller v. City of Oakland*, both decided by the Ninth Circuit Court of Appeals, demonstrate the importance of a reasonable woman standard for both sexual harassment and stalking claims. The incidents that resulted in these two lawsuits took place in California before it became the first state to enact a stalking statute, and therefore a stalking remedy was not available to either of the women who sued their employers for sexual harassment. Sexual harassment is a form of sex discrimination for which the law holds the employer, rather than the person engaging in the conduct, responsible. Stalking is now a crime, and in some states a civil wrong, for which the law holds the stalker personally responsible. Analysis of these two cases in terms of sexual harassment and stalking illustrates the importance of adopting a reasonable woman standard for both kinds of harm. In these workplace cases, a sexual harassment remedy is not necessarily enough because the stalker himself is not held legally culpable. Only through a claim of stalking can there be criminal sanctions and a protective order requiring the stalker to leave his target alone.

The Love-Struck Stalker: *Ellison v. Brady*

Ellison, decided in 1991, was the first case in which a court explicitly adopted a feminist reasonable woman standard of care for hostile environment sexual harassment. The facts involve a male worker who was romantically obsessed with a female worker whom he hardly knew. Kerry Ellison and her harasser-stalker, Sterling Gray, both worked as revenue agents for the Internal Revenue Service (IRS) at the San Mateo, California, office. As the court noted, "the two co-workers never became friends, and they did not work closely together." Revenue agents often lunched together in groups. One day, when no one else was in the office, Ellison accepted Gray's invitation to lunch. They stopped by Gray's house to pick up his son's forgotten lunch, and Gray gave Ellison a tour of the house.

After the lunch, Gray "started to pester" Ellison, hanging around her desk and asking her unnecessary questions. A few months later Gray asked Ellison out for a drink, which she declined; the next week he asked her to lunch, which she also declined. Gray then handed Ellison a note that said: "I cried over you last night and I'm totally drained today. I have never been in such constant term oil [*sic*]. Thank you for talking with me. I could not stand to feel your hatred for another day."

The note shocked and frightened Ellison. When she left the room, Gray followed her and "demanded that she talk to him." Instead, Ellison left the building. Ellison then had a male coworker tell Gray that she was not interested in him and that Gray should leave her alone.

Ellison did not see Gray again because she started training out of state. While she was away, she received a three-page, single-spaced letter from Gray, which Ellison described as "twenty times, a hundred times weirder" than the other note. Gray wrote, in part:

> I know that you are worth knowing with or without sex. . . . Leaving aside the hassles and disasters of recent weeks. I have enjoyed you so much over these past few months. Watching you. Experiencing you from O so far away. Admiring your style and elan. . . . Don't you think it odd that two people who never even talked together, alone, are striking off such intense sparks. . . . I will [write] another letter in the near future.

As soon as she received this letter, Ellison phoned her supervisor about her fear of Gray. Ellison asked that either she or Gray be transferred from San Mateo. Her supervisor told Gray to leave Ellison alone. Before Ellison returned from her training, Gray transferred to the San Francisco office. A short time later Gray filed a union grievance, seeking to transfer back to San Mateo. The union and the IRS agreed to allow him to return in four months, on condition that he leave Ellison alone. When Ellison learned that Gray would be returning, she was frantic. She filed a sexual harassment claim against the IRS and was permitted to transfer temporarily to San Francisco when Gray returned. Gray tried to have joint counseling with Ellison and wrote her another note that still suggested they had a special relationship.

Ellison's sexual harassment claim against her employer was for hostile work environment under Title VII. Therefore, the issue was whether Gray's conduct "was sufficiently severe or pervasive to alter the conditions of [Ellison's] employment and create an abusive working environment." The federal trial judge dismissed Ellison's case. He concluded that she had not made out a valid claim of sexual harassment because Gray's conduct was "isolated and genuinely trivial." On appeal to the Ninth Circuit Court of Appeals, the trial judge's decision was reversed, and Ellison's case was remanded for trial. Judge Robert Beezer, writing for the two-person majority, expressly rejected the "reasonable person" perspective adopted by the Sixth Circuit in *Rabidue v.*

Osceola Refining Co. In *Rabidue,* the court decided that pornographic pinups and sexual and sexist remarks had only a *de minimis* effect on women employees. In stark contrast, the *Ellison* majority opinion expressly evaluated the conduct from the reasonable woman's perspective. The majority explained:

> We realize that there is a broad range of viewpoints among women as a group, but we believe that many women share common concerns which men do not necessarily share. For example, because women are disproportionately victims of rape and sexual assault, women have a stronger incentive to be concerned with sexual behavior. Women who are victims of mild forms of sexual harassment may understandably worry whether a harasser's conduct is merely a prelude to violent sexual assault. Men, who are rarely victims of sexual assault, may view sexual conduct in a vacuum without a full appreciation of the social setting or the underlying threat of violence that a woman may perceive.

The *Ellison* majority critiqued the reasonable person standard in hostile environment sexual harassment cases, saying that it was "adopt[ing] the perspective of a reasonable woman primarily because we believe that a sex-blind reasonable person standard tends to be male-biased and tends to systematically ignore the experiences of women." The court pointed out that the reasonable woman standard does not unfairly benefit women or "establish a higher level of protection for women than men." Rather, "a gender-conscious examination of sexual harassment enables women to participate in the workplace on an equal footing with men. By acknowledging and not trivializing the effects of sexual harassment on reasonable women, courts can work towards ensuring that neither men nor women have to 'run the gauntlet of sexual abuse in return for the privilege of being allowed to work and make a living.'"

Finally, the *Ellison* majority applied their new reasonable woman standard in this case, noting that it made a difference here because the perspectives of Ellison and Gray differed significantly. As the court so aptly put it: "Analyzing the facts from the alleged harasser's viewpoint, Gray could be portrayed as a modern-day Cyrano de Bergerac wishing no more than to woo Ellison with his words." Further, because there was no evidence that Gray felt ill will toward Ellison, "it is not difficult to see why the district court characterized Gray's conduct as isolated and trivial." The *Ellison* majority went on to point out that her perspective was quite different:

> Ellison, however, did not consider the acts to be trivial. Gray's first note shocked and frightened her. After receiving the three-page letter, she became really upset and frightened again. . . . We believe that a reasonable woman could have had a similar reaction. After receiving the first bizarre note from Gray, a person she barely knew, Ellison asked a co-worker to tell Gray to leave her alone. Despite her request, Gray sent her a long, passionate, disturbing letter. He told her he had been "watching" and "experiencing" her; he made repeated references to sex; he said he would write again. Ellison had no way of knowing what he would do next. A reasonable woman could consider Gray's conduct, as alleged by Ellison, sufficiently severe and pervasive to alter a condition of employment and create an abusive working condition.

The *Ellison* majority's opinion demonstrates that you don't have to be a woman to be able to understand and apply the reasonable woman standard. Here, two male judges clearly empathized with how a woman might feel, while also recognizing that many men would not be frightened by comparable letters from a woman.

While the *Ellison* opinion perceptively acknowledges the need for a reasonable woman standard, it fails to recognize that this standard is appropriate in all sex-based hostile environment cases, regardless of the gender of the parties. The majority states that "where male employees allege that co-workers engage in conduct which creates a hostile environment, the appropriate . . . perspective would be that of a reasonable man." Instead, for both sexual harassment and stalking, the reasonable woman should be the standard in *all* cases. No one, male or female, should behave as Gray did; and no one, male or female, should have to endure this kind of unwelcome, intrusive conduct.

Ellison was a sexual harassment case, but it could just as well be considered criminal stalking. The conduct that the court said "shocked and frightened" Ellison involved repeated and unwelcome communications that would fit the definition of stalking *if* the requisite intent and proof that her fear was reasonable were established. However, Ellison would have faced two obstacles in making out a violation of most states' stalking statutes. First, many stalking statutes would require that she prove Gray either intended to frighten her or knew she would be frightened by his letters. This case demonstrates how such statutory requirements fail to consider adequately the harm that a love-struck stalker can unintentionally inflict on his target. Gray didn't want to hurt Ellison; he wanted to make love to her. Nevertheless, as the *Ellison* majority astutely noted, his unwelcome amorous pursuit caused Ellison severe distress—distress that no one should have to endure. To feel safe, Ellison was given no alternative but to transfer to another town. Statutes that require a mental animus on the part of a stalker fail to account adequately for the harm that mostly male stalkers inflict on their mostly female targets.

Ellison also might have faced difficulties in proving that Gray's conduct toward her fulfilled most states' requirement that her fear or apprehension be "reasonable." Under a reasonable person/man standard, writing two letters, neither of which includes explicitly threatening language, may not be fear-inducing. The reality is that for many men, such conduct would be no more than annoying. But even for men who would be frightened by such conduct, their fear wouldn't be viewed as credible, because they are not supposed to be frightened by mere words. In contrast, many women would be genuinely concerned that such unwelcome attentions could escalate into a physical assault, and that the attack likely would include sexual violence. Furthermore, if required to examine the conduct from a reasonable woman's perspective, the judges and juries are likely to be able to understand why a woman would experience fear in this context. But *no one* should have to endure this kind of intrusive behavior. Therefore, a reasonable woman's fear should be the standard to which everyone accused of stalking is held, regardless of society's gender-based expectations of the stalkers or their targets.

The *Ellison* facts provide a good example of the need for stalking laws and the limits of existing stalking laws. Most likely, Ellison's appropriate first step would have been to obtain a stalking protective order against Gray, mandating that he leave her alone. However, unless the reasonable woman's perspective were applied to legitimate her subjective feelings of terror, Ellison quite likely would not have been able to obtain such an order. As a result, Gray's behavior would not have been deemed unlawful. Without a stalking protective order's clear message that continuing to pursue Ellison would lead to criminal sanctions, Gray, in his besotted state, might not have had sufficient notice or incentive to stop. And without an order, it would have been difficult to convict Gray if he had continued to stalk her. It also seems probable that had Ellison's employer been notified that a stalking order was in effect, it would have dealt with Gray more decisively. Under a stalking statute that evaluated Gray's conduct and Ellison's perceptions from a reasonable woman's perspective, a judge would have issued a stalking order and, had Gray persisted, would have found him guilty of stalking; it is much less certain that a "neutral," reasonable person statute would have led to the same result.

No Such Thing as an Unlisted Number: *Fuller v. City of Oakland*

Fuller v. City of Oakland, decided in 1995, is another Ninth Circuit Court of Appeals opinion involving hostile environment sexual harassment. Written by Judge Cecil Poole for a unanimous three-judge panel, it involves harassment and stalking conduct that is much more egregious than what happened in *Ellison*. The harasser-stalker and his target were both police officers who, in the course of working for the city of Oakland, became romantically involved. Patricia Fuller and Antonio Romero had a consensual sexual relationship for a few months in 1986. Unfortunately, when Fuller no longer wanted to be involved with Romero, he refused to accept her decision and stalked her. Judge Poole noted: "By September 1986, Fuller no longer wished to continue the relationship. What followed is a disturbing tale." Considering that it involved erratic and threatening behavior from a man who was usually armed with a gun, most women would also find it terrifying.

When Fuller told Romero she no longer wanted an intimate relationship, he made it clear that he wanted the relationship to continue. He both openly and secretly stalked Fuller. Romero called her at home and at work. He also wrote her and "track[ed] her down on her beat." In addition, Romero tried to get one of Fuller's friends from out of state to help him get back with Fuller. Over a four-month period, he called her friend several times and told the friend that Fuller was dating someone he didn't approve of and was engaging in lesbian activity.

During the entire time Fuller was stalked, her phone numbers were unlisted. However, they were included in her Oakland Police Department personnel file. The phone stalking began in earnest after Fuller ended her relationship with Romero. She began to get up to twenty-five hang-up calls a day, but *only* on her days off. When she changed her phone number, the calls continued. Even when she moved residences and changed her number again, the calls continued unabated. In

January the calls continued only on her nights off, after her work schedule had changed.

In early March, Fuller began dating another police officer. A week later, seven months after Fuller had broken off her relationship with Romero, he called and finally acknowledged that she no longer wanted to see him and apologized for bothering her. The next night he called her at work in a drunken state and threatened to commit suicide. He called again the next day to "apologize." In reaction, Fuller changed her phone number again. This infuriated Romero. A few days later, the following occurred as Fuller approached her parked car near the police station parking lot:

> Romero drove up beside her and confronted her about changing her phone number. As she neared her car, he pulled up at an angle so as to prevent her from leaving, and when she got in her car he held her door open and demanded her new phone number. [Fuller] finally told him the number because it was apparent Romero would not allow her to leave until she did.

A short time later, when Fuller and her boyfriend were walking toward her car, Romero drove toward them in his police car, stopped, "spun out and sped off squealing his tires."

When Romero found out that Fuller's boyfriend was visiting her at home, he angrily phoned about her new relationship. Fuller told him to stop calling her, to leave her alone, and to mind his own business. Again, she changed her unlisted number. Nevertheless, Romero ignored Fuller's demands and called her the next week, claiming he came across her new number "inadvertently" while going through police personnel files.

A terrifying incident occurred in July 1987. While Fuller was driving her boyfriend home, Romero came speeding at them in an unmarked police car. Fuller had to swerve to avoid a head-on collision. When asked about the incident later, Romero lied both to Fuller and to the police investigator. After this incident, Romero for the most part left Fuller alone.

Three months later Romero was appointed to a position with supervisory authority over Fuller. Considering his past conduct toward her, it is not surprising that she was afraid of what he would do to her. In fact, she refused to file a complaint against him "because she feared for her safety." However, other officers reported his conduct to the police chief, who assigned someone to begin an internal affairs investigation. The investigation lasted from October 1987 until May 1988. The investigator concluded that Fuller was lying even though "none of the documents gathered . . . gave him reason to believe Fuller was untruthful." He found corroboration for his belief when he placed a tap on Romero's phone shortly *after* Romero was informed that he was being investigated. When Romero's phone records for that time showed no calls to Fuller, the investigator recommended closing the case. At that point, he had not interviewed Romero or any of the many available witnesses. He reluctantly kept the investigation going but did not interview Romero until two months later, just after Fuller filed a complaint with the Equal Employment Opportunity Commission. The investigation dragged on. Even after interviewing Fuller's friend from out of state, who confirmed Fuller's version of what happened and who said Romero's calls made her scared for Fuller and were "disturbing," the investigator filed a final report that declared Fuller's concerns "unfounded." This meant his investigation proved that Fuller's version of what happened was false. The police chief approved of this report.

Based on the outcome of the investigation Fuller "reported feeling ostracized and afraid . . . because visible isolation on the beat endangers an officer's safety." She went on disability leave after developing a "severe stress disorder." When her psychiatrist recommended that on her return she should not be supervised by Romero, the Oakland Police Department ignored this recommendation. "Rather than face this prospect, she resigned."

Fuller then sued the city of Oakland for hostile environment sexual harassment. Federal district court judge Marilyn Patel found that Fuller's version of what happened, including the numerous incidents of stalking by Romero, was credible. Nevertheless, Judge Patel found:

> Even measured against this reasonable woman standard, plaintiff has failed to carry her burden of proving that Romero's conduct . . . was sufficiently severe and pervasive to create a hostile work environment. Although Romero's behavior towards plaintiff was disturbing, the most egregious of this conduct occurred before Romero was in a supervisory position over plaintiff.

Judge Patel then concluded that "while plaintiff may have been uncomfortable having contact with a person with whom she had had a romantic relationship, this discomfort does not constitute sexual harassment."

What an extraordinary failure on Judge Patel's part to recognize what made Fuller "uncomfortable." This case isn't about discomfort with working with one's former lover. Fuller's present supervisor had previously stalked her for months, forcibly detained her and coerced her into giving him her phone number, misused his position to obtain her phone number, threatened to kill himself over her, and assaulted her and her boyfriend with his car. This is a case where the boss—a man with a gun, who knows how to use it—has previously terrorized his now-subordinate former lover.

On appeal, the three male appellate judges disagreed with Judge Patel's application of the reasonable woman standard. Judge Poole's opinion noted that the two major incidents—Romero's running Fuller off the road and his forcing her to give him her unlisted number—were "sufficiently extreme such that Fuller would no longer know what to expect next from Romero, and [was] reasonably . . . concerned that he might do anything at any time." The other stalking behavior "would reasonably lead Fuller to believe that, no matter how much she tried, she couldn't escape Romero."

Judge Poole then concluded: "Taken together, the fear that Romero might do anything and the fact she couldn't escape would lead a reasonable woman to feel her working environment had been altered." Judge Poole found the city's response to be woefully inadequate. The court chastised the city for blaming the victim rather than the harasser, noting that "harassment is to be remedied through actions targeted at the *harasser*, not the victim" (emphasis added). The appellate court concluded that because the city failed to respond properly to Romero's harassment, it should be found liable.

Fuller even more than *Ellison* highlights that the decision makers' gender isn't as important as their willingness to consider seriously how certain kinds of harassing conduct affect reasonable women. It is ironic and disappointing that a female judge failed properly to apply the reasonable woman standard. But this shouldn't be viewed as particularly surprising, because the law has always treated the male perspective as the norm. Until *Ellison*, as rape law demonstrates, even a reasonable woman standard meant what a man viewed as reasonable female behavior. Without explicitly giving meaningful content to term *reasonable woman*, its purpose of assuring that women's perspectives will receive adequate consideration when the harm involved is gendered will not be fulfilled. Misapplications will continue unless decision makers are adequately informed that the reasonable woman is someone who expects to be treated with respect for her bodily integrity and free agency.

Fuller demonstrates the need for stalking laws. None existed when these events occurred. Today, however, Fuller still might have faced an uphill battle. Romero could argue that any stalking remedy she sought was not based on reasonable fear. He could assert from a male perspective that his behavior was reasonable and her fear was groundless. His selfish, proprietary, and obsessive refusal to leave Fuller alone would be justified by their consensual intimate relationship, which from his perspective gave him a right to continue to pursue her. He could claim he wasn't trying to hurt her, he was just trying to get her back.

The law must not allow men like Romero to get away with mistreating women this way. It is outrageous that Romero was promoted and Fuller was forced to quit. Until a woman's reasonable reactions are explicitly considered, the Romeros of the world will continue to terrorize women with impunity. In this case, had a stalking remedy been available, Romero's unreasonable conduct and Fuller's reasonable fear should have justified convicting Romero of the crime of stalking. But given that Judge Patel was able to conclude that Romero's behavior was not sexual harassment, it is likely he would not have been convicted of stalking either. Unless and until the reasonable woman standard defines stalking, the law will allow some men to stalk and terrorize women, and to get promoted for good measure.

Stalking and Domestic Homicide

More than 30 percent of all women murdered in America are killed by their husbands, ex-husbands, boyfriends, or ex-boyfriends. As many as 90 percent of these women are stalked when they leave or try to leave the relationship. All too often, when a battered woman leaves, her batterer continues to hound and threaten her. Unlike celebrity stalking, the stalking of former intimates receives little publicity—even when the stalking and harassment end in homicide. Our male-biased civil and criminal legal systems have failed to protect these "intimate targets" when they leave, just as they have failed to respond adequately to violence in an existing intimate relationship.

When men stalk their former intimates, the law doesn't really take the behavior seriously. This negligence stems at least in part from the presumption of male possessory rights over certain women and of the woman's implicit responsibility for "causing" the man's behavior. Add to this the law's obstinate refusal to recognize the legitimacy of women's fear when they are threatened and stalked by violent former partners, and it becomes obvious why present stalking law is inadequate to protect many of these women. The diminution of the seriousness of the conduct of stalking intimates runs counter to the reality: men who stalk their former wives or girlfriends frequently escalate the threats and harassment to more violent acts, such as assault, rape, and murder.

"Sorry, Lady"

Her father's description of what happened to Kristin Lardner shows the pervasive flaws in the legal response to intimate stalking. In April 1992, Lardner broke up with Michael Cartier; six weeks later he shot her three times, killing her. They had dated for two and a half months. When she told him the relationship was over, he became angry and violent. As she walked away, he followed, grabbed, and beat her, then left her bleeding on the sidewalk. During the next few weeks, Cartier repeatedly called and followed Lardner, threatening her. On May 11, Lardner decided to go to court. When she went to the police station to file the complaint, an officer showed her Cartier's arrest record. As George Lardner explained in "The Stalking of Kristen," she told her friends later, "You won't believe the size of this guy's police record. He's killed cats. He's beat up ex-girl-friends. Breaking and enterings." The next day she appeared in court to get a one-week temporary restraining order.

The officer Lardner spoke with drafted a complaint charging Cartier with assault and battery, larceny, intimidation of a witness, and violation of the domestic abuse law and submitted it for issuance of a summons for arrest. However, the summons wasn't issued, nor was the information communicated to the judge who issued the temporary restraining order. Cartier violated the order, and Kristin filed a complaint. The next day, she went with friends to the hearing for the permanent restraining order. As a friend told Kristin's father, "It was her understanding that as soon as she got the permanent restraining order, he was going to be surrendered" for violating probation. The judge did not review the complaint, nor did he inquire into Cartier's police record. The hearing lasted five minutes, with the judge merely ordering Cartier to avoid any contact with Lardner and to stay at least two hundred yards away from her. Two weeks later, Cartier ambushed Lardner as she walked down a "busy, sunlit sidewalk" and shot her. He ran into an alley, then ran back and shot her twice more—in the head. Later that day, he returned home and shot himself.

Certainly, Cartier's violent and twisted history, combined with his beating and stalking of Lardner, would seem more than enough to cause a reasonable woman to be afraid. But the law failed to address that reasonable fear. Would the present stalking laws have prevented Kristin Lardner's stalking and death? Based on news reports, it's not likely. In February 1999, Mary Pontarolo and Margaret Hobart wrote an article in the *Seattle Times* about the serious problem of stalking and murder by estranged intimates. They described the recent murders of three women by the men who had been stalking them. Each of these women had gone to the police and obtained a stalking protection order or had the stalker arrested. Nevertheless, these men were not arrested for violating the protection orders, and their targets died.

Similarly, in September 1996, Brent LaLonde wrote in the *Columbus Dispatch* about the stalking death of twenty-four-year-old Toia Roberts at the hands of her twenty-two-year-old former boyfriend Edward Lee. Lee had stalked Roberts for six months—ever since she broke up with him—before he shot her ten times while she slept. Even with the sparse facts set out in the news story, it is impossible to grasp why Lee was not in custody, unless his behavior was considered trivial because it was "just" a domestic dispute. According to the article:

> "We have filed charges against him several times, but nothing ever gets done with it," [Toia's brother] Allan Roberts said. "We've been Downtown so many times we've lost count."
>
> Records in Municipal Court show Lee was charged with felonious assault in October 1995. He was accused of striking Toia Roberts and breaking her jaw.
>
> He'd also been charged with domestic violence, criminal damaging and criminal endangering during the past two years.

About a month before he killed her, Lee had fired shots at Toia's house, compelling her to stay with her mother. The police did nothing.

These all-too-common scenarios show how the deeply embedded male bias in the law continues to treat intimate stalkers more leniently than is warranted. The law still measures both the behavior of the stalker and the response of the target by a male standard. An unexamined presumption remains that stalking by former intimates is a form of "domestic dispute" and thus not the justice system's business. In general, it's hard to get someone arrested for stalking, even for violation of a stalking protection order, and harder still to get a conviction. As in rape cases, when the stalker is a former intimate, the threshold for arrest and conviction is higher, as is the difficulty in stopping the stalker.

Stalking laws must incorporate the reasonable woman standard both for measuring the reasonableness of the woman's fear (including the context of prior violence and threats in a relationship) and for the reasonableness of the man's behavior. Thus, if a reasonable woman would or should know that engaging in the conduct would cause fear in the target, the stalker would be liable. This second factor might at least begin to hold men accountable for their own violence and obsessions—if a reasonable woman wouldn't behave that way, neither should a man. Maybe then fewer women would die at the hands of their "intimate stalkers."

Sometimes the Stalker Loses Too

As in *Fuller*, *Commonwealth v. Stonehouse* involved two police officers who had a brief intimate relationship. Like Patricia Fuller, Carol Stonehouse broke off the relationship. The *Stonehouse* case doesn't describe what was happening in the workplace, only outside it, although Stonehouse continued to work at the same police station throughout. William Welsh obsessively pursued Stonehouse: for approximately three years he stalked, threatened, and assaulted Stonehouse and repeatedly vandalized and burglarized her home and car. Stonehouse changed her locks, called the police, filed complaints, went to court, and moved, but Welsh continued to stalk and assault her.

The court summarized Welsh's "vandalism and harassment" after Stonehouse broke up with him in 1980, saying:

[S]he dated another police officer briefly. Several times, that officer's car tires were flattened. . . . Welsh . . . responded to [Stonehouse's] conversation in a bar with another man by wrecking [her] apartment. Welsh threw food on the floors and walls, cut up [her] clothes, tore the curtains from the windows, urinated on and sliced the bed, ripped the wires out of the television, and soaked [her] shoes and clothes in hot water. [Stonehouse] did not call the police immediately because she did not think she could prove that Welsh had damaged her apartment. Later that night, Welsh returned and [she] called the police. . . . The police knew Welsh, so they did not make a report. They insisted that [Stonehouse] serve as the arresting officer. [She] wrote her own report and also approached Internal Affairs with the problem, with no result. [Stonehouse] filed a complaint with a magistrate regarding this incident. Upon [her] return from the magistrate's office, she encountered Welsh coming out of her apartment, and he threatened to kill her. The magistrate knew Welsh, so Welsh was only required to stay away from [Stonehouse] for thirty days, after helping her clean the apartment, and replacing her clothes and drapes and the money he had taken.

We can look at the facts of the case and think that Welsh might have been stopped if Stonehouse had had recourse to a stalking statute. Welsh's conduct would surely constitute stalking under present statutes, so Stonehouse could have obtained a stalking protective order against him. Right? But Welsh did far more than just follow and telephone Stonehouse. He repeatedly assaulted her, broke into her apartment to vandalize it or terrorize her, stole from her, threatened and attempted to kill her—yet the police did nothing and the court did not much more. Welsh's acts were in themselves serious criminal offenses, but he was never arrested or charged.

Would a stalking statute have made any difference? Perhaps. If it explicitly incorporated the reasonable woman standard we propose, a stalking statute might have counteracted the extreme male bias against "interfering" with "domestic disputes" (particularly when the accused is another police officer) so that Stonehouse's more-than-reasonable fear would have been recognized and responded to. Under such a statute, Welsh's conduct would have to be considered aggravated stalking—a felony.

In fact, Stonehouse did have a brief respite after going to court and getting the thirty-day restraining order, which indicates that stronger legal action might have stopped the conduct. However, after the respite, Welsh resumed his stalking and harassment. He called Stonehouse at least twenty times a day and followed her everywhere. She finally stopped going out socially at all for eight or nine months in 1982. "Welsh always seemed to know where [she] was going, and, in fact, at one time he tapped her telephone."

In addition to essentially imprisoning Stonehouse in her home, Welsh "would not permit her to leave the city." To briefly escape the constant harassment and threats, Stonehouse made secret plans with a woman friend to spend a few days out of town. After their first day at the beach, the women left their motel to find Welsh on the road, following them. They returned to Pittsburgh. As the court put it; "There was no escape for [Stonehouse] from this man, no safe refuge."

How true. Stonehouse had another brief respite after a court ordered Welsh to stop harassing her for sixty days; but the charges and order were dismissed because Welsh did not, during that interval harass Stonehouse, only the man she was dating and his ex-wife. So the violent stalking continued. For example, Stonehouse went out with a woman friend on New Year's Eve, 1982. Welsh followed them, threw drinks in Stonehouse's face, and threatened to kill her. The women fled to the friend's house but Welsh followed, forced his way in, then pulled Stonehouse's hair and spit on her. He later drove her off the road. Returning home, she found devastation:

> There were seventeen knife slashes in [her] waterbed. . . . Drapes had been slashed or torn off the windows and stuffed into the toilet. . . . [Her] clothes were soaking in the bathtub with beet juice and hot water. Cleaning supplies, cold cream, lotion, food and potting soil were smeared all over the walls, windows, floors, mirrors and rugs. Curtain rods and racks were torn off the walls. The back door was off its hinges and every closet was emptied, every piece of furniture upset.

Three months later, Stonehouse shot and killed Welsh in the immediate aftermath of a particularly violent attack, during which he kept repeating, "You're done now," and she thought he was turning to shoot her. Stonehouse was convicted of second-degree murder. Her conviction was not reversed until many years later, when it reached the state supreme court. Even then, the majority of the court did not seem to accept that her belief in imminent deadly harm was reasonable. The substance of the murder trial and the gender bias that prevented Stonehouse from successfully claiming self-defense is discussed in chapter 11.

Stonehouse and the other intimate stalking/homicide cases discussed here demonstrate the serious need for prompt and definitive action to protect women in similar situations. If a stalker's conduct would cause a reasonable woman to be afraid for her safety, she should be able to get an immediate protective order. If the stalker violates that order, he should be arrested and incarcerated. Otherwise, many more women will live in terror and be killed.

PART IV

Domestic Homicide

Indeed, if woman had no existence save in the fiction written by men, one would imagine her a person of the utmost importance; very various; heroic and mean; splendid and sordid; infinitely beautiful and hideous in the extreme; as great as a man, some think even greater. But this is woman in fiction. In fact . . . she was locked up, beaten and flung about the room.

—Virginia Woolf, *A Room of One's Own*

9

Slips in a Dangerous Game

> Men . . . strive to control women, albeit with variable success;
> women struggle to resist coercion and to maintain their choices.
> There is brinksmanship and risk of disaster in any such contest,
> and homicides by spouses of either sex may be considered the slips
> in this dangerous game.
>
> —R. Emerson Dobash and Russell P. Dobash,
> "Violence against Women"

The Spectrum of Domestic Violence

Both men who kill their domestic partners and women who kill their batterers represent extreme outcomes of male violence against women. Male violence against women all too frequently culminates in severe injury or death. The law of domestic homicide reveals in a particularly gruesome way the disparity between the law's treatment of men and women. To generalize broadly, the experiences, perceptions, and actions of men and women differ significantly when it comes to violence in intimate relationships. Yet the male view is the presumptive norm. As a result, the legal system often doesn't take it seriously when men assault, threaten, and stalk their intimates and former intimates, even though many of these women are ultimately killed. In the much less frequent cases in which women kill their batterers, the extreme danger these women experienced is still largely disregarded. As a result, many of these women must prove they suffer from a debilitating psychological syndrome in order to explain their actions.

How our legal system frames the issues and defines the crimes and defenses in domestic homicide tends to perpetuate deadly violence against women. In prosecution of domestic homicides, both female decedents and female defendants bear the brunt of responsibility and blame. Nancy Gibbs quotes Michael Dowd, director of the Pace University Battered Women's Justice Center, as saying their studies found that the average sentence for a woman who kills an intimate is fifteen to twenty years; while for a man, it is two to six years. Although much progress has been made during the past twenty years, only drastic law reform can achieve justice for women and stem the persistent tide of deadly male violence against women. Using our reasonable woman standard for domestic homicides could play a vital role in that necessary reformation.

We advocate explicitly making women—and their gendered experience—the measure of how men treat women. The reasonable woman standard would hold men accountable for their own actions instead of letting violent men, and too often, the law, blame the woman. Further, the reasonable woman would provide a standard for judging women's responses to men's violence against them, including homicide. As a subsidiary, where necessary to enlighten the jury, the reasonable woman standard would also measure the actions of women that purportedly precipitate male violence. Using this woman-defined standard would legally require men to conform to the more controlled and empathetic societal expectations associated with women.

Chapters 10 and 11 focus on the two extreme consequences of domestic violence: men killing women out of jealousy and need to control, and women killing their violent partners in self-defense. We refer to both types of killings as "domestic homicide," and to the relationship as that of either "intimates" or "domestic partners." Although these types of killings differ significantly, they often stem from the same source—men's violence against their intimates, escalating to the point where one or both of them ends up dead. How the law treats these two extreme, deadly outcomes of male violence strongly influences the extent to which society and law condone and perpetuate that violence.

Domestic violence came to public attention in the mid-1970s. Before then it was largely invisible, considered a purely private matter, ignored by the police. Since the 1970s, many changes have been effectuated through direct support of domestic violence victims, political action, and education. Today, battered women have resources available to help them challenge and escape the violence. A vast, excellent literature exists concerning men's violence against women and women's responses to that violence. Nevertheless, men continue to assault and kill their intimates at an alarming rate: one-third to one-half of all female homicide victims in the United States are killed by an intimate, most often after the woman leaves, or decides to leave, the relationship.

In a comprehensive study of intimate homicides written up by Jan Chaiken, the U.S. Department of Justice Bureau of Justice Statistics found an overall decline in the number and percentage of intimate killings between 1976 and 1996. However, the decline was far greater among male victims. In 1976, the study recorded 1,357 men killed by intimates; in 1996, the number dropped dramatically to 516, a *62 percent* decline. During the same time frame, the number of female victims declined from 1,600 reported in 1976 to 1,326 in 1996, a decline of only 17 percent. Something is terribly wrong with this picture.

In addition to the gender disparity in intimate homicide rates, studies show that the motives of men and women who kill their intimates differ significantly. Most domestic homicides culminate years of male emotional and physical violence in attempts to control their intimates. Men generally act out of jealousy and the need to control, whereas women usually kill intimates to protect themselves or others. As Emerson and Russell Dobash describe it:

> When the woman dies, it is usually the final and most extreme form of violence at the hands of her male partner. When the man dies, it is rarely the final act in a relationship in which she has repeatedly beaten him. Instead, it is often an act of self-defence or a reaction to a history of the man's repeated attacks.

Further, men not infrequently commit suicide after killing their intimates, the struggle for control thus ending in two deaths. Therefore, getting such men to behave like a reasonable woman might in some cases save two lives. Consider the January 1999 intimate homicide–suicide reported by Littice Bacon-Blood and Michael Perlstein in the *New Orleans Times-Picayune*:

> [A] month ago, the owner of the Prytania Theatre was arrested for terrorizing his estranged girlfriend—a debutante-turned–New Orleans police officer—allegedly by dousing her with pepper spray, putting a gun to her head and threatening to take her life and his own.
>
> On Friday, Christopher Riley made good on his threat, police said, fatally shooting off-duty officer Gifford Darling Riess in her Uptown apartment, then turning the gun on himself after exchanging shots with another officer who happened onto the scene. Riess, 24, was found on

the bedroom floor . . . , shot in the head and chest, police said. The violence erupted at about noon after Riley, 31, violated a restraining order by forcing his way into Riess' apartment.

The legal system did not take the kidnap, assault, and threats against Gifford Riess seriously, even though she was a police officer and an upper-class white woman. After that incident, Riley was charged only with misdemeanor assault and released on $5,000 bail. Only the day before the murder–suicide—after Riess had filed a civil complaint detailing the assault—was the charge upgraded to felony kidnapping and assault. Even then, the police did not take Riley, a prominent and visible businessman, into custody. Had the justice system viewed the initial "incident" seriously, by measuring Riley's actions against how a reasonable woman would have acted, and therefore convicted Riley of serious crimes, both Riess and Riley might still be alive.

Legal standards defined by male behavior and prerogatives mean that women just can't win. Even the relatively enlightened admission of "battered woman syndrome" evidence in cases of women prosecuted for killing their batterers frequently pathologizes the women. Most courts admit the evidence only for the subjective part of the self-defense standard—whether the defendant herself believed she was in life-threatening danger. By allowing this evidence in primarily to explain why she didn't "just" leave, that she had "learned helplessness" from years of violence, many courts treat battered women as less-than-rational actors. This demeans women and fails to do them justice. A few jurisdictions go further, allowing evidence about patterns of domestic violence in general, and in that particular relationship, to be considered in judging the reasonableness of the woman's actions. This is close to what we advocate. The basic question should be whether killing a violent intimate after brutal and escalating assaults and life-threatening behavior constitutes justifiable homicide—that is, whether a reasonable woman in similar circumstances would have responded with deadly force.

Too often, the law still "understands" how men can kill in jealous rage but not how women can kill their batterers while legitimately defending themselves and others, usually against that same kind of jealous rage. As a result of the profound bias of this legal structure, judges and jurors do not place the responsibility for domestic homicide where it belongs—on the violent man. Instead, the law still tends to blame women both when they are killed and when they kill in self-defense.

Why People Kill Their Intimates

Studies of men who kill their intimates show a common pattern of abuse escalating to death threats and, finally, death—particularly when the victim attempts to leave or in fact leaves her abuser. A comprehensive study of domestic homicide data by Dobash and Dobash found that, although the rates across cultures varied significantly, in every society for which they had a sample of intimate homicides the story was the same: "men kill their intimates out of jealous, proprietary, violent responses to her real or imagined infidelity or desertion." Martha Mahoney, in her groundbreaking work "Legal Images of Battered Women: Redefining the Issue of Separation," points out that more than half of domestic homicides are committed after the victim has left the relationship, "when the batterer's quest for control becomes lethal."

Less frequently, the batterer's lethal quest for control culminates in the woman killing him. When a woman kills her batterer, it is often after her attempts to stop the violence—such as calling the police, obtaining restraining orders, and leaving the relationship—have failed. After the batterer has hunted her down and brought her "home," threatening her with death if she ever tries to leave again, the woman reasonably comes to believe that she must kill or be killed. In fact, the rate of women's killing their batterers declines in proportion to their access to safe "escape routes," to legal and extralegal resource availability. Angela Browne and Kirk Williams found a direct correlation between increased availability of resources for battered women and a decline in women killing their intimates. This supports our view that women do not generally kill their intimates unless they reasonably believe there is no other solution to their situation. Unfortunately, there is no similar correlation between resource availability and male-perpetrated homicides.

That the frequency of men killing their intimates has changed little during the past twenty years, despite increased public awareness and resource availability, can be attributed in large part to our legal system. Much of the law's ineffectiveness stems from the continuing legal emphasis on the female victim's conduct. The law thus fails to make violent men take responsibility for stopping the violence by controlling their own behavior. Instead, the system places the victims in a deadly double bind because the male-biased inquiry focuses on her instead of him, asking, "Why *didn't* she leave?" when she kills him and "Why *did* she leave, and provoke him so?" when he kills her for escaping. The law should shift its perspective and ask instead, "Why didn't he let her go?" The law should presume that a man has no right to hurt or kill a woman simply because he had an intimate relationship with her.

Domestic violence and its most extreme expression, domestic homicide, are *not* inevitable: Men who batter their intimates usually manage to contain their anger in other contexts, with other people. Knowing there are serious legal consequences, such men usually exercise self-control even in the face of highly "provocative" actions such as being fired, insulted, or losing a fiercely contested game.

This capacity for self-control also exists in the domestic context. Variance in domestic homicide rates between cultures and within cultures over time proves this. For example, according to the research of Margo Wilson and Martin Daly described in their article "Who Kills Whom in Spouse Killings?" women in the United States are five to ten times more likely to be killed by their husbands than are European women. This difference, among other factors, shows that men killing their intimates is not biologically predetermined.

Mary Koss and her colleagues in *No Safe Haven* reviewed fifty-two studies of male violence against women in the home, workplace, and community. After careful analysis, they found that "the most influential victim precipitant is being female," concluding that "the victimization of women may be better understood as the outcome of male behavior." Particular women do *not* cause violence against themselves— they do not "do something wrong" or subconsciously want to be hurt. Instead, male *batterers* control whether and when they attack their intimates. These men hurt and kill their intimates *because they are women.*

Homicide law developed in an era in which women were not legal persons at all and men essentially owned their wives and daughters. Under English, and subsequently American, law a man's ownership of his wife included the right to chastise her and even, under certain circumstances, to kill her. William Blackstone's *Commentaries on the Laws of England*, which both described and continues to influence Anglo-American law, stated that because a wife was property she had no corresponding right to kill her lord and master, for adultery or even in self-defense.

The law has changed surprisingly little since: it continues to define the legitimacy of actions by a male standard that makes women responsible for domestic peace. Thus, for any breaches of that peace the woman is presumed to be at fault. This is the true double bind, because the law holds women at fault both when they are killed and when they kill their batterers.

The Law of Domestic Homicide

Under prevailing legal rationales, intimate relationships *by their very nature* legitimate unchecked male anger and violence. Women may not engage in lawful behavior, such as leaving, without risking death at the hands of the men who purportedly love them. At the same time, women may not kill their batterers, even when a reasonable woman in the circumstances would believe she had no other recourse—that it was kill or be killed. For men, the law generally treats violence against an intimate as *more* permissible than violence against an acquaintance or a stranger. The law often treats men who batter or kill intimates, which is especially cowardly and despicable behavior, as less criminal than men who kill strangers. The law tends to sympathize with him and blame her. For women, the law treats violence against an intimate as a greater crime than violence against an acquaintance or a stranger. When she kills him, again the law tends to blame her. When women kill men, even after years of battering, the law still often sympathizes with the men.

Men who kill their intimates often claim provocation or extreme emotional disturbance caused by the victim's actions. They assert that a reasonable "person" in similar circumstances would have lost control and killed. Successful assertion of this claim mitigates the crime, reducing murder to manslaughter or first-degree to second-degree murder. Justice demands that the law find *no* mitigating circumstances. Instead, even as the provocation defense in intimate homicides becomes more restrictive, the same woman blaming and male bias emerge as the foundation for new defenses, such as the "rough sex" defense. In these cases, men claim that the death was an accidental outcome of the decedent's craving for heightened orgasm by choking, thus explaining away rape, battery, and strangulation as *her* sexual perversity.

When women kill their batterers, justice demands that they be found not guilty. However, many women who claim self-defense fail to meet the male-defined legal standard for that defense, particularly the "imminence" and "proportionality" elements. Although many jurisdictions have begun to use a "situated reasonable person" standard in self-defense cases, the law of self-defense remains circumscribed by traditional male behavior. Thus, the law of self-defense frequently limits women to claiming provocation, extreme emotional disturbance, or diminished capacity. This is true even when a reasonable woman would have believed she had to use deadly force in defense of herself or others. In jurisdictions that admit evidence of domestic violence and that have modified the legal standard for claims of self-defense, some women are found innocent; however, many jurisdictions simply do not go far enough, so many innocent women spend years in jail.

When men kill their intimates, justice demands that most of them be severely punished. It is men, not women, who most often engage in extreme violence against their current and former intimates, including aggravated assault, rape, stalking, torture, deadly threats, and homicide. However, the law criminalizing violence typically presumes that perpetrators and victims are male strangers of approximately equal size and strength. This is just not the case for male-on-female violence. Typically, men are stronger and larger than women, and the violence often erupts in a relationship of trust and love, or at least at the end of one. Frequently, children are involved, and social expectations, economic constraints, and threats of greater violence place the victim in ongoing proximity to the violent intimate and hinder her ability to leave. Concomitantly, women who kill their batterers are usually physically weaker and justifiably frightened, so they cannot protect themselves on equal physical terms and must resort to weapons against fists.

For crimes in which men are equally or predominantly the victims, the law focuses on the acts and intentions of the accused. Robbery, common assault, and killings of non-intimates all fit in this category. In such crimes, the behavior of the victim is rarely examined unless the accused claims that the victim precipitated the crime by his own *unlawful* behavior, such as a previous assault. However, when male violence is about control, masculinity, dominance—in woman abuse—the law scrutinizes the victim's conduct. The legal system looks at who "started it," frequently equating a woman's emotional "violence" with physical assault or swallowing improbable and totally unsubstantiated claims that the woman demanded "rough sex" *after breaking off the relationship*, thereby precipitating her own death.

According to the law in many states, a woman may provoke her own death without either threatening or causing physical harm: she "starts it" by, apparently, threatening or causing emotional or dignitary harm. Both judicial decisions and statutes regularly consider lawful behavior such as leaving, having an affair, insulting a man's virility, or mere arguing to be legally adequate provocation for deadly violence against a female intimate. The carefully "neutral" language in *United States v. Paul* shows how emotional and physical violence are conflated in intimate homicides. Describing the night Michael Paul killed his wife, the court said:

> On July 18, 1992, Darlene Paul *died during a fight with her husband* Michael Paul at their home on the Gila River Indian Reservation. Paul claims his wife came home drunk around one o'clock in the morning. According to Paul, Darlene wouldn't tell him where their 2 1/2 year old son, Joshua, was. An argument *ensued* during which the two *traded personal insults and accusations leading to violence*. During *the fight*, Paul strangled Darlene and banged her head against the ground. Believing he killed her, Paul took a shower to wash blood off himself and changed into new clothes. He then went to his mother's house, told her he thought he killed Darlene, and instructed her to call the police to come pick him up. (Emphasis added)

Note the language: Darlene Paul "died during a fight" after "trad[ing] personal insults and accusations." The implication is that a "fair fight" unfortunately ended in accidental death. But Michael Paul did not have any physical injuries, so how was it "a fight"? The court clearly equates emotional "violence" such as insults and accusations with physical attack. In reality, Michael Paul beat and choked his wife to death, essentially because she came home late and argued with him.

As in *United States v. Paul*, once "precipitated," domestic violence and homicide involve a grossly unfair fight, quite unlike the theoretical "fair" bar or street fight. Not only are women less physically and socially equipped to fight than men, but such attacks also usually occur in private, against someone who is isolated and, supposedly, a loved one. Yet the law gives this cowardly and despicable behavior special treatment, assigning much of the blame to the female victim.

Gendered legal standards and assumptions prevent judges and juries from placing domestic homicides in the spectrum of violence by which men subordinate women. Passion/provocation claims rest on the belief that the victim caused her own death by failing to be a proper wife or girlfriend—if she had not misbehaved, he wouldn't have killed her, so his violent response was "reasonable." Similarly, when a battered woman kills in reasonable fear of serious injury or death, the law presumes that she somehow created the situation by failing to be a proper wife or girlfriend—if she had not misbehaved, or if she had just left, he would not have beaten her and she would not have killed him, so her violent response was, per se, unreasonable. Either way, it's really her fault.

In fact, men disproportionately kill women when they leave a relationship, or try to. Many of these women had used all available means to protect themselves. In January 1999, Janet Burkitt and Anne Koch described a typical domestic homicide for the *Seattle Times*:

> [Gertrudes Lamson] filed for a protection order and a divorce from Victor Lamson in September. The divorce was to be final this week, friends say. When he tracked her down two weeks ago at the home of a girlfriend in Bothell, Gertrudes Lamson called the police.
>
> But on Saturday, two days after Victor Lamson pleaded not guilty . . . to violating a protection order and stalking his wife, Gertrudes Lamson, 50, was fatally shot. . . .
>
> In her petition for a protection order, Gertrudes Lamson wrote that her husband told her that if she left him, "both of us are going to die." "I'm scared even going to sleep sometimes when we've had an argument because I'm afraid he'll kill me while I'm asleep," she wrote.

Her friends described Gertrudes Lamson as a strong woman determined to leave her husband. She was a highly respected nursing supervisor at a Seattle hospital. She did everything right, yet she was murdered. Her husband was, apparently, not willing to let her go. Unlike many such cases, Victor Lamson didn't escape responsibility through a manslaughter plea. In June, Lamson pleaded guilty to first-degree murder, signing documents, according to a report by Ian Ith, "in which he didn't specifically admit he shot his wife but agreed that the evidence was stacked against him." Even in this case, however, Lamson's public defender described the murder as "a tragic situation."

While cases like that of Victor Lamson indicate some progression in the law, Gertrudes Lamson is still dead even though she did everything "right." And, sadly, the great majority of men who kill their intimates plead guilty to or are convicted only of voluntary manslaughter.

When women kill their batterers, they too are often convicted of manslaughter. On the surface, that seems equitable, but it's not. This is not a crime of passion, but rather an act of self-defense against the man's violence. Normally, consent to the injury is not a defense to a crime involving serious bodily harm, and for lesser injury consent is ineffective if induced by force, duress, or deception. Despite this general rule of law, the law presumes a kind of shadow consent when it comes to men's violence against women who are or were intimates.

When a battered woman kills, there is an underlying assumption that she somehow consented to the violence leading to the homicide: she should have called the police; she should have or could have just left. The focus is not on what the batterer did to her and its profound unlawfulness but on her and how she erred. If she stayed, it must mean that she *at least* consented to the violence against her. In fact, most women who kill their batterers have previously tried to leave and have been prevented or caught and threatened with death for any further attempts to leave. And even if a battered woman has never tried to leave, her failure to escape does not equate to consent to violence against her.

At its most basic, the law presumes a woman's consent and moral responsibility in both types of domestic homicide because she agreed to "belong" to a man with whom she has or had a relationship. The unexamined assumption remains that she is his property. The reasonable person in the domestic homicide context embodies and perpetuates this profound male bias.

Domestic Homicide and the Reasonable Woman

In a comprehensive review of studies of male violence against women in *No Safe Haven*, Mary Koss and her colleagues found that such violence is inextricably linked with power inequalities—social, legal, economic, physical—and functionally serves to maintain male dominance and female subordination. The structure and application of the law has imposed a view of the world that devalues women's experiences and perspectives and fails to respect women's well-being. As they put it: "Cultural norms and expectations play critical roles in promoting and shaping male violence against women, minimizing or covering up its harmful effects, and preventing the development of effective policies and programs designed to prevent such violence." Law as it now exists supports, and to some extent creates, these cultural norms and expectations.

Lack of respect for women's well-being and autonomy underlies what is wrong with the current law of domestic homicide. The reasonable woman standard and perspective can help explain women's experiences to judges and juries. However, we do not argue that women should be held to a different standard from men. Instead, the legal system must give women's experience precedence over that of men by holding both women and men to the reasonable woman standard. When deciding if someone was provoked sufficiently to warrant a verdict of manslaughter instead of murder, the decision maker would consider the behavior of the killer, as well as his perception of the victim, in context of the reasonable woman standard. Applying a reasonable woman standard in passion/provocation homicides would essentially abolish the defense, because only the rarest (and thus not reasonable by community standards) woman kills in a jealous rage, for "honor," or due to humiliation. Thus, only serious physical violence would legally constitute provocation so as to reduce the offense to voluntary manslaughter. Killing one's intimate in a jealous, possessive rage would be seen as the heinous, unmitigated crime that it is.

With regard to the other extreme outcome of domestic violence, we would have the decision maker judge the battered woman who kills her batterer by how a reasonable woman would have perceived the situation and acted. Rather than focusing on "why didn't she leave," the law would focus on the batterer's violent behavior and the very real threat he posed, whether she stayed or left. This change in perspective and legal standard will help dismantle the pervasive, unexamined biases that continue to rationalize and accept grotesque violence against women as inevitable or incited.

We want passion/provocation homicides to be treated as the brutal and unwarranted crimes that they are; at the same time, we want women who kill their violent intimates in self-defense to go free. Some may claim that we are asking to have it both ways; that, to be consistent, both types of killing must be treated either more seriously or less seriously. But that view denies the reality of male violence against women, which is the ultimate "cause" of most intimate homicides, whether the decedent is the man or the woman. To stop the killing, the precipitating violence must cease, *and that can happen only when men—and the law—stop blaming women for men's unchecked jealousy, anger, and violence.* Courts must view male violence against women and its deadly consequences from a woman-based perspective by making the reasonable woman the measure of men's behavior.

10

"Provoked" Intimate Homicide

Defendant's aunt testified that defendant stated that he hit the victim "with his fist." . . .

The first officers on the scene noticed bruises on the victim's arms and chest near the collar bone. Dr. S. J. Jones, the parish coroner who examined the victim before she was removed from her home, testified that "the patient had multiple points of trauma, in many places; contusions about the . . . face . . . and also on the arms . . . there were marks on the back of the neck which appeared to be . . . marks that would be compatible with finger marks on the neck." On cross-examination, Dr. Jones testified that there were "many injuries" to the victim's head which "wouldn't have occurred in a single fall to the floor . . . there are many bruises, many violent bruises and injuries to this head—all about the head." Dr. Jones further testified that the cause of death "was either one or two things . . . either one was sufficient . . . manual strangulation or trauma, generalized, multiple points of trauma to the head."
—*State ex rel. Lawrence* (1990),
Chief Justice Calogero, dissenting

Despite this evidence, the majority of the Louisiana Supreme Court held that "the evidence clearly proves that the crime resulted from sudden passion and heat of blood." The court went on to explain: "Although taller and heavier than his wife and a trained soldier, David Lawrence does not fit the stereotype of the wifebeater who finally goes too far. It was his wife who attacked him and backed him into the kitchen." Therefore, the court reversed Lawrence's conviction for second-degree murder, remanding the case to the trial court for sentencing on manslaughter.

According to the law in many states, as long as the killer is a man and the breaking point was his intimate taunting him, having an affair, screaming, attempting to leave him, leaving him, or even arguing with him, it isn't really murder. Instead, because a reasonable *person* might have been so provoked that *he* would kill, it's manslaughter, and he often gets only probation or a relatively short sentence. Where the killing is particularly gruesome, intimate provocation still commonly mitigates the severity of the crime or penalty so that it is reduced from first- to second-degree murder or from a capital to non-capital sentence.

Elizabeth Rapaport calls this the "domestic discount," by which the law of homicide treats men who are "provoked" to kill women less seriously than other, similarly violent criminals. These almost entirely male-perpetrated killings are often exceptionally brutal. Pam Belluck, in a *New York Times* article on a study of woman-killing, reported that in these cases women "are very likely to be punched and hit and burned and thrown out of windows" in violence that "sp[eaks] of enormous rage." Nevertheless, the law often concludes that these women victims provoked the rage and consequently their own deaths.

When a woman leaves or otherwise challenges the man's hegemony, the law assumes that she did something wrong, thereby persistently retaining vestiges of male property rights over women. The law views adultery, "desertion," and other exercises of autonomy by women as profound violations of male rights and honor. Thus, judges and juries "understand" passion/provocation killings of intimates and see them as somehow reasonable, because some ordinary men in such circumstances would be likely to lose control and kill. However, when a woman kills out of sexual jealousy, a similar honor violation is not presumed. The outcome in the (very) rare cases when a woman kills her adulterous husband highlight the gendered foundation for passion/provocation killing.

For example, in September 1998, Shirley Quick was released to a halfway house after spending twenty-three years in prison for killing her estranged husband. There was evidence that he had asked her to bring his handgun to the mobile home where he was living. By Shirley Quick's account, when she arrived he came to the door zipping up his pants. An editorial in the *Lakeland (Florida) Ledger* on July 20, 1998, quoted her as saying: "His shirt was open. I started to come in and he blocked me and I saw, in side vision, this girl; she was naked, going down the hallway." Quick shot him four times, killing him. She was convicted of first-degree murder—an inconceivable outcome had the genders been switched, particularly in 1975. For such "simple" pro-voked homicides, men are almost invariably charged only with second-degree murder or voluntary manslaughter. In 1975, a man might well have not even been charged.

In this chapter we argue that, when determining whether a killing was sufficiently "provoked" to reduce the crime from murder to manslaughter, the relevant inquiry should be whether the provocation was such that a reasonable *woman* would have become enraged, lost control, and killed. Just as the jury in 1975 did not make such a deter-mination in finding Shirley Quick guilty of first-degree murder, modern juries applying the reasonable woman standard would not do so for a male defendant. Under a reasonable woman standard, such a claim of mitigation would not even be permitted. The reasonable woman stan-dard applied to *men's* behavior would drastically limit legally con-doned domestic violence and passion/provocation homicide by shifting the analysis to the man's behavior and expecting him to control his vio-lent impulses.

Holding defendants to a reasonable woman standard would essen-tially revoke the domestic discount, making the law treat this most ex-treme form of domestic violence seriously. Furthermore, under our rea-sonable woman standard, the law would no longer permit *anyone* to claim that an intimate's lawful act ever constitutes provocation for deadly violence. Under our proposed reasonable woman standard, nothing short of actual or imminent serious bodily harm would be legally adequate provocation. Passion/provocation homicides would no longer receive special treatment, nor would the killers be given spe-cial understanding.

The Law of "Crimes of Passion"

Homicide law varies from state to state, so "the law" cannot be accu-rately generalized for all jurisdictions. With that caveat, certain com-mon features can be stated. A person who purposely, knowingly, reck-lessly, or negligently causes the death of another human being is guilty of criminal homicide; that homicide may constitute murder or the lesser crime of manslaughter. Most states further divide murder into first- and second-degree murder. The degrees of homicide depend upon the killer's mental state when the crime was committed and, at a more fundamental level, what mental states the legal system deems more culpable.

The most serious level of homicide, first-degree murder, is generally defined as criminal homicide committed purposely or knowingly, with premeditation, or under circumstances showing extreme indifference to the value of human life (commonly called "malice murder"). Additionally, a person who kills another, even accidentally, while committing a felony such as robbery, rape, kidnapping, arson, and felonious escape is guilty of first-degree murder. Some states have made extreme domestic violence a felony, but none that we know of includes felonious domestic violence as a foundation for felony murder. Wouldn't that make a difference—if an accidental killing during felonious domestic violence constituted first-degree murder. As a general rule, a person who kills another without premeditation, malice, or while committing a felony is guilty of second-degree murder.

Generally, a person who intentionally kills another is guilty of the reduced charge of voluntary manslaughter if the killer lost control of himself as a result of legally sufficient provocation by the victim. In common-law jurisdictions, where the appellate courts create homicide law, the test is whether (1) a "reasonable person" in the circumstances would have been so provoked that "he" would lose control and kill; (2) a reasonable person so provoked would not have "cooled off" and regained emotional control in the interval between the provocation and the killing; (3) the killer was in fact provoked; and (4) the killer did not cool off during that interval.

In states where homicide is defined by statute, the test varies. However, most jurisdictions have adopted statutes based on the American Law Institute's Model Penal Code, under which homicide constitutes manslaughter when it is "committed under the influence of extreme mental or emotional disturbance for which there is reasonable explanation or excuse." Generally, reasonableness is viewed from the perspective of "a person in the actor's situation under the circumstances as the actor believes them to be," which in many states is a largely subjective standard. However, some states, such as Oregon, have reintroduced an objective element, requiring in addition to the subjective test that the "reasonableness of the explanation for the disturbance shall be determined from the standpoint of an ordinary person."

We use the term *passion/provocation homicide* as best describing the crime's antecedents and justifications, despite the differing standards in common-law and statutory jurisdictions. In essence, when men kill women who are or have been intimates, the ancient presumptions of women as property and of male honor all too often determine the outcome. As Victoria Nourse notes in "Passion's Progress":

> The important point to see here is that the provoked killer's claim for our compassion is . . . a claim of authority and a demand for our concurrence. The defendant . . . asks that we share his judgments of emotional blame. . . . He asks us to embrace him . . . as one who rightly sets the emotional terms of blame and wrongdoing *vis-a-vis* his victim.

In the 1700s, the law established certain categories of behavior as inherently provocative: being seriously assaulted, observing the assault of a friend or family member, illegal arrest, and finding one's *wife* in the act of adultery. Until the 1900s, if a defendant became enraged and killed in response to one of these unlawful acts, there was no inquiry into whether that provocation was objectively sufficient to cause his loss of control. Because the provocation was categorically sufficient, he was guilty only of manslaughter. In particular, adultery was seen as the greatest violation of a man's property. Sometimes killing an adulterous wife or her lover was considered to be justifiable homicide, akin to self-defense. To date, only one state has fully rejected the fundamental assumption of adultery as per se provocation: Maryland in 1997 set out by statute that "the discovery of one's spouse engaged in sexual intercourse . . . does not constitute legally adequate provocation for the purpose of mitigating a killing from the crime of murder to voluntary manslaughter."

The legal doctrine of manslaughter evolved, formally incorporating an objective test that measured the individual killer's actions against how a reasonable man might behave in similar circumstances. The objective part of the test places some boundaries on what provocation is deemed adequate. Nonetheless, this community-based "reasonable man," and later, "reasonable person," standard embodies traditional gender expectations and hierarchies. Because these many assumptions about "normal" or "reasonable" behavior remain unexamined, our law fails to recognize or confront the gendered nature of deadly violence against women. Thus, ironically, in the passion/provocation context, the evolution from the categorical provocation of finding one's wife committing adultery to the "objective" inquiry served primarily to *expand* the scope of adequate provocation. Intimate provocation spiraled out from observing one's wife in an adulterous union, to discovery that she had committed adultery, to the belief that she was committing or would commit adultery, to finding that she wanted to leave, was leaving, or had left.

In an apparent attempt to establish a more neutral, fair standard, the Model Penal Code replaced the common-law manslaughter doctrine with the more subjective test of "extreme emotional disturbance." The code has been adopted at least in part by a majority of states. Ironically, Victoria Nourse found in a comprehensive study, that in "reform" jurisdictions more men are excused than in common-law jurisdictions because they subjectively experienced uncontrolled, killing rage, even if that "extreme emotional disturbance" was not objectively reasonable. Thus, today, in many states, male rage excuses and justifies itself by its very existence. Yet the vast majority of people, including men, are capable of controlling their violent emotions and actions. True fairness demands that aberrant men be held accountable for their violence, particularly against their intimates.

The Reasonable Woman and Passion/Provocation Homicide

The doctrine of provocation, or "crime of passion," which reduces a homicide to manslaughter, is implicitly male-oriented. What constitute provocations are typically related to male experiences, such as aggravated assault, mutual combat, and finding one's wife committing adultery. Surely, women discover their husbands' adultery with comparable or even greater frequency. However, these women almost never go into a rage, losing control and killing their unfaithful spouse. Shirley Quick's is one of only a handful of reported cases of women's killing in a jealous rage. "Reasonable provocation," which reduces murder to the lesser offense of manslaughter and thus results in much less severe punishment, is that which would cause an ordinary man/person to lose "his" self-control. It is male.

In the context of sexual jealousy, provocation was originally limited to the circumstance of a man catching his wife in the act of adultery. However, in modern times courts have extended the scope of such provocation to include a woman is simply leaving, or trying to leave, her spouse or partner. Such provocation means that she may be stalked, kidnapped, stabbed or shot repeatedly, mutilated, battered to death, and because an ordinary "person" might react similarly under the circumstances the killer can claim mitigating circumstances. After all, she was so provoking.

The law of passion/provocation homicide looks at the *victim's* behavior through the male gaze. The law looks away from the volitional nature of the killer's anger and violence, ignoring the fact that most of these men are quite capable of refraining from violent rage in contexts where society deems it impermissible, such as in the workplace. The biased law, like the killer, thus fails to confront the underlying issues of jealousy and the struggle for control of the victim that culminated in her death—the ultimate act of control. And violent men are not compelled to take responsibility for their own actions. Because only the men themselves can stop their violence against women, the issue of legal responsibility for homicide affects thousands of women who are battered and terrorized and who daily face the danger of death.

When the victim of male violence is male, most courts require that provocation occur shortly before the killing. There can be little or no time for "cooling off" from the provocation, and the provocation must be extreme and unlawful. Yet, when men kill women intimates, courts have sometimes extended the cooling-off time period to weeks with the creative concept of "cumulative provocation." And they hold that a woman's lawful, reasonable conduct, such as screaming or saying that she is getting a divorce, would so provoke a reasonable "person" that "he" would kill.

The very existence of this type of provocation as a legal doctrine, let alone the common result of manslaughter rather than murder convictions for these homicides, accepts without challenge the assumption that men understandably react with anger and violence to certain lawful acts, as long as the acts are committed by their women intimates. Thus, the law of manslaughter conflates male anger and violence against women—his right to feel that way and act on it—and implicitly understands it. By doing so, the law sanctions a man's belief that his intimate *caused* his rage, that no real man could control his reaction to such upsetting behavior, and that he had to kill her. In stark contrast, the law refuses to conflate a woman's terror and violence or to grasp her understandable and reasonable belief in the necessity of violent self-protection. This is true even in circumstances where the law would not doubt that a man faced with the same violence and threat by anyone, or a woman confronted similarly by a stranger, acted in self-defense.

The doctrine of passion/provocation killings is anomalous in the law of homicide: in most jurisdictions, sufficient provocations involve some form of unlawful assault. Leaving a spouse or even adultery is not unlawful, and even if it were, neither is an assault under any legal standard. Rather, leaving and adultery are manifestations of female autonomy—manifestations that male-dominated society deems harmful and thus provocative. It is outrageously misogynistic that when a woman leaves her intimate, the law "understands" if he kills her, yet when a woman kills her batterer because he will not let her leave alive, the fact that she *didn't* leave increases her legal culpability.

Cases, research studies, and news articles demonstrate that men often assert passion/provocation in killing their partners or former partners, and that women almost never do. A careful search of reported decisions and news reports unearthed very few cases in which a woman claimed passion/provocation for killing her adulterous husband. As Mary Koss and her colleagues described in *No Safe Haven*:

> In a study of both men and women who killed their partners, men most frequently gave as a reason their "inability to accept what they perceived to be a rejection of them or their role of dominance over their eventual victim." . . . a walk-out or threat of separation was especially provoking, representing an "intolerable desertion, rejection, or abandonment." In killing their women partners, men in this study believed they were reacting to a previous offense against them (i.e., leaving) on the part of their wives.

Now that women are legal persons, rather than men's property, mitigation based on those premises serves no purpose. Fairness to the dead woman is more important than fairness to the killer. Joshua Dressler asserts a bizarre kind of equality that, unlike in the past, women can now claim passion/provocation homicide. How comforting—women now have official permission to react to separation with anger and deadly violence, just like men. This false and perverse equality which permits women to claim passion/provocation misses the basic point: women almost never kill their intimates out of jealousy or anger about rejection, and most importantly, the law should not condone acting that way. It is bad social policy to legitimate this kind of provocation, regardless of gender. Jealousy and possessiveness should never mitigate the severity of anyone's crimes. Adding insult to injury, in practice, because of gender bias, the law looks askance at women who kill men, even if the standard is officially nongendered.

What if reasonable provocation were determined by what would cause a "reasonable" or "ordinary" *woman* to lose self-control such that *she* would kill? A court could still consider whether the killer was so provoked by the victim's behavior as to reduce the crime to manslaughter. However, it would cease to do so within the context of male-defined aggression, of offended male sexual pride, or of a man's presumed sexual ownership of "his" woman. Instead, men would have to behave as a reasonable woman would under the circumstances. This would counterbalance the implicit but highly questionable belief that an ordinary man would be so enraged by adultery that he would kill. Concomitantly, it would counterbalance the belief that a woman should know that having an affair or leaving is likely to provoke such a response, and therefore that she assumes the risk—that she is to blame.

Such a paradigm shift would recognize and legitimate broader truths. Even though most people who are so provoked are men, *most men do not kill women intimates when they leave or commit adultery.* The small percentage of men who do not take responsibility for their rage and violence, who hurt and kill their intimates, define a perverse legal norm. Instead, the law should presume that civilized people do not kill in a jealous rage and a desperate need to control, and the law should severely sanction people who do.

The Cases

The stories of passion/provocation killings reach from before the founding of our legal system to the present day. Women are murdered by their past or present partners in every state in America, and in every state, courts drastically reduce sentences because women "provoke" their violent deaths through their autonomous acts. Women who are confused, women who are afraid, women who are angry, women who are calm are murdered every day for making, or trying to make, choices about their own lives that their killers and the judicial system view as somehow harmful or unacceptable.

It is not uncommon for men who kill intimates to have previously stalked and made death threats. However, such actions, which as a rule show premeditation, are viewed differently in domestic homicides. Despite their often extreme brutality, these homicides are rarely viewed as having been committed recklessly, in circumstances indicating extreme indifference to the value of human life. And previous domestic violence, no matter how severe, is frequently excluded from trial evidence as too prejudicial to the accused and is notably absent from the underlying felonies in felony murder.

The cases discussed in this section are representative of pervasive and usually unexpressed gender biases. Some are so egregious that they make the bias visible without overt expression. Others openly state the fundamental sexism that defines the law of passion/provocation killings. These types of cases remain common. Applying the reasonable woman standard in these cases will ultimately eliminate the claim that a woman provokes her own death by engaging in lawful—even if extremely upsetting—behavior. The reasonable woman can change the focus so that the antiwoman bias is seen clearly and simultaneously can reshape the law to respect women's physical integrity, safety, and autonomy.

One of these cases involves a particularly brutal killing in which the sentence was reduced from death to life imprisonment, because the killer had been so disturbed about his ex-girlfriend's moving out months before he killed her. His "extreme emotional disturbance" was shown by his stalking the victim and his refusal to accept her leaving; that is, his ongoing injury of her and his inability to control his own emotions mitigated the crime. Although we do not support the death penalty, we reject minimizing the seriousness of certain killings based on gender and relationship. Such male self-referential analysis paradoxically treats the extreme brutality in intimate homicides as proof that the killer is less culpable.

Instead, the basic presumption in passion/provocation killings should be that the victim's behavior was not unreasonable, and that the killer is responsible for his own anger and his own violent acts. The reasonable woman can also overtly and specifically change the legal standard that excuses male violence and sexual jealousy. If the jury must determine whether the facts and circumstances were sufficient to arouse the passions of the *ordinary reasonable woman,* claims of intimate provocation will become a rarity and eventually disappear entirely. If a reasonable woman would not have killed in those circumstances, it should not be a mitigating circumstance for a man to do so.

"There Are Murders and There Are Murders"

When passion/provocation homicide cases actually go to trial, rather than being resolved by plea agreement, state trial courts do not issue written decisions. And in criminal cases, only the defendant may appeal an adverse trial verdict (with very limited exceptions). Not surprisingly, only a fraction of passion/provocation cases are appealed, thereby resulting in published opinions. With the common verdict of voluntary manslaughter and a minimal sentence, these "provoked" killers rarely appeal—they know they got off light.

As a result, the relative dearth of published appellate opinions presenting the classic passion/provocation defense can be misleading. As statistics and news reports demonstrate, each year men kill thousands of women in intimate homicides. Therefore, we drew the following stories of "provoked" intimate homicides from news stories rather than from appellate cases.

Some of these homicides were controversial, either locally or nationally, but many seem to have garnered little attention. Yet all are shockingly typical. They represent common intimate homicides that rarely appear as published cases, and they highlight deep societal and legal assumptions about such killings. For example, fairly cursory search on Nexis (an on-line news database) limited to a one-year period pulled up hundreds of similar passion/provocation homicides in which the killer either pleaded guilty to or was convicted of voluntary manslaughter. Almost none of these cases was appealed, and many never went to trial. Often the controversies about these cases arise primarily because the judges make such patently biased statements to the press.

A 1989 Oregon case involved clear judicial bias and apparent inability to perceive wife beating as "real" violence. Javier Romero Blanco fatally stabbed his estranged wife and her fifteen-year-old son outside the apartment they had shared. Carmela Mendosa Mejia and her son had returned from a battered women's shelter to collect their belongings. Romero found them in the parking lot and stabbed Mendosa thirteen times and her son ten times with a filed-down steak knife. They both bled to death.

The initial news report foreshadowed the legal outcome in this case, referring to the murders as "a domestic disagreement [that] took a violent turn," preceded by "the woman and her son [becoming] involved in a physical altercation with Romero." Romero assaulted Mendosa and her son as they attempted to escape him. He stabbed them both dozens of times in the back. Presumably, when the victims resisted, screamed, and tried to run away, Romero's assault on them became a "physical altercation," and they became blameworthy.

The prosecution initially charged Romero with two counts of aggravated murder, each of which has a minimum sentence of thirty years without parole and a possible death penalty. Although "the victims had moved from the apartment they shared with [Romero] because he was physically abusing Carmela," Romero was allowed to plead guilty to lesser charges of intentional murder *because he lacked a violent history* and was not considered likely to commit future acts of violence. And then he received extremely light sentences for those crimes. As the judge put it, justifying the concurrent ten-year minimum terms imposed instead of the twenty-year minimum recommended by the prosecutor, "there are murders and there are murders." That is, wife killing—even estranged wife and stepson killing—is not really murder.

A Pennsylvania case that generated national controversy involved similar judicial bias and bluntness about that bias. The *Peacock* case was an almost "classic" crime of passion killing: after Kenneth Peacock returned home unexpectedly to discover his wife in bed with another man, he killed her. We argue that even such classic categorical provocation should not be legally sufficient, because a wife's adultery is no longer an invasion of a man's property, and a reasonable woman would not lose control and kill in such circumstances.

Aside from the court's presumption that Kenneth Peacock was, per se, sufficiently provoked, this case is particularly egregious because there was a long interval between the provocation and the homicide. When men kill men, such a cooling-off period nullifies the claim of reasonable provocation. Not so in this case. After chasing his wife's lover away with a gun, Peacock drank and argued with his wife, Sandra, for more than four hours. He then shot her in the head with a hunting rifle.

Domestic homicides like this rarely get much media attention, even when the accused is given a lenient plea agreement. However, the *Peacock* case is notable for the very light sentence imposed—contrary even to the prosecutor's relatively mild sentence recommendation—and for the judge's comments at the sentencing hearing.

Kenneth Peacock pleaded guilty to voluntary manslaughter and was sentenced to eighteen months in prison, with work release. At sentencing, the judge stated that he would prefer not sending Peacock to prison at all, because "I seriously wonder how many men married five, four years would have the strength to walk away without inflicting some corporal punishment." Apparently, this judge considered *capital* punishment the appropriate corporal punishment for adultery.

The prosecution team said that they agreed to the lesser plea and recommended a light sentence because Peacock had no criminal record and no history of domestic violence. But in an interview after the sentence was announced, Sandra Peacock's mother described a pattern of jealousy, threats, and violence by Peacock. A few years before he killed her, Peacock severely beat his wife. She left him but eventually returned. According to her mother, "It was just the one time he really beat her. The other times, he just hit her once." Sandra Peacock's mother thus minimized the violence, saying the beatings weren't serious, except maybe once. The judge minimized the seriousness of Peacock's deadly violence by characterizing shooting an adulterous wife in the head as corporal punishment.

A shocking 1997 California case adds a cultural defense element to the standard male bias in wife killings. A superior court judge held the killing to be *involuntary* manslaughter when Jae-Whoa Chung and Sung Soo Choi, both Korean missionaries, stomped Chung's wife, Kyung-Ja, to death. They claimed they were performing a "demon-cleansing ritual" to save her from the demons that possessed her. The men testified that these demons were making her arrogant and disobedient to her husband. So, naturally, the demons must be exorcised, even if she died in the process.

According to Ann O'Neill's report in the *Los Angeles Times,* the defendants' "religious zeal led them to repeatedly crush Chung's abdomen and chest with their hands and feet—conduct that was reckless but not malicious, the judge determined." Most jurisdictions define involuntary manslaughter as an unintentional killing resulting from a lawful act performed "in an unlawful manner, and without due caution and circumspection." Most also define voluntary manslaughter as killing resulting from "ordinary" recklessness, and second-degree murder as homicide committed with extreme recklessness or with the intent to inflict grievous bodily injury.

The autopsy showed that Kyung-Ja Chung had sixteen broken ribs; the muscles in her thighs were so damaged that the tissue had died; internal organs were displaced and crushed; and a vein leading to her heart was torn. However, because the defendants sincerely believed they were exorcising demons, the judge found that the men were engaging in a lawful act without due caution—they acted with the lawful intention of removing the demons of disobedience. "Demon cleansing" by stomping is a lawful act? Disobedience equals demonic possession? These men crushed and stomped Kyung-Ja Chung to death because she was asserting her autonomy and personhood. Her terribly brutal and prolonged death was held to be involuntary (woman)slaughter. In some ways, this killing seems paradigmatic of why men kill intimates.

Asking how a reasonable woman would perceive and behave in similar circumstances changes the language, its syntax, and its meaning, erasing the false image of neutrality and reason.

A False Parity: The "Domestic Dispute"

Many domestic homicide cases trivialize domestic violence and obscure the profound gender disparity with regard to physical strength and aggression. Commonly, this is accomplished by calling the conflict a "domestic dispute," which glosses over the issue of who is the aggressor and who has more ability to inflict injury. Such domestic imagery also implies private, consensual conduct that is better kept behind closed doors and out of the public realm. The mild, neutral term *domestic dispute* also denies the brutal reality that women are overwhelmingly the victims of domestic violence—that men hurt women. It is not a fair fight. This euphemism represents and reinforces a male-defined paradigm while making a pretense of neutrality. In that sense, it is comparable to the patently male "reasonable person" in domestic homicide law.

The problems inherent to using this terminology to explain and rationalize male violence against women are evident in many domestic homicide cases. For example, explaining why the defendant's driving to his ex-wife's house with a gun, chasing her down the street, and shooting her and their twenty-two-month-old daughter was not consistent with "cold" deliberation, the Florida Supreme Court in *Santos v. State* said his violence stemmed from "an ongoing, highly emotional domestic dispute with Irma and her family." The court concluded that the "unrebutted expert testimony . . . that this *dispute* severely deranged him" was "entirely consistent with a crime of irrational, heated passion brought on by a *domestic dispute*" (emphasis added). In other words, it was reasonable for him to be unreasonable. The court went on to cite as examples six other Florida domestic homicide cases standing for that principle, all involving men killing women. Seemingly, the moral is that if some women were not so difficult, some men wouldn't lose it and kill them. Why, then, if the genders were reversed, would a woman's "irrational, heated passion" be considered anomalous?

Often the bias emanates from juries who are asked to apply the traditional provocation standards. In a 1997 intimate homicide case in Tennessee, the judge appeared to disagree stringently with the jury's verdict of voluntary manslaughter instead of first-degree murder. According to staff reporters in the article "Boyfriend Gets Full Six-Year Term in Domestic Killing," when giving Terry McGee the maximum possible sentence the judge called domestic violence "a plague on our society." McGee had been convicted of domestic violence five times during the ten years before he killed his girlfriend "during an argument." McGee claimed that he tripped while carrying his SKS assault rifle and that it went off accidentally, striking Jacquelyn Sims. Nonetheless, jurors found that McGee killed Sims in a state of passion and "under enough provocation to lead a reasonable person to act in an irrational manner." What was the provocation? Was it the "argument"? Apparently, the jury ignored McGee's proven violent history and accepted that "reasonable persons" shoot their intimates during "arguments."

Another striking example of how euphemisms distort reality and reason involved a "domestic dispute" over the volume of the stereo. In *State v. Shannon*, Shannon was convicted of murdering his girlfriend, but the appellate court remanded the case with different manslaughter instructions based on a specific legal issue. However, when viewed critically, the facts don't indicate that manslaughter instructions were merited at all. The court seems to say that a domestic dispute escalated into a crime of passion killing, but it fails to analyze whether the provocation was legally sufficient. Adequate provocation appears to be (1) turning up the stereo and (2) scratching one's attacker when assaulted.

As the court put it, Shannon and his girlfriend "got involved in a domestic dispute" while high on alcohol and crack cocaine. Shannon testified that the victim turned up the stereo volume, and when he turned it down, she would turn it back up. Shannon became increasingly angry. "The dispute escalated to a physical altercation in which apparently both the victim and defendant participated (as evinced by the scratch marks found on defendant's body after he was arrested)." He finally choked her to death, ending the "dispute."

Consider the skewed logic. Turning up the stereo constitutes adequate reason to assault an intimate. Scratch marks show equal participation—even though scratching is not life-threatening. An intimate's turning up the stereo and "participating" in a "physical altercation" is sufficient provocation for manslaughter. Therefore, "this is the kind of case in which it is appropriate to submit heat-of-passion manslaughter." Again, transpose the genders of the killer and the victim, or make the victim a male friend, and the responsibility suddenly falls where it belongs—on the killer. Surely, a reasonable woman would not kill her partner in such circumstances.

Blinders on Justice: *People v. Berry*

People v. Berry is a striking case on many levels. We include it as a paradigmatic case of passion/provocation homicide, exemplifying the way many trial courts still approach passion/provocation homicides. *Berry* shows how far a court will stretch the limits on the time frame and the acts that constitute "reasonable provocation" in domestic homicides so that the crime is reduced to voluntary manslaughter. Although *Berry* was decided in 1976, it remains a legal precedent for passion/provocation killing. Moreover, many criminal law textbooks include it to demonstrate the fluidity of the "cooling-off" requirement, so it forms a basic part of what lawyers know about passion/provocation homicide.

Twenty-year-old Rachel Pessah married Albert Berry, aged forty-six. Three days later she returned to Israel, where she became involved with another man. When she returned to California two months later, she told Berry that she loved someone else and wanted a divorce. They continued living together for a volatile two weeks. Their arguments escalated until one day Berry choked Pessah unconscious with a phone cord; two hours later he sent her to the hospital by taxi. When she was released from the hospital, Pessah went to the police to report the assault. The police issued a warrant for Berry's arrest. Three days later, Berry returned to the apartment. He subsequently stated that he wanted to talk with her, but she was out. He slept there, waiting until she returned, twenty hours later. When she did, he choked her to death with a phone cord.

When told this way, Berry's killing of Pessah does not come across as sympathetic, unexpected, or less blameworthy because of her infidelity. At trial, Berry was found guilty of first-degree murder for killing his estranged wife. The California Supreme Court reversed his conviction on appeal, saying, "Defendant's testimony chronicles a two-week period of provocatory conduct by his wife Rachel that could arouse a passion of jealousy, pain and sexual rage in an ordinary man of average disposition such as to cause him to act rashly from this passion."

The state supreme court empathized entirely with Berry, characterizing the interval between Pessah's return from Israel and the killing as "tormenting" for him. As the court put it—based on Berry's testimony—Pessah "alternately taunted Berry with her [other sexual] involvement . . . and at the same time sexually excited him, indicating her desire to remain with him." She was a bad woman who got what she deserved.

In addition to Berry, the appropriately named Dr. Blinder testified as an expert witness about Rachel Pessah, whom he knew solely through Berry's description. His analytic focus on the victim made overt what is usually covert. Although passion/provocation cases consistently focus on what the victim did to upset the killer, and thereby the victim's at least partial responsibility for her own death, they don't usually clinically diagnose the decedent as wanting and intentionally provoking her own death.

Dr. Martin Blinder testified that a suicidal impulse drove Rachel Pessah to aggravate the increasingly dangerous situation with Berry over a period of two weeks. As he described it; "She did this by sexually arousing him and taunting him into jealous rages in an unconscious desire to provoke him into killing her and thus consummating her desire for suicide." Berry was not entirely ignored in Dr. Blinder's testimony: he was the victim of Rachel Pessah's suicidal impulse. Her provocative behavior over the two weeks prior to her death put Berry in "a state of uncontrollable rage" in which he was "completely under the sway of passion." He couldn't help killing her.

No other testimony supported Dr. Blinder's assessment of Rachel Pessah's mental state. No evidence was introduced to show why this evidence was relevant, let alone reliable. Nevertheless, the court accepted Blinder's suicidal provocation theory without examination or dissenting opinion. According to standard legal rules, only the victim's actions, their effect on the killer, and their probable effect on a reasonable person are relevant to a provocation claim and thus admissible in evidence. The victim's state of mind is considered only in specific circumstances, inapplicable in *Berry*.

Blinder's postmortem psychoanalysis of Pessah should never have been admitted into evidence. It was a particularly egregious manifestation of the belief that women *make* men hurt them because they *want* it. Further, Blinder's diagnosis of Pessah as pathologically provocative and suicidal clearly implied that she wanted Berry to kill her. In this view, Berry did her a favor. The court's admission of this testimony and adoption of the male-biased reasoning are noteworthy in how openly they pathologize and blame the female victim.

Positing a different scenario further illuminates the male bias in *Berry*. For example, if the prosecution had wanted to introduce evidence showing that Rachael Pessah acted "erratically" because she was terrified of Berry and believed that he would kill her if she left, such evidence would not have been admissible. To the lay observer, that evidence would seem relevant to his criminal intent to harm her, and thus to whether he committed first- or second-degree murder rather than voluntary manslaughter. But to the law it is often irrelevant and inadmissible or excluded as too prejudicial to the defendant.

Compare the approach taken by the Pennsylvania Supreme Court in *Commonwealth v. Myers*, a 1992 domestic homicide case. The court excluded evidence of prior serious battering and the victim's fear that her husband would kill her. Shortly before the woman's death by multiple stab wounds, her husband "terribly beat [her] up, her face and eye were all terribly bruised, and her tooth was chipped." She had been extremely fearful of him, as evidenced by statements to others and by her behavior.

Even in a "normal" passion/provocation case, one would think such evidence would be relevant to intent and therefore admissible. In *Myers*, excluding evidence of the defendant's prior violence against the decedent was even harder to comprehend: Myers claimed that *she* had attacked *him*, and he had killed her in self-defense. Normally, the victim's state of mind is relevant when the accused claims self-defense. For example, state-of-mind evidence would be admissible to show that the victim was afraid of the defendant and therefore would not have attacked him. Also, evidence that the defendant had severely battered the decedent previously would tend to show that she had not been the first aggressor when he killed her.

The contrast between the *Berry* and *Myers* cases shows the elastic way in which courts approach admissibility of state-of-mind evidence in passion/provocation homicides. When, as in *Berry*, the victim's purported state of mind shores up the defendant's case, it is often admitted. When it would undermine the defendant's claim, as in *Myers*, it is not.

Another aspect of passion/provocation homicides in which courts tend to be loose with the general rules concerning voluntary manslaughter and biased toward the defendant, is the "cooling-off" time. *Berry* is frequently cited, and criticized, for its extremely elastic interpretation of the cooling-off requirement. Most courts require that a relatively short interval—usually only a few minutes—occur between the provocation and the killing. However, like the expanded scope of provocation and the variable admissibility of evidence of the victim's state of mind, many courts stretch the cooling-off time when men kill their intimates. The basic rationale for manslaughter is that the killings involve lesser criminal intent because they arise out of uncontrollable impulse, without deliberation and without time to regain control. Otherwise, a reasonable man would "cool off" enough to control himself and refrain from killing.

Nevertheless, the court in *Berry* found that, in the circumstances, a reasonable "person" would not have "cooled down," although Berry waited for *twenty hours* for Pessah to return home before he killed her. When she arrived, they had a very brief interaction, during which even Berry did not claim that she was sexually or otherwise provocative. According to Berry's testimony, when Pessah saw him in the apartment, "she said, 'I suppose you have come here to kill me.' [Berry] responded, 'yes,' changed his response to 'no,' and then again to 'yes,' and finally stated 'I have really come to talk to you.' Rachel began screaming." He grabbed her; she kept screaming; they struggled; and then Berry strangled her with a telephone cord. Because of Pessah's "long course of provocatory conduct" and because she screamed, a three-day interval plus twenty hours of waiting was not enough time for a reasonable person to cool down. Rachael Pessah couldn't even express fear—presumably, anything she did or said at that point would have been wrong.

Instead of focusing on Berry's violent behavior preceding the homicide, such as his choking Pessah into unconsciousness days earlier, putting her into the hospital, or the fact that he deliberately sought out a confrontation by lying in wait for her, the court focused on what she did "wrong." And even what she did right, such as going to the police and swearing out a warrant for his arrest, was not seen as contradicting Dr. Blinder's theory that she wanted Berry to kill her.

Berry illustrates a common misconception about "provoked" men who kill their intimates. Courts often view such men as not inherently violent, as posing no threat to society. Apparently, this particular woman was unusually aggravating—a "bad" wife—and thus the violent reaction would not be provoked by a more pliant, submissive, "good" wife.

This mistaken and prevalent assumption by the courts ignores the relevance of the man's previous violence against his homicide victim, as well as his violence against previous, and most likely future, intimates. When Berry strangled Pessah, a warrant was out to arrest him for choking her to unconsciousness days before. Furthermore, he had threatened his first wife with a knife and destroyed property belonging to a girlfriend. He was, in fact, a person with violent propensities, someone who was likely to act violently against intimates.

Stalking Shows *His* Distress, Lessening the Crime: *Farinas v. State*

In 1990 the Florida Supreme Court decided *Farinas v. State*, which demonstrated a level of sympathy toward the killer's emotional disturbance similar to that expressed in *Berry*, although the homicide was more heinous. Because the "extreme emotional disturbance" standard is quite subjective in Florida, there is no discussion of provocation by the victim. In *Farinas*, the killer's emotional state is entirely self-referential and thus self-justifying. However, the traditional assumptions surrounding passion/provocation homicide permeate the opinion.

Alberto Farinas stalked his former girlfriend, Elsidia Landin, for two months before he killed her. Just before the murder, Farinas went to her parents' house looking for her and broke in when her father told him to leave. Landin refused to talk to him, so Farinas lay in wait until she drove off with her father and sister. Farinas followed until she had dropped her father off at work, then tried to force her off the road until she stopped the car. He then reached into her car, took the keys, ordered her to get out, grabbed her arm, and dragged her to his car. He sped away. When he stopped at a traffic light, Landin jumped out of the car, running and screaming for help. Farinas gave chase, shooting her in the back and paralyzing her. She lay on the ground, bleeding, pleading with him to stop. He shot her in the head twice, *unjamming the gun three times in order to do so*. In this horrific fashion, Farinas essentially executed her for leaving him.

At trial, Farinas was convicted of first-degree murder and given the death penalty. On appeal, however, the court's empathy with him was palpable—as was its lack of empathy with the victim. So, despite finding aggravating factors and that the defendant committed the felonies of burglary and kidnapping during the murder, the appellate court reduced his sentence to life in prison. Why? Because Farinas had become so extremely disturbed during the two months since the victim, Elsidia Landin, left him, and was particularly so on the day he kidnapped and shot her.

The appellate court's opinion exemplifies particularly egregious passion/provocation homicide verdicts, in which the reasonable person is male and the victim is made the culprit, thereby reducing the severity of the crime. Although the crime was not reduced to voluntary manslaughter because Farinas had committed other felonies in addition to aggravated murder, the state supreme court clearly saw the situation through the eyes of a rejected lover and thus viewed the crime as less serious. This case also highlights the underlying bias through a dissenting opinion, which to some extent represents the reasonable woman standard as we would apply it.

According to the appellate court majority, Farinas killed in a state of extreme emotional distress, so the homicide was not premeditated murder, worthy of the most serious penalty. That is, Farinas's drawn-out, self-perpetuating distress, manifested by his harassing and stalking Landin over a period of two months, his fury when he was prevented from talking with her earlier in the day, and his intense jealousy all made the offense lesser and somehow showed that the murder wasn't planned. The court doesn't cite any behavior on Landin's part that provoked Farinas—other than leaving him—yet gives great credence to his distress in a way that validates the reasonableness of wounded male masculinity.

This near reverence for "cold" calculation as the *sine qua non* of first-degree, premeditated murder exists almost solely in the domestic homicide context. People get angry, upset, jealous all the time, but it is only when the victim is a female intimate that the validity of the emotion is not questioned, that the imperative of controlling one's own emotions is trivialized. People usually do not kill without any emotion. For killings of non-intimates, courts regularly find that "premeditation" can occur seconds before the act; yet for killings of intimates, hours, even months of demonstrated intent do not show premeditation.

Substituting a different victim, with an equally distressed killer, shows the deep legal bias. For example, imagine that Farinas was fired from a job to which he was quite attached. Over a period of two months he confronts his former supervisor, "Mary Smith," demanding to be reinstated, but she refuses to discuss it. Farinas's masculinity is profoundly wounded because someone else has his job and because a woman fired him. He manifests extreme emotional distress by harassing and stalking Smith over a period of two months, reacting in fury when prevented by her family from talking with her, and expressing intense jealousy of his replacement at work. He then follows and kills Smith, just as Landin was killed. It is almost impossible to conceive of a court finding that his manifest emotional distress lessened or mitigated the crime.

The dissenting opinion rightly points out that while Farinas may have been prompted by jealousy, he clearly planned the crime. He stalked Landin, followed and blocked her car, and kidnapped her at gunpoint. "When she jumped out of the car at a stop light, he chased her and shot her in the back. He then walked up to her as she lay immobilized and executed her by firing two shots into the back of her head, but not before his gun had jammed three times." As he kidnapped her, Farinas told Landin he would kill her before seeing her in the arms of another man. How could the homicide not have been premeditated? Outside the domestic homicide context, courts typically find that a plan may form minutes or even seconds before the killing, and that the homicide is therefore intentional or premeditated, often meriting capital punishment.

Prepared for Deadly Rage: *Moye v. State*

A 1985 New York case offers another extreme example of the self-referential nature of emotional disturbance claims in certain jurisdictions. In *People v. Moye,* the defendant carried a carving knife to a planned sexual encounter. He used that knife to decapitate and eviscerate Gloria Blocken when she laughed at him and told him to leave after he couldn't get an erection. New York's highest court held that the defendant's "savage acts of mutilating and decapitating his victim, coupled with his statements . . . that 'something snapped' inside him when she mocked and taunted him" showed the necessary loss of self-control for the defense of extreme emotional disturbance.

The victim's ridicule of Willis Moye and taunts about his impotence constituted sufficient explanation or excuse for his disturbed emotional state. Therefore, the court held that the offense was mitigated, so the jury should have received instructions on extreme emotional disturbance and had the option of finding Moye guilty of the lesser charge of voluntary manslaughter.

Moye and Blocken were not presently or formerly married, living together, or dating. They had met only twice when Moye killed her. Moye had visited Blocken because he had a problem with impotence, and a friend had told him "if anybody can get you an erection, it would be Gloria Blocken." He met her briefly, and they set up a time for him to go to her apartment for sex. Before leaving he drank heavily, despite the fact that drinking increased his difficulty in getting an erection. He also put a carving knife in his pocket.

Moye appears to have fulfilled the subjective element of extreme emotional disturbance under the New York statute—he was very upset and "lost it." However, he set himself up for the emotional disturbance by drinking heavily and seemed to prepare himself to act on that disturbance by taking a carving knife to Blocken's apartment. Further, Blocken's ridicule of his impotence does not seem to meet the threshold requirement that there be a reasonable explanation or excuse for the emotional disturbance. This case reveals what seems to be a core value in intimate provocation cases: male sexual pride. That pride is injured when a woman rejects a man sexually—by committing adultery, by saying she doesn't love him or like him sexually, by leaving, by laughing. And injuries to that pride constitute per se adequate provocation.

If the reasonable woman standard were applied in cases like *Farinas* and *Moye*, the killer's emotional disturbance and his consequent acts would be viewed in light of whether a reasonable woman would react similarly in the circumstances—which, most likely, she would not.

A Real Crime of Passion: "Rough Sex"

Beginning in the late 1980s, a new variant on provoked homicides appeared. These cases involve women's dying by strangulation after trying to end a dating relationship. In each case, the defendant claimed the victim asked for "rough sex" and it got out of control. She died accidentally, as a result of her own aberrant sexual practices. These cases resulted in convictions for criminally negligent homicide or voluntary manslaughter.

A critical comment by Senator Alfonse D'Amato on the jury's verdict in a 1988 case shows the connection between "traditional" passion/provocation homicide and the newer "rough sex" cases. A *Newsday* article by Alvin Bessent reported that D'Amato decried the verdict of criminally negligent homicide, saying Joseph Porto *should have been convicted of manslaughter instead.* Manslaughter? What was the reasonable provocation?

Seventeen-year-old Kathleen Holland disappeared one afternoon in 1986. Her boyfriend, nineteen-year-old Joseph Porto, joined the intensive search for Kathleen, seemingly quite distressed and worried about her. When they found her body, strangled, bloody, and bruised, the police caught him in a lie and he confessed. Porto confessed on videotape and in writing that he strangled her in a rage because she broke up with him.

At trial, Porto recanted. He said instead that it was a terrible accident: Holland had died during rough sex. Holland had wanted to enhance her sexual pleasure by having a rope tied around her neck. She told him to pull the rope tighter and tighter, until she lost consciousness and died. Explaining why he'd confessed, Porto said he fabricated the story because he was "too embarrassed" to admit the truth. He also denied that Holland was trying to break off their relationship.

Previously, one of Holland's friends had witnessed Porto repeatedly punching her in the face. A few days before she was killed, Holland told another friend that Porto had been stalking her and had run her off the road because she was trying to end their relationship.

A few hours before the murder, a coworker overheard Holland talking to Porto, during which she said: "It's over, Joe. . . . I can't see you any more. Please stop this." Porto kept calling her at work until she agreed to see him "just for an hour." The judge excluded this testimony, as well as other evidence of Porto's history of violence against intimates.

Holland's body was clothed when found, which contradicted Porto's contention that she died during rough sex. Further, her face was badly bruised, and there was blood on her clothing. Nevertheless, the jury bought his story and sentenced him to one and one-third to four years in prison. He was released thirty months later.

In 1994, Gerald Ardito was convicted of manslaughter for strangling a former girlfriend and sentenced to eight to twenty-five years in prison. Marie Daniele had been in a relationship with Ardito but had broken it off, although she continued to see him occasionally "because she felt sorry for him." Like Porto, Ardito claimed that Daniele died accidentally during rough sex. Also as in the *Porto* case, the judge helped Ardito by excluding apparently relevant and credible evidence of prior violence in the relationship.

Only two months before Daniele's death, she ran outside at approximately 2:50 A.M., screaming for help, waking at least three people. According to the report "Advance Ruling Denied on Scope of Rebuttal" in the *New York Law Journal:*

> At least one witness saw [Ardito] with his hands on Daniele's throat, and another chased [him] with a baseball bat. Yet another called 911 and Daniele's screams could be heard on the tape of that call. The victim declined to press charges after this incident. The District Attorney noted that there were indications by the defense that [Ardito] and Marie Daniele had engaged in "erotic asphyxia" before the murder and that defendant would defend on the theory that Daniele had died accidentally during "rough sex." Thus, the prosecutor argued that the uncharged February assault would be relevant and probative insofar as it would establish [Ardito's] motive and intent in the homicide and refute defense claims of mistake, accident or rough sex.

Nevertheless, the court found "the evidence 'too ambiguous' to justify its admission on the People's direct case." Further, "its probative value was 'slight' compared with 'the extremely prejudicial effect' it would have."

The chief medical examiner described Daniele's death as "an absolute text book example of manual strangulation." He also stated that the injuries were inconsistent with accidental death due to sexual asphyxia, since the compression of her neck had to continue for a minute or more after she went limp and lost consciousness, and he knew of no basis for sexual gratification by compressing the neck of an unconscious person.

In both of these cases, the victim was found culpable for inviting her own death. And in a most grotesquely offensive way—she died because she liked violent sex. She died in relentless pursuit of the ultimate orgasm! Despite contradictory evidence and a lack of corroborating evidence, Porto and Ardito both got off light in the circumstances. Try to imagine a woman claiming "rough sex" as a defense for killing a former intimate, let alone succeeding in it. Under the reasonable woman standard, the judge and jury would see these defendants for what they are and convict them accordingly. Even if the victims *had* engaged in consensual "rough sex," a reasonable woman would not continue strangling an unconscious sexual partner unless she wanted to kill him. A reasonable woman would be unlikely to engage in sexual strangulation of her partner, consensual or not. In such cases, the reasonable woman standard should also be applied to the victim's conduct: Would a reasonable woman in similar circumstances ask for rough sex? That would make more obviously relevant any evidence that might support or rebut the defendant's claim. Otherwise, the defendant kills his victim twice—first killing her and then her reputation.

On the Importance of Words

At its most basic level, the reasonable woman standard in passion/provocation homicides is about changing the language and the reality reflected and created by that language. Although all methods have low success rates, studies have found that the most effective way to reduce domestic violence is to reeducate violent men, to make them take responsibility for their own emotions and actions. Part of taking responsibility means suffering legal consequences for their violence.

In a letter to the editor in the *Irish Times*, Dr. Harry Ferguson eloquently expressed the essence of what we want to achieve by the "language and justice making" of a reasonable woman standard:

[A recent article] informed us that the first marriage of Patricia Mc-Gauley, who was slain by [Michael] Bambrick, was "characterised by violence," and that she and Bambrick "regularly fought about, drinking and about Bambrick getting a job." . . .

The use of such language blurs the lines of responsibility and implies that somehow these women were culpable in their own demise because of a supposed propensity to enter "violent relationships."

Abused women do not in fact live in relationships "characterised by violence," but with violent men who make decisions to abuse and violate them. Unless our language and justice making fully and unequivocably reflect the reality of abusive men's total and absolute responsibility for their behaviour, violent men will continue to manipulate the system and even the most heinous crimes against women will go on being minimised and downgraded by the criminal justice system.

Our language and justice system must change to reflect unequivocally that men who batter and kill their intimates are fully responsible for their own violence. The women who "provoke" men who kill them are not "partially responsible"; they do not somehow deserve retribution for emotionally injuring men. We believe that our reasonable woman standard would help prevent many of "the most heinous crimes against women" and transform the system so that, when committed, those crimes are treated with the seriousness they warrant. The reasonable woman standard places the focus where it belongs—on the killer—and ceases blaming the victim for his violent behavior.

At the same time, this standard may allow a glimpse of the murdered woman as an autonomous person, so that her voice is heard, her life and physical integrity valued. By judging the intimate killer's behavior in terms of the reasonable woman, the victim's behavior is no longer seen through a male-defined perspective. She is then the reasonable woman who left, rather than the upsetting, unfaithful betrayer of a reasonable man whom she drove to irrationality.

11

When Battered Women Kill

Husband and wife, in the language of the law, are styled *baron* and *feme*. . . . If the feme kills her baron, it is regarded by the laws as a[n] atrocious crime, as she not only breaks through the restraints of humanity and conjugal affection, but throws off all subjection to the authority of her husband.

. . . The law denominates her crime [of killing her husband] a species of treason, and condemns her to the same punishment as if she had killed the king. And for every species of treason . . . the sentence of women was to be drawn and burnt alive.

—William Blackstone, *Commentaries on the Laws of England*

American law derives almost entirely from the law of England in the eighteenth century. As this quote from Blackstone shows clearly, that legal paradigm did not recognize self-defense by a woman against her "lord and master," father or husband. Men ruled the kingdoms of their homes: even the poorest peasant could go home and beat or kill his wife, and only rarely would the law intervene. If a wife (or daughter) attempted to defend herself, it was she who was culpable. Self-defense simply did not apply to women within the private, domestic realm; instead, killing a husband was tantamount to treason, regardless of the circumstances.

Although this underlying rationale is now unacknowledged, in many ways the law still equates husband-killing with treason: such killing is presumed unreasonable, and the woman is seen as morally responsible for the man's violence against her. The law of self-defense is framed in terms of how men "reasonably" respond to the violence of other men; women killing men isn't part of the picture. The basic terms are skewed so that women who kill their batterers rarely fit the male-defined standard of a justifiable killing. And because at a subterranean level the law equates husband killing with treason, women are held to a *higher* standard for asserting self-defense than a man would be in the same circumstances.

Consider the case of *Commonwealth v. Stonehouse*. Carol Stonehouse, a police cadet, had a brief affair with William Welsh, a married police officer. Big mistake. After she finally succeeded in breaking up with him, he stalked and threatened her relentlessly for years. She changed her locks, called the police, went to court, changed her behavior so as not to "antagonize" him, moved—but she could not stop him from stalking and assaulting her. Welsh repeatedly broke into her home and trashed her belongings, breaking things and cutting up and urinating on her clothes and furniture. Almost daily Welsh let the air out of her car tires and followed her. He burglarized her home, beat her, and threatened to kill her if she didn't return to him. He broke into her car, hid in the backseat, and then sprang on her, holding a knife to her throat, threatening to kill her—then saying he wouldn't kill her, *yet*.

Finally, Welsh appeared in Stonehouse's kitchen pointing a .357 Magnum at her head. They struggled and he knocked her down, beating her head against the floor, screaming that he would kill her. When she managed to grab her own gun, he ran away. As Stonehouse watched from the porch, she saw him turn back. Believing Welsh was turning to shoot her, she shot and killed him.

This is an almost textbook case of self-defense: anyone, male or female, in such circumstances would have felt in reasonable fear of severe bodily harm or death. However, Stonehouse encountered the inverse of the domestic discount—we'll call it the domestic mark up: she was convicted of third-degree murder and sentenced to seven to fourteen years in prison. Even the court that reversed her conviction saw Stonehouse as blameworthy for having been involved in a brief sexual relationship with Welsh. In a well-intentioned but essentially irrational analysis, the court trotted out the battered woman syndrome to explain *why she didn't leave* and why she overreacted to the threat he posed. In short, because she had an affair with Welsh, killing him could only have been a result of "learned helplessness," which would explain her subjective belief that she had to kill him, even though the risk was not objectively reasonable.

Perhaps the most striking aspect of this case consists in the divergent views of the majority, the concurring opinion, and the short but vicious dissent. These three views encapsulate what is so wrong with the present law of domestic homicide when women kill their batterers or stalkers. Thus, the case of Carol Stonehouse is a major focus of this chapter.

Often, men who kill women intimates do so after a separation or divorce or when it appears the woman has decided to leave. Commentators have noted the reality, and often the severity, of risk involved in leaving a violent and threatening man, including the potential for reprisals. Mary Koss and her colleagues in *No Safe Haven* found: "Homicide case histories suggest that attempting to terminate a relationship with a violent partner, or even discussing the possibility of termination, can lead to severe aggression or reprisal." Similarly, Lenore Walker points out in *Terrifying Love* that "separation creates a period of unprecedented danger in battering situations, a danger often not recognized by others." Walker's premise is illustrated by *Stonehouse* and numerous other cases of women who, after leaving or trying to leave, killed their batterers. *Stonehouse* shows that even extreme and blatant danger over a period of years is often not recognized for what it is, simply because an intimate relationship once existed.

Under current law, a reasonable *person's* legitimate fear of death or severe injury by an abusive partner or former partner often doesn't count when *she* finally kills *him*. The law doesn't accept that her fear is reasonable because it is not consistent with the male-combat model, and it threatens the long-established balance of power between men and women in intimate relationships. Even, as in *Stonehouse*, when the homicide fits into the traditional model of self-defense, the existence of a past or present intimate relationship distorts how courts and juries see the defendant: the law fails to recognize the actual, objective risk the decedent posed, even when the threat was quite obvious. When the threat is more subtle, the law often disregards the objective danger as perceived by the woman. The law thereby disregards the fact that battered women become sensitized to signs of impending violence as a matter of safety, if not survival, and are thus able to assess the risk more accurately than an outsider could. Women in these situations just can't win. By modifying self-defense law to incorporate our proposed reasonable woman standard, some of the women who ultimately kill their batterers might finally begin to be treated fairly.

We are not alone in advocating changes in the law of self-defense to incorporate the realities of domestic violence. Our argument in many ways covers well-trodden ground. While not inconsistent with many proposed innovations, our reasonable woman standard attempts pragmatically to "recalibrate" the legal standard so that it will encompass the experience of women and their right to personal safety and autonomy.

The Law of Self-Defense

> Gender-neutral measures that equate the potential of an unarmed man and an unarmed woman to seriously harm, physically menace, or physically control an opposite sex partner run the risk of equating "fender benders" with head-on collisions.
>
> —Mary P. Koss et al., *No Safe Haven*

Under both judge-made and statutory law, a criminal defendant charged with homicide or assault and battery may invoke self-defense to justify the use of physical force against another under certain circumstances. Unlike passion/provocation claims, a successful claim of self-defense results in acquittal rather than mitigation to the lesser crime of manslaughter. Killing in self-defense is deemed justified: the killing is not morally blameworthy because it was the best alternative available, the killer did not "start it," and self-preservation is fully justified.

A successful claim of self-defense for a homicide requires reasonable belief of an imminent danger of severe bodily harm or death and that deadly force is necessary to avoid the danger. The standard for determining whether the defendant's use of physical force in a particular instance was in fact reasonable varies by jurisdiction. Most determine reasonableness on an objective basis, with the standard often phrased in terms of what a "reasonable person" or "person of ordinary firmness" would have done in the defendant's situation.

In general, the crime of murder is defined as a killing committed purposely, knowingly, or "recklessly under circumstances manifesting extreme indifference to the value of human life." According to the Model Penal Code, which has been enacted in whole or in part by most states, "the use of force upon or toward another person is justifiable when the actor believes that such force is immediately necessary for the purpose of protecting himself against the use of unlawful force by such other person on the present occasion." However, for deadly force to be justifiable, the actor must believe "that such force is necessary to protect himself [or a third person] against death, serious bodily harm, kidnapping or sexual intercourse compelled by force or threat." The use of deadly force must be necessary: the actor must not be able to avoid using such force "with complete safety by retreating or by . . . complying with a demand that he abstain from any action that he has no duty to take." However, one does not generally have a duty to retreat from one's home or workplace.

The "equal-force" element of a self-defense claim invokes the male code of combat. A person may use deadly force only to protect against deadly force and usually may use only an equivalent weapon. The equal-force rule also requires that the danger be "imminent" for the response to be reasonable. Essentially, it is self-defense if you "fight fair," with similar weapons and in the heat of combat. The concepts of imminence and proportionality stem from a stereotypical idea of how men should combat violent aggressors of approximately equal strength and fighting ability.

By definition, the traditional standard of self-defense rarely fits battered women who kill. Women are rarely able to respond with equal force against their batterers' attacks—typically, women are physically weaker than men and discouraged from learning how to fight. Furthermore, the cumulative and volatile nature of male violence against women intimates expands the time frame or "zone" of deadly threat, and a woman who has been the target of a batterer's violence over time recognizes that zone of danger.

The proportionality and imminence requirements and the male standard by which they are measured virtually preclude traditional self-defense for most battered women who kill their violent partners. For example, a 1995 U.S. Department of Justice study, *Spouse Murder Defendants,* determined (with unexplained criteria) that 44 percent of women accused of murdering their husbands had been threatened with a weapon or physically assaulted at or around the time of the murder. Of these, 56 percent were convicted. This greater than 50-percent conviction rate for women killing in such circumstances is extreme and unjust. And it doesn't even take into account the fact that the measure of simultaneous assault or threat probably excluded many cases in which women killed in response to life-threatening violence. Not surprisingly, in states that relax the imminence and equal-force requirements when battered women kill and admit evidence on domestic violence and its consequences, more women are found to have killed in self-defense.

Most woman are physically smaller and weaker than men so cannot defend themselves "appropriately" under this male standard. Most women are simply unable to protect themselves against physical assaults without a weapon. Further, as the Washington Supreme Court noted in *State v. Wanrow*, "women suffer from a conspicuous lack of access to training in . . . those skills necessary to effectively repel a male assailant without resorting to the use of deadly weapons." Given the disparity in size, threat, and training, use of a weapon in most circumstances where the batterer is unarmed should be considered "proportional." A reasonable woman standard would allow for this.

When women kill their intimates, whether in confrontational or nonconfrontational settings, they encounter difficulties with the male-defined standard of self-defense. Elizabeth Schneider aptly summarized the problem in "Describing and Changing: Women's Self-Defense Work and the Problem of Expert Testimony on Battering," saying:

> Gender-bias pervades the entire criminal process with respect to battered women who kill. Gender-bias in perceptions of appropriate self-defense, and the legal standard of self-defense, the broader problem of choice of defense, and the need for expert testimony on battering are all interrelated. . . . And, of course, the substance of the defense necessarily shapes the content of any testimony, particularly expert testimony, that might be proffered in support of that defense.

In assessing self-defense claims, some states have adopted a more subjective formulation under which "a person employing protective force may estimate the necessity thereof under the circumstances as he believes them to be when the force is used, without retreating, surrendering possession, doing any other act which he has no legal duty to do or abstaining from any lawful action." However, most states still require that the perceived danger of death or serious bodily harm be objectively reasonable—that a reasonable person would have acted in the same way under the circumstances and that the force used was proportional to that of the threat. For example, it would not usually be proportional to shoot or stab an unarmed man.

At least in theory, battered women who kill would fare better under the more subjective Model Penal Code standard, but even that isn't sufficient to overcome the profoundly male-based assumptions of what is legitimate self-defense. The current self-defense paradigm of a man engaging in approximately equal combat with an aggressor or defending his home or castle against another man or men simply doesn't encompass a woman killing her "lord and master" in self-defense or defense of her children. The law must be deliberately reconstructed to build a new paradigm in which women are truly persons.

Battered women who kill are often limited to pleading incapacity or provocation because the circumstances of the homicide don't fit into the narrow confines of self-defense law. Even when permitted to go forward with a self-defense claim, many women do not succeed. Over the past decade, a majority of jurisdictions have begun to accept expert testimony on the "battered woman syndrome" and evidence concerning the history of violence by the decedent. This has enabled battered women to successfully claim self-defense in certain circumstances. However, using the battered woman syndrome as a defense has troublesome implications. In practice, the battered woman syndrome defense echoes the old incapacity defense—she was acting out of learned helplessness rather than necessity—and fails to adequately consider the terrible experiences and choices these women face. This pathologizing of battered women who kill denies the serious political implications of violence against women and the harsh reality battered women encounter when they try to leave.

When Battered Women Assert Self-Defense

There is a common, but quite false, notion that battered women usually kill their abusers while the men are asleep, intoxicated, or otherwise off guard. Although such killings do occur, women rarely kill their batterers outside violent or life-threatening confrontations. When battered women kill, it is often in the face of escalating violence and death threats. We argue that these women reasonably believe they must resort to deadly force in order to save their own lives or the lives of their children. Yet this type of domestic homicide rarely fits into the supposedly nongendered standard of self-defense.

Reading the popular press, one might think that battered women have become vigilantes out of control, that because they have an "abuse excuse," women kill their intimates instead of just leaving. Some fear that admitting the decedent's acts of violence into evidence would mean that no man is safe—a groundless fear. Women comprise more than 75 percent of the victims of intimate homicides. And as the battered woman defense has gained acceptance, the rate at which women kill their intimates has dramatically *decreased*.

In fact, most courts take a narrow approach to introduction of evidence about domestic violence in cases where battered women kill their abusers, allowing the evidence only in the form of expert testimony on battered woman syndrome. They treat this evidence as a special exception to determine whether the battered woman defendant suffers from a psychological infirmity. For example, in 1993 the New York court in *People v. Rossakis* admitted expert testimony on battered woman syndrome but formally held that it constituted "psychiatric evidence." Thus, the defendant had to submit to psychiatric examination and give statutory notice to the state. According to the court, her act of perceived self-defense was objectively *un*reasonable; the only question was whether her psychiatric disability mitigated her offense.

Not only does placing domestic violence evidence within the constraints of the battered woman syndrome pathologize women and minimize the actual harm inflicted by batterers, but in its most narrow applications, the syndrome emphasis denies women the right even to claim self-defense. When battered woman syndrome evidence is used in its strictest sense, only a woman whose behavior fits the narrow framework of the syndrome benefits. She must have been assaulted repeatedly, economically dependent on her abuser, passive and fearful with low self-esteem—in short, she did not and could not fight back. Narrowly applied, the battered woman syndrome puts battered women who kill in a double-bind—learned helplessness explains why she had to kill him, but her act of killing him denies such helplessness. Women in certain racial groups and social classes have particular difficulty in using the battered woman syndrome effectively—based partly on stereotypes and partly on gritty reality, many of these women do not seem sufficiently helpless, which compounds the essential paradox of "helpless" women being decisive enough to kill.

For many women who kill their batterers, it was the only way to get away alive. Far from suffering learned helplessness, many of these battered women are active survivors who are most at risk when they assert their right to safety and autonomy, when they are, in a sense, most powerful. Perhaps it would be more apt to say that the legal and social systems have learned helplessness and so fail to protect women and to hold men responsible for their own violence.

The great majority of battered women who kill do so in the midst of a dangerous confrontation. For them, battered woman syndrome evidence can become a negative. Many women who kill their violent partners demonstrate significant resourcefulness and strength. Because they are not helpless, they go to prison when they should go free. More appropriately, the law should redefine the standard of self-defense and allow evidence concerning the decedent's violence to demonstrate the actual reasonableness of the battered woman's perception and actions.

A 1993 *Time* magazine story by Nancy Gibbs told what happened to one young woman who apparently didn't seem sufficiently helpless to the court. Shalanda Burt was serving a sentence of seventeen years in prison for shooting her abusive boyfriend, James Fairley. She was nineteen and three months pregnant when she killed him. Burt voiced the plight of many battered women who kill, saying: "After the law turns you away, society closes its doors on you, and you find yourself trapped in a life with someone capable of homicide. What choice in the end was I given?" The article described some of the violence Fairley had inflicted on Burt, and the system's failure to help her:

> A week after she delivered their first baby, James raped her and ripped her stitches. Several times she tried to leave or get help. "I would have a bloody mouth and a swollen face. All the police would do is give me a card with a deputy's name on it and tell me it was a 'lovers' quarrel.' The battered women's shelter was full. All they could offer was a counselor on the phone."

Burt's experience provides an example of the often perverse "equal treatment" of men and women in a battering situation. "Two weeks before the shooting, the police arrested them both: him for aggravated assault because she was pregnant, her for assault with a deadly missile and violently resisting arrest. She had thrown a bottle at his truck." In other words, he beat her up and she fought back or retaliated. But she was found equally, or more, culpable. Given the many previous times the police had refused to arrest Fairley, she thought it grossly unfair that they tried to arrest her, and she resisted. Not only that: "Her bail was $10,000; his was $3,000."

> He was back home before she was, so she sent the baby to stay with relatives while she tried to raise bail. The end came on a Christmas weekend.

After a particularly vicious beating, he followed her to her aunt's house. When he came at her again, she shot him. "They say I'm a violent person, but I'm not. I didn't want revenge. I just wanted out."

The system failed Burt again, in the form of her female public defender, who told her to accept a plea bargain and seventeen years. Burt says, "I wanted to fight. But she said I'd get life or the electric chair."

The *apparent* helplessness of some battered women reflects the reality of their situations—facing daily life-threatening violence with grossly inadequate resources for safely leaving. Without a safe place to stay, police responsiveness and protection, employment and educational opportunities, child care, and financial and legal support, these women literally have no way out. But it doesn't mean these women are innately helpless. Rather, it means there is no one helping them. In fact, a growing body of research indicates that women in assaultive relationships show a high degree of resourcefulness and persistence in their responses to their violent situations and their attempts to stay alive.

When a battered woman attempts to fight back, escape, or contact the authorities, the batterer frequently escalates the abuse and threats of worse to come. These threats often extend to her children and to close family members who might help her. Further, the law is often ineffectual. For example, in a U.S. Department of Justice study, Marianne Zawitz estimated that nearly 90 percent of women killed by intimates had previously called the police, and that half of these had called five or more times.

A reasonable woman might believe that she must kill her batterer, using a knife against his fists or even shooting him while he sleeps because of his greater strength, history of violence, and promises to kill her if she leaves. Yet courts routinely deny such women the right to assert a claim of self-defense at all: the jury never gets to consider whether she acted in self-defense, whether her action was reasonable. In retaining the narrow, male-defined model of self-defense, our legal system denies women justice and legal equality because they don't kill as men kill and because they *do* kill as men kill. This is the fundamental double bind: she must be feminine and passive and kill "like a girl," but if she does, she is seen as psychologically damaged and still often ends up in prison; if she kills as a man would kill, she is aberrant and per se unreasonable, and she goes to prison. Either way, she loses.

Damned If She Does: Commonwealth v. Stonehouse

Commonwealth v. Stonehouse, mentioned in the beginning of this chapter, demonstrates the depth of the law's unexamined bias and moral blame against women. Despite egregious facts and strong evidence that Stonehouse met the traditional standard of self-defense, the court seemed to believe the killing could be seen as "reasonable" only if Stonehouse suffered from battered woman syndrome. The court went on at length about how otherwise she would have left, or at least would have taken effective action in response to the "domestic disturbances." The majority opinion doesn't seem to notice that Stonehouse "left" years before, and that she had done everything possible to stop the decedent's violent assaults and harassment. She was not in a relationship with the decedent in any way—except as the target of his stalking and assaults. Nevertheless, Stonehouse was morally culpable because she had briefly dated the decedent years before, even though he had repeatedly committed serious violent crimes against her person and her property after the termination of their relationship.

This case is also remarkable for the minority opinions. The concurring opinion effectively argues that Stonehouse was entirely reasonable in killing Welsh by *any* standard of self-defense, and that the evidence about Welsh's threats and assaults was relevant to the reasonableness of Stonehouse's belief in the need to shoot in self-defense. At the other end of the spectrum, in a scathing dissent, two justices argue that Stonehouse could *not* be found to have acted in self-defense under any standard, and that she was lucky to have the Pennsylvania Supreme Court acting as her defense attorneys.

But in fact, Carol Stonehouse did everything right. She called the police; they did nothing. She went to court; the magistrate told her she should just move. She moved; Welsh found her. After a while, to avoid "provoking" Welsh, Stonehouse stopped going out at all, except to work. But he continued with his insane campaign of harassment. In the weeks leading up to the homicide, Welsh threatened to kill Stonehouse more than once, and he seemed to have completely lost control of himself. Stonehouse was terrified. The system had completely failed to help. She ultimately shot him, in circumstances in which she clearly feared imminent severe bodily harm or death, and in which any reasonable woman—in fact, any reasonable man/person—would have felt the same. Nonetheless, she was convicted of murder.

The events leading up to this shooting are horrendous. For about three years Welsh stalked, threatened, and assaulted Stonehouse, repeatedly breaking into and vandalizing her home and car. He called her frequently, usually saying: "You deserve to die" and "You ruined my life and you're going to pay for it." These were not idle threats. Welsh brutally assaulted Stonehouse a number of times and both threatened and tried to kill her. The court described a few of the incidents:

> Welsh began calling [her] at least twenty times a day. . . . She agreed to meet with him to make it clear that she did not want to see him any more. . . . Welsh drove . . . to a shopping center where he dragged her out of the car and then repeatedly attempted to run over her with the car. Failing to run over [Stonehouse], Welsh finally jumped out of the car and punched her, breaking her nose and rendering her semi-conscious. [She] recalled seeing flashing red lights at the scene, but no arrest was made. . . .
>
> One night . . . at the end of 1981, Welsh turned on the gas in [Stonehouse's] apartment. [She] became quite ill, but Welsh woke her in the morning with all the windows open, saying "I couldn't do it to you this time, you bitch. I'll do it the next time." He also . . . stole her car.

Despite Welsh's repeated serious crimes against Stonehouse, the police refused to do anything. They told her that she should handle it herself. The attacks escalated.

> In January of 1982, Welsh entered [Stonehouse's] apartment in the middle of the night and threatened to "slice up" [her] face. When asked if she had done anything to provoke this attack, [Stonehouse] replied, "No. I wasn't going out. I was trying not to provoke him. . . ." The same night, Welsh put a gun to [Stonehouse's] head and threatened to blow her brains out. [She] was so terrorized by Welsh that she fled early one morning . . . to her sister's home, certain that Welsh was going to kill her. Welsh called [her] there day and night and showed up at the door . . . cursed and threatened [her] sister. . . . [Stonehouse] reluctantly returned after telling her sister about her life insurance policies and bank accounts.

Notice the court's casual reference to Stonehouse being asked "if she had done anything to provoke this attack." He broke into her apartment *in the middle of the night*, with a knife and a gun, and threatened to "slice up" her face and "blow her brains out." That is burglary, a class-A felony. What would have been adequate provocation for that?

Going out? If Stonehouse had never had an affair with Welsh, the question would never have been asked.

In May 1982, Stonehouse moved again. "By June of 1982, Welsh returned to his more destructive behavior and kicked in the back door of [Stonehouse's] apartment, accusing [her] of having affairs with other men. Welsh also kicked in the front door to [her] apartment. This was done numerous times according to [her] landlord." Neighbors constantly saw Welsh driving around the neighborhood in a van, watching Stonehouse's apartment through binoculars, and were regularly awakened by Welsh pounding on Stonehouse's doors and shouting obscenities.

On New Year's Eve in 1982, Stonehouse went out with a woman friend. After hunting her down and dragging her outside, "Welsh ran her car off the road, took her glasses, beat her head against the inside of her car and spit on her again, saying, 'Wait till you get home. Wait till you get home.'" What she found at home was wreckage and defilement.

Welsh threatened to throw acid on her face. He continued to break into her apartment, follow her, watch her, phone her, and pound her doors day and night. During most of his many phone calls, Welsh would say: "You deserve to die" and "You ruined my life and you're going to pay for it." On the night before the shooting, as Stonehouse drove to a woman friend's house, Welsh followed, tailgating and bumping the rear of her car at traffic lights.

Around 5 A.M. the next morning, Stonehouse returned home. An old friend and neighbor, Steve Owens, also went to her apartment, apparently out of concern for her. Shortly thereafter Welsh began kicking and battering the front door. Stonehouse knew Welsh could break down the door, so she got her gun and let him in. Welsh took the gun from her, but she and Owens were able to retrieve it. "Owens testified that Welsh appeared to be 'wild-eyed' and was not 'the person that I had known.' Welsh immediately left, and within seconds, Welsh threw a brick through the window of [Stonehouse's] car, prompting a neighbor to remark to her son: 'He really looks like he's mad today.'" Stonehouse called the police. As they waited for the police to arrive, Owens went out for cigarettes. After Owens left, Welsh returned.

As [Stonehouse] stood at the kitchen sink, Welsh suddenly appeared in her kitchen pointing a .357 Magnum revolver within six inches of her face. Welsh told [Stonehouse] she was going to die, and she begged him not to kill her as she tried to get her hand on the gun to get it away from her head. [Stonehouse] stated at trial that "He was crazy. He didn't even know who I was in his eyes. I never saw him like that." Welsh backed [Stonehouse] into her bedroom, and when she tripped, he beat her on the back of her head and neck with the gun. Welsh kicked [her] and continued to tell her she was "done now." [She] crawled toward Welsh convinced she would die but still trying to prevent him from shooting her in the face. [Stonehouse] was able to locate her gun, and suddenly Welsh disappeared.

[Stonehouse] knew Welsh would return because he always returned, so she stepped out onto the back porch to look for him, not wanting to be caught with her guard down. As she leaned over the railing, [she] saw Welsh on the ground below aiming his gun at her. Believing that she heard a shot, [Stonehouse] fired her gun twice. One of the bullets entered Welsh at the top of his right shoulder and exited near his clavicle, severing a major artery. At the time of his death, Welsh's blood alcohol level was .14.

. . . she called the police twice after discharging her gun, and was found on her porch in a state of hysteria when the police arrived. Welsh was found dead beside his van with the fingers of his left hand wrapped around the grip and trigger of a .357 Magnum revolver that had not been fired. . . . [Stonehouse] consistently stated to the police, "He shot at me. I shot at him."

The trial court instructed the jury on self-defense, saying: "You may find the defendant guilty only if you're satisfied beyond a reasonable doubt that she did not reasonably believe that the use of deadly force was then and there necessary to protect herself against death or serious bodily injury." The court also described the standard for voluntary manslaughter, saying, "if the defendant believed it was necessary to use deadly force to protect herself from death or serious bodily injury but her belief was unreasonable, then the degree of homicide would not rise higher than voluntary manslaughter."

Under Pennsylvania law, when the defendant raises a supportable claim of self-defense, the prosecution must disprove self-defense beyond a reasonable doubt, that (1) the defendant did not reasonably believe that he or she was in danger of death or serious bodily injury; (2) the defendant provoked the use of force; or (3) the defendant had a duty to retreat and retreat was possible with complete safety. The trial court properly determined that Stonehouse had no duty to retreat from her home. And although the prosecutor tried to prove that Stonehouse "deliberately provoked Welsh's attacks by talking with and dating other men," the Pennsylvania Supreme Court noted, "Nor was there any serious contention that appellant provoked the attack on her by Welsh on the morning of March 17." Thus, the sole issue for the jury was whether Stonehouse reasonably believed that she was in imminent danger.

At a fundamental level, it doesn't seem that *any* evidence other than the previous death threats and Welsh's actions just before the shooting would be necessary to find that Stonehouse killed Welsh in self-defense. Even if Welsh did not in fact shoot at Stonehouse before she shot him, he "was found dead beside his van with the fingers of his left hand wrapped around the grip and trigger of a .357 Magnum revolver," which he had held to her head moments before. Who would *not* have been in reasonable fear of imminent death or serious bodily injury? Add to that three years of virtually continuous assaults, burglary, vandalism, and death threats, and it seems obvious that any person, of any gender, class, race, or age, would have felt the same.

Nonetheless, the jury convicted Carol Stonehouse of third-degree murder and sentenced her to a term of seven to fourteen years in prison. Apparently, the jury did not even think that Stonehouse *un*reasonably believed that deadly force was necessary in that context. That is why we call it the domestic markup—once a woman has had an intimate relationship with a man, however brief, her testimony about his acts against her and her own response and emotions are by definition not credible. "She should have left."

The Pennsylvania Supreme Court ultimately reversed Stonehouse's conviction, reaching the right result for the wrong reason. The court based the reversal on a well-intended but essentially bizarre discussion of the battered woman syndrome—to explain why Stonehouse didn't leave. This case had nothing to do with any syndrome. Stonehouse was not involved in a relationship with Welsh—she broke up with him years before. His constant death threats, assaults, and vandalism induced a completely legitimate, rational, and reasonable fear for her life and safety.

The supreme court held that the jury instructions were erroneous in that, where there has been physical abuse over a long period of time, the reasonableness of a defendant's fear of death or serious injury at the time of a killing must be considered in the context of the defendant's familiarity with the victim's past behavior. "Thus, the jury should have been apprised of the fact that the abuse [Stonehouse] suffered for three years was to be considered by the jury with respect to the reasonableness of [her] fear of imminent danger of death or serious bodily injury." So far, so good.

However, the majority went on to find that the trial court should have considered expert testimony on battered woman syndrome, stating:

> It is widely acknowledged that commonly held beliefs about battered women are subject to myths that ultimately place the blame for battering on the battered victim. For example, battered women are generally considered to be masochists who derive pleasure from being abused. This myth was exploited by the prosecutor in the instant case when he asked [Stonehouse] if she was "a willing participant in the activities that went on between [her] and William Welsh," and when he stressed to the jury in his closing argument that if appellant had truly been an innocent victim she could have put an end to the relationship. Similarly, this myth was given credence by the Superior Court which determined that [Stonehouse's] assertion of self-defense was unreasonable because of "[t]he continued relationship between [Stonehouse] and the victim." These "blame the victim" myths enable juries to remain oblivious to the fact that battering is not acceptable behavior, and such myths do not begin to address why battered women remain in battering relationships.

This is all very well, in the proper context. However, Stonehouse was not by any means a "willing participant," nor was there a "continued relationship," nor did she "remain in a battering relationship." It is almost as if the supreme court, like the prosecutor and the appellate court, could not see the objective facts in this case. For example, the majority stated: "Expert testimony would reveal that battered women view batterers 'as omnipotent in terms of their ability to survey their women's activities,' and that there are reasons for battered women's reluctance to seek help from others, such as fear, embarrassment, and the inability of police to respond in ways that are helpful to the battered women."

In fact, Welsh stalked and harassed Stonehouse so pervasively that it can only be described as "omnipotent" or "omnipresent" surveillance of her activities. And in fact, Stonehouse repeatedly sought to end the harassment, by filing police reports, going to the police department's internal affairs office, going to court, and moving. She didn't demonstrate any false or learned helplessness—the system utterly failed her, by treating Welsh's vicious assaults, burglaries, vandalism, and threats as "domestic disturbances." The system—not Stonehouse—suffered from learned helplessness. What was missing in this case was evidence concerning the three years of violent, threatening acts by Welsh and the distinct escalation manifested in his use of a revolver the day he died. Expert testimony could have rebutted the myth that Stonehouse, simply by being a former intimate, somehow precipitated the assaults or "wanted it," but testimony on battered woman syndrome would have been simply irrelevant.

Justice Zappala, in his concurring opinion, gets it right. He points out that Stonehouse did not argue that expert testimony on battered woman syndrome should have been admitted. She argued instead that Welsh's previous violence against her was relevant to the reasonableness of her actions. Justice Zappala makes a similar argument, stating that while the "jury heard extensive testimony about the victim's violent nature and the abusive relationship," they were not instructed to consider that history of abuse in "determining whether [Stonehouse's] belief that she was in imminent danger of serious bodily injury or death prior to the shooting was reasonable." According to Justice Zappala: "No more harmful omission is conceivable. . . . For this reason alone, I believe a new trial is warranted."

In contrast, Justice Nix wrote a brief and scornful dissent, saying: "The appellant here is a uniquely fortunate litigant in that the Supreme Court of this Commonwealth has elected to serve as her counsel." He saw no error in the decisions of the lower courts and argued that because Stonehouse did not raise battered woman syndrome on appeal, it should not have been considered. He further ignored what she did argue, as emphasized in Justice Zappala's concurrence. As far as Justice Nix was concerned, Stonehouse was guilty of murder, and she got what she deserved.

Stonehouse argued throughout her appeal—as we do—that the jury should have been instructed to consider the cumulative abuse and history of violence and threat with regard to her "reasonable apprehension" of death or severe bodily harm. She argued that her attorney had erred in failing to request jury instructions requiring the jury to consider the cumulative effects of psychological and physical abuse when assessing the reasonableness of a battered person's fear of imminent danger of death or serious bodily harm with respect to a claim of self-defense.

Our use of the reasonable woman would by definition require that the history of violence be admissible as evidence and that the jury be instructed to consider that history in determining the reasonableness of the accused's fear of imminent death or serious bodily harm. The decision maker would ask whether a reasonable woman would have feared imminent death in those circumstances and responded in the way the accused did. The reasonable woman standard would also apply to the decedent's behavior; the jury would be told to consider whether a reasonable woman would have done what *he* did. The reasonable woman standard would most likely have enabled Stonehouse to be found not guilty in the first place, instead of suffering years in prison and appealing to the state's highest court before she was finally released.

Sometimes They Get It (Almost) Right

In some jurisdictions, the legal system is starting to get it right when it comes to battered women killing in self-defense. The justice system seems to be gradually accepting the reality and seriousness of domestic violence and is beginning to see it from a woman's perspective. Some courts' admission of "syndrome" evidence in self-defense claims to establish the dangerousness of the situation and the objective reasonableness of the woman's fear takes the woman's perspective into account. This is related to what we and others advocate, and it certainly results in more battered women successfully claiming self-defense. However, the focus still remains largely on the woman and why she didn't leave, rather than on the decedent's unjustifiable deadly violence.

In *People v. Humphrey*, the California Supreme Court held that battered woman syndrome evidence was relevant and admissible concerning the defendant's credibility. Making the classic argument at trial, the prosecutor urged the jury not to believe Evelyn Humphrey's testimony that the decedent had shot at her the night before the killing, saying that "if this defendant truly believed that the victim had shot at her, on that night, she would have left." On appeal, the court held that evidence on battering, by dispelling commonly held misconceptions about battered women, would have assisted the jury in objectively analyzing the defendant's claim of self-defense.

The court explained that expert testimony would help dispel the ordinary layperson's perception that a woman in a battering relationship can leave at any time and would counter the jury members' "commonsense" conclusions that if the beatings were really that bad, Humphrey would have left her husband much earlier. Further, in the court's view, if the jury understood Humphrey's conduct in light of battered woman syndrome evidence, they might well have concluded that her version of what happened was sufficiently credible to warrant acquittal because, on the facts as she related them, she acted in self-defense.

Similarly, in *State v. Kelly*, the New Jersey Supreme Court reversed the trial court, saying:

> Depending on its content, the expert's testimony might also enable the jury to find that the battered wife, because of the prior beatings, numerous beatings, as often as once a week, for seven years, from the day they were married to the day he died, *is particularly able to predict accurately the likely extent of violence in any attack on her. That conclusion could significantly affect the jury's evaluation of the reasonableness of defendant's fear for her life.* (Emphasis added.)

A news report in February 1998 showed a promising trend for battered women who kill, at least when they have obvious physical injuries. Reporter Marlys Duran described how the prosecution agreed to dismiss a second-degree murder charge against Patricia Lopez for the fatal stabbing of Guadalupe Gonzalez. Taking an innovative approach, Lopez's attorneys sat down with the prosecutors and laid out their evidence that she had acted in self-defense. That evidence included photos taken in the county jail three days after the homicide, showing Lopez with a black eye, cut lip, bruises, and choke marks. Through an interpreter, Lopez described what happened. Three years before, she had left Mexico to escape Gonzalez, but he tracked her down in 1997 and they began living together again. A few months later, Lopez killed him. The district attorney explained that

> she gave prosecutors this account: Lopez and Gonzalez were arguing when he began slapping her, and she slapped him back. Enraged, he began hitting her with a fist and told her he would kill her. Lopez fled to the kitchen, where Gonzalez pinned her against the sink, choking her with one hand and hitting her with the other. She reached back and grabbed a knife from a dish drainer and stabbed Gonzalez in the lower back. Gonzalez let go of Lopez's throat but kept hitting her. She then stabbed him in the heart. She tried to revive him and called 911.

So, after seven months in jail, Lopez was free. While much better than spending years in prison, it seems unjust that Lopez was even charged under the circumstances, or at least that she was not questioned and released much sooner.

These cases show that some courts and even prosecutors have made progress toward achieving justice for battered women who kill. Using the reasonable woman standard is compatible with these approaches but would go further by placing the woman's actions in their appropriate political and social context.

The Reasonable Woman and Self-Defense

Our reasonable woman standard potentially addresses a broad range of gender bias as it affects battered women who kill. It redefines what is appropriate self-defense, changes the legal standard to reflect women's experience in the context of intimate violence, and creates a basis for admission of expert testimony to show that the woman responded reasonably to an abnormal, life-threatening situation. The reasonable woman would also hold men to a standard of conduct that respects the physical integrity and well-being of women. The history of assaults and threats in the particular case, as well as expert testimony concerning the patterns of intimate violence, would be relevant and admissible to show reasonableness of fear by those who kill their batterers. Admission of such evidence would, as it has in many cases where battered woman syndrome evidence was admitted, also dispel some myths that damage the defendant's credibility. However, unlike the present syndrome-based approach, it would do so without pathologizing her.

Most unarmed women are unlikely to put their intimates in fear of violent rape, severe bodily harm, or death by sheer physical menace. Yet, as Koss and her colleagues note, "the aspect of physical menace—the ability of a potential assailant to do damage, coupled with a perception of their willingness to do so—is a powerful dynamic in assaultive male-to-female interactions." For a reasonable woman it may justify deadly force, which typically would not be with her fists. Therefore, the reasonable woman standard would change the proportionality and imminence requirements to take into account the relative size and strength of the parties involved and the context of violence and threat. It would look at the history of violence through the woman's eyes.

In cases where women kill their violent partners, expert testimony and specific jury instructions help establish the conduct and reactions of the reasonable woman, such as the reasonableness of her belief that deadly force was necessary to protect herself from imminent harm and the proportionality of that force. What is meant by a "reasonable woman" will require explication. To avoid putting another name to stereotypes that perpetuate subordination, the behavioral standard must be defined by experts and instructions, as well as described by the individual woman. Otherwise, women face the risk of being held to a definition of reasonableness that is defined in terms of male privilege.

Applying the reasonable woman standard does not mean that all women who kill their batterers will go free. For women who kill their batterers outside of a violent confrontation or even while the batterer is asleep, the reasonable woman standard would only broaden the scope of inquiry and the relevance of the decedent's violence. To prevail in her claim of self-defense, the woman would have to establish that she believed he would kill or seriously injure her when he awoke, and that a reasonable woman in her circumstances would have believed she had no other choice but to kill.

Asking whether the reasonable woman would have acted as the defendant did, with a self-defense standard defined in terms inclusive of women's experience, in a sense asks whether her act was reasonable in response to his conduct. However, to elicit a fuller examination of the bias inherent in the law of self-defense and the treatment of intimate violence, we should also ask whether his violence and threats were reasonable responses to her conduct. Thus, we also advocate that the decedent's behavior be judged by a reasonable woman standard. The judge and jury would evaluate whether the decedent's behavior, and how it affected the accused, was reasonable. If a reasonable woman would not engage in such nondefensive violence, it would be viewed in its true light as unlawful criminal behavior.

A recent comprehensive study by the U.S. Department of Justice and of Health and Human Services, assessing the validity of battered woman syndrome testimony, determined that expert testimony about "battering and its effects" was a more useful construct, applicable to a much broader range of criminal cases involving battered women. As the study put it, "understanding an individual's appraisal of a situation as dangerous involves consideration of the actual threat behavior, the dangerousness of the situation, and the resources at hand for responding to that threat." We wholeheartedly agree with the study's conclusion that "battering and its effects" testimony should supplant the "battered woman syndrome" testimony. We would take it a step further, however, so that the issue is not only battering and its effects but also the objective reality and dangerousness of violence against women. Applying the reasonable woman standard—to her behavior *and* to his—emphatically states that women are entitled to physical safety and personal autonomy.

PART V

Rape

... it was the professor's statement about the mental, moral and physical inferiority of women ... How to explain the anger of the professors? Why were they angry? For when it came to analysing the impression left by these books there was always an element of heat. This heat took many forms; it showed itself in satire, in sentiment, in curiosity, in reprobation. But there was another element which was often present and could not immediately be identified. Anger, I called it. But it was anger that had gone underground and mixed itself with all kinds of other emotions. To judge from its odd effects, it was anger disguised and complex, not anger simple and open.   —Virginia Woolf, *A Room of One's Own*

12

Rape and the Use and Misuse
of the Reasonable Woman

I wish I had just said no. I mean I could've, and I did for once but
then I just let it go.
                    —Sixteen-year-old Jenny, quoted in Tracy Higgins and
                              Deborah Tolman, "Law, Cultural Media(tion),
                                and Desire in the Lives of Adolescent Girls"

Just saying "no" to sex in our society is not enough to make
unwanted intercourse rape under the laws of most states. Jenny's viewing unwanted sex as her fault despite her saying no is typical. Maria T's
case, as described in *People v. May*, further illustrates the law's problem with "no."

Maria, a divorcée with three children, testified about how she was
raped. She and defendant William May went to a bar, where they
drank and played pool. They then went to another bar, had more
drinks, and, as night approached, drove to May's apartment. When
they entered May's apartment, he told Maria to go to the bedroom and
undress. He then went to the kitchen, where she followed him, grabbed
a knife, and told him no. May took the knife from her. He slapped her
face, grabbed her by the arm, and took her to the bedroom, where he
once again ordered her to undress. This time she didn't say no but
"stood there for awhile." Then, because she was frightened, she took
her clothes off and got on May's bed.

May also undressed and got on the bed. Maria tried to get up but he
hit her again. May then put his penis in her mouth and his mouth on
her vagina, telling her to get his penis "nice and hard." She began to
suck on it, feeling she "had no choice." May continued to hit her with
both his open hand and his closed fist, while licking and biting her

221

vagina. Maria responded by vomiting. While oral intercourse continued, the phone rang. When May left the room to answer it, Maria got dressed and escaped from the apartment. She called a friend and got a ride to her car.

The defendant told a completely different story, one of prostitution in return for cocaine. The jury believed Maria T., finding May guilty of forcible oral copulation and assault with intent to commit rape. He was sentenced to concurrent six- and eight-year terms, with an additional year for each of his three prior felony convictions. The court of appeals viewed Maria as less credible, but since it could not substitute its view of the facts for the jury's, it instead applied male rape law with a vengeance. It concluded that, *even assuming the truth of Maria's testimony*, her lack of consent "could reasonably have been misinterpreted." Further, the court implied that she probably really *did* consent, or she would have just left. The court summed up its rationale:

> Maria's behavior in willingly accompanying him to the apartment after several hours of merriment, her failure to escape when presented with the opportunity, and her lack of verbal objection while in the bedroom could reasonably have been misinterpreted by May as the conduct of someone playing games rather than resisting his advances. . . . Thus, there was unquestionably evidence substantial enough to permit a jury to find that the defendant had a good faith, albeit mistaken, belief that Maria consented to the sexual acts he performed.

In short, no doesn't mean no, slapping and punching a woman into submission doesn't mean she isn't willing, and vomiting indicates pleasure and voluntary agreement. To this court, as to many, a "reasonable" woman would have never been in that situation—intoxicated and in a man's apartment—and if she had been, she would have resisted strenuously enough (even after being hit) that her conduct could not "reasonably have been misinterpreted" as "someone playing games" rather than saying no.

Rape and the reasonable woman have a long-standing and problematic relationship. In the context of rape, the reasonable woman is a male construct that has been used against women. The male gaze defines what a reasonable woman would, or would not do. For rape law, the reasonable woman standard focuses on the victim and is defined by how men want women's behavior to be perceived: women want to be seduced and to have their verbal and physical resistance overcome;

women's behavior and clothing indicate willingness to engage in sexual intercourse; and women don't tell the truth about sex.

Webster's Third New International Dictionary defines consent as "capable, deliberate, and voluntary agreement to or concurrence in some action." But that is not how consent is defined when it comes to rape. Although some of the more severe manifestations have disappeared, the fundamental, centuries-old, male-biased presumptions underlying the rape law remain. Despite the frequency with which men commit violence against other men, our law and society do not thereby conclude that men like or want to be beaten, nor that men provoke the violence by their appearance, "merriment," or failure to repeatedly communicate their nonconsent. However, the law presumes these very things about women in many contexts, perhaps most dramatically in its definition of how reasonable women communicate nonconsent in rape law.

In this chapter we redefine the reasonable woman standard for rape law, framing it from a woman's perspective and demanding that women be treated with respect for their bodily integrity and free agency. We argue that when it comes to sex, instead of measuring women's behavior by how men would like reasonable women to behave, men must be held to the standard of how women would like men to behave. From a reasonable woman's perspective, sexual penetration without a woman's consent is rape. Furthermore, from a reasonable woman's perspective, when a woman indicates her lack of consent by word, such as no, or by conduct, such as pushing away, crying, or trying to leave, a man's failure to stop constitutes rape. Finally, from a reasonable woman's perspective, a woman's clothing, line of work, marital status, sexual history, degree of intoxication, or actions such as accompanying a man in his car or to his room or to the park, and kissing or petting do not indicate consent to sex in and of themselves. When it comes to sex, men who fail to abide by the standards that reasonable women view as appropriate should be held legally accountable.

Our analysis in this chapter owes much to the work of Susan Estrich in her law review article "Rape" and her book *Real Rape*. We view her writings as definitive on how the male norm affects the law of rape. Estrich notes that to address unwanted sex adequately, law and social norms must change to treat all sex without a woman's consent as criminal—as rape. Estrich persuasively asserts that when it comes to sex, if a woman says no and a man nevertheless proceeds to have sex with her, he commits the crime of rape. Application of our reasonable woman standard complements this basic legal change. Under our version of the reasonable woman, rape depends on the determination of what women, not men, consider to be consent and nonconsent. For our reasonable woman, no clearly means no and requires the man to stop!

Estrich demonstrates that, despite the law's claim of equal treatment of all rapes, in application the law has created two categories of nonconsensual sex. One category—"real rape"—involves gang rapists, men who use or threaten to use deadly weapons, and, most importantly, strangers. Real rape makes sex without a woman's consent a crime. However, even for real rape, an exception to the consent requirement often exists when a woman's behavior or dress is deemed "provocative."

The other category—"simple rape" or "acquaintance rape"—involves rape by someone the woman knows and who does not use a weapon or significant physical force against her. In a simple rape, a woman can be subjected to sex without her consent and in the face of her protests. A man will rarely be found guilty of simple rape unless he forcibly overcomes the woman's physical resistance. Thus, "appropriate" men are given broad sexual access to women with whom they are acquainted, regardless of the women's wishes. "Appropriate" men form a continuum from intimates and former intimates to neighbors, coworkers, and casual acquaintances. In addition, there exist at least two categories of women for whom nonconsent remains irrelevant: prostitutes and wives. That's why it was important for the defendant May, in the case described at the beginning of this chapter, to convince the jury that Maria was a prostitute. He apparently convinced the appellate court, and therefore her nonconsent was irrelevant.

The vast majority of rape survivors (outside of prison) are women. And the vast majority of women who are raped know their rapist. A survey of eight thousand women and eight thousand men by Patricia Tjaden and colleagues indicated that 86 percent of the rapes reported by the women surveyed were perpetrated by people they knew. Most commonly the rapists were intimates or former intimates. In contrast, strangers committed 60 percent of the rapes against men. Thus, as is true of almost everything else about rape, the long-standing myth that strangers commit most rapes represents men's experience with and perceptions of rape (almost always by other men), not women's.

These rape statistics almost certainly do not account for all the non-consensual sexual contacts the women surveyed experienced. When men they know pressure women into sex against their will and against their verbal nonconsent, many women accept the social and legal norms that don't treat this as rape. But a fundamental aspect of human dignity should be that *no one should be required to engage in sex against her (or his) will.* The goal of redefining the reasonable woman standard in rape law is to better assure that what the law treats as "just sex" is, in fact, based on mutual desire.

Estrich dismantles the false premises underlying the distinctions between "real" and "simple" rape. A woman's demonstrated wishes should determine whether sexual conduct is rape, regardless of what kind of relationship she has with the man involved. The focus should not be on what men want to believe women want but rather on whether the accused's conduct was reasonable in the sense of respecting a woman's words and bodily integrity. As Estrich put it in "Rape":

> I recognize that both men and women in our society have long accepted norms of male aggressiveness and female passivity which lead to a restricted understanding of rape. And I do not propose, nor do I think it feasible, to punish all of the acts of sexual intercourse that could be termed coerced. But lines can be drawn between these two alternatives. The law should be understood to prohibit claims and threats to secure sex that would be prohibited by extortion law and fraud or false pretenses law as a means to secure money. The law should evaluate the conduct of "reasonable" men, not according to a Playboy-macho philosophy that says "no means yes," but by according respect to a woman's words. If in 1986 silence does not negate consent, at least crying and saying "no" should.
>
> Traditionally, the law has done more than reflect the restrictive and sexist views of our society; it has legitimized and contributed to them. In the same way, a law that rejected those views and respected female autonomy might do more than reflect the changes in our society; it might even push them forward a bit.

More than a decade has passed since Estrich wrote those words. We argue that, today, no should always mean no, and often silence or conduct such as crying, pushing away, and trying to leave should negate consent as well. Further, rape law for the new millennium should require affirmative indications that sex is mutually desired.

The Law of Rape

Generally, rape is defined as carnal knowledge or sexual intercourse, by means of force, without the consent or against the will of the survivor. Further, in many jurisdictions, resistance on the part of the survivor is an additional necessary element of the crime of rape. The force, consent, and resistance elements are only officially waived where the woman is unconscious or otherwise deemed incapable of giving consent. However, in application these elements of the crime are often impliedly satisfied for "real rape" but strictly enforced for "simple rape."

Until recently, it was standard to portray rape survivors as responsible for their own rape. While the most severe aspects of the "she asked for it" defense have been diminished by increased awareness and legal changes, the law of rape still differs significantly from other crimes against the person. Contrast the law of rape with robbery, which is generally defined as a felonious and forcible taking of goods or money from the person of another by violence or by putting the victim in fear. The requisite force may be either actual or constructive, such as threatening words and gestures. The victim does not have to show overt physical violence; even a "slight tug" on the arm to take the property or grabbing a purse and running away constitutes sufficient force. As Morris Ploscowe aptly wrote in 1951:

> It is one thing . . . to say that such persons were terribly careless and quite another to state categorically: "When a woman drinks with a man to the point of intoxication, she practically invites him to take advantage of her person. She should not be permitted to yell when she is sober, 'I was raped!'" A man who flashes a roll of hundred dollar bills is also probably courting trouble, yet no one suggests that he cannot later cry, "I was robbed!"

A reasonable woman might be "terribly careless" or naive and still be raped. If she were merely robbed—not raped *and* robbed—she would have presumed rights of possession and freedom from offensive touching. A woman who visits a recent acquaintance to have a drink and is then robbed does not have to prove she didn't consent to the taking; her presence in the robber's home does not have to be justified. A robbery does not become a gift because the victim was drunk, dressed expensively, or voluntarily associated with the robber. But when it comes to rape, any acquaintance can point to intoxication, manner of dress, and the mere fact that they know each other, and the law will accept that as evidence of consent to intercourse. The profoundly male bias underlying rape law requires radical measures to make it consistent with other crimes against the person, such as robbery and nonsexual assault. Substituting our reasonable woman standard for the existing one would facilitate this.

Women, Sex, and the Male Gaze

Historically, the law has viewed women to be particularly lacking in credibility when they allege rape, and even more so when the woman knows her rapist. Unlike primarily male-on-male crimes, the law of rape involved—and still does involve, to a lesser extent—special rules, including requirements for corroboration and prompt complaint, cautionary instructions, and nonconsent as an element of the crime.

These special rules stemmed from the law's overt mistrust of women, in order to protect innocent men from vindictive, lying women. Renowned evidence scholar John Wigmore, in his treatise *Evidence in Trials at Common Law*, argued that women in general, and sexually active women in particular, were unreliable witnesses in sex cases because "the unchaste mentality . . . finds incidental but direct expression in the narration of imaginary sex incidents in which [she] is the heroine or the victim." Many jurisdictions still require a cautionary instruction in sexual offense cases—unlike any other crime. The judge tells the jury that rape/sexual assault is an allegation easily made and difficult to disprove, and that the survivor's testimony therefore requires more careful scrutiny than that of other witnesses. In short, in rape, unlike in any other crime against a person, the complainant is presumed to be lying, or at least to not be very credible.

As in provoked homicide, in many acquaintance rape cases the focus remains on the survivor's conduct, rather than on that of the accused rapist. At a deep level, our law holds women responsible for their own sexual purity and availability. Men may somehow presume consent from women they know, despite express nonconsent and resistance. The legal system does not treat acquaintance rape as real rape: trial judges have characterized acquaintance rape as "friendly rape," "felonious gallantry," and "assault with failure to please." In "Rape," Susan Estrich said, while the focus is on the female victim, the judgment of her actions is entirely male. If the issue were what the defendant knew, thought, or intended as to key elements of the offense, this perspective might be understandable; yet the issue has instead been the appropriateness of the woman's behavior, according to male standards of appropriate female behavior.

As part of this judgment of appropriate female behavior, the rules of evidence have historically singled out rape complainants for special treatment. Their characters were put on trial. Traditionally, courts regularly admitted into evidence rape survivors' sexual history as an exception to the general rule that evidence of a person's character, character traits, or propensity to act in a certain way is not admissible. Until enactment of its rape shield rule, the Federal Rules of Evidence admitted prior sexual history under the exception for "evidence of a pertinent trait of character of the victim of the crime offered by an accused." When Congress enacted the federal rape shield rule, the reasons cited included protecting the privacy of rape survivors, preventing the degradation and humiliation of survivors, and encouraging rape survivors to come forward. Without rape shield rules, survivors often accurately described their experience at the trial as being raped a second time.

Largely as a result of feminist challenges to the sexist and demeaning treatment of rape complainants, most jurisdictions have passed rape shield statutes that exclude evidence of the survivor's prior sexual history—with certain exceptions. The most troublesome exception is that, even under the rape shield rules, previous sexual relations between the survivor and the accused are admissible to show that she consented on the occasion at issue as well. That is, once a woman has engaged in sexual relations with a man, she is forever presumed to be sexually available to him.

When a woman is sexually assaulted, the inquiry focuses on her behavior. After determining whether sexual conduct occurred, most courts still look to what she did to precipitate or prevent the sexual intercourse. If she knows her attacker, the woman must have resisted strongly enough to show her lack of consent. Saying no, pleading, struggling, trying to leave, being forcibly restrained are often not enough—she must act with "earnest resistance," as a reasonable woman would under the circumstances. This "reasonable woman" is, in fact, a "real man" ready to do battle, man to man. Further, she must be found to belong on the correct side of the virgin/whore dichotomy. If she falls into one of the many categories of "bad women," the onus will fall on her even in stranger or other "real" rapes.

Contrast the rape of a man to that of a woman. When a man is sexually assaulted, the justice system does not ask whether he consented, whether he "really wanted it," or whether he communicated his lack of consent to his attacker. The system also does not ask whether he was intoxicated, what he was wearing, or why he was hitchhiking or walking alone late at night. Rather, a man's lack of consent is assumed, based upon the coercive or violent circumstances of the attack.

Unrapeable Women

Courts and jurors tend to assume that a woman raped by a stranger did not consent—unless she is a prostitute or was dressed like she was "looking for trouble." However, when the survivor isn't attacked by a total stranger, consent is often presumed. Some women are unrapeable. She may be bad or black or his wife or the kind of woman or girl who was looking for trouble or a "good time." Consider the 1981 "statutory rape" case of *Michael M. v. Superior Court.* The following dialogue comes verbatim from the trial transcript in this case and involves the questioning of the survivor:

> Q. Now, after you met the defendant [at the bus stop], what happened?
> A. We walked down to the railroad tracks.
> Q. What happened at the railroad tracks?
> A. We were drinking at the railroad tracks and we walked over to the bush and he started kissing me and stuff, and I was kissing him back, too, at first. Then, I was telling him to stop—
> Q. Yes.
> A. —and I was telling him to slow down and stop. He said, "Okay, okay." But then he just kept doing it. . . . We was laying there and we were kissing each other, and then he asked me if I wanted to walk over to the park; so we walked over to the park and we sat down on a bench and then he started kissing me again and we were laying on the bench. And he told me to take my pants off.

I said, "No," and I was trying to get up and he hit me back down on the bench and then I just said to myself, "Forget it," and I let him do what he wanted to . . .

Q. *Did you have sexual intercourse with the defendant?*

A. Yeah. . . .

Q. You said he hit you?

A. Yeah [in the face with his fist]. . . .

Q. As a result of that, did you have bruises or any kind of injury?

A. Yeah. . . . I had bruises.

Q. Did he hit you one time or did he hit you more than once?

A. He hit me about two or three times.

Michael M. was decided by the United States Supreme Court. The rape survivor, Sharon, was sixteen, a minor, and by statute deemed incapable of consent. Nevertheless, in upholding the constitutionality of convicting the defendant Michael under a gender-specific statutory rape statute, Supreme Court Justice Harry Blackmun viewed Michael as the victim of mutually desired sex where the woman unjustly cried "rape." Justice Blackmun noted that

[their] nonacquaintance with each other before the incident; their drinking; . . . their *foreplay,* in which she willingly participated and seemed to have encouraged; and the closeness in their ages . . . are factors that should make this an unattractive [case] to prosecute at all, and especially to prosecute as a felony. . . . [Nevertheless] the facts, I reluctantly conclude, may fit the crime [of statutory rape]. (Emphasis added.)

For Blackmun, a reasonable woman who acted as Sharon did would have viewed the sexual intercourse as just sex, not rape. By kissing him, she engaged in "foreplay." And for a girl like her, a few slugs in the face were foreplay as well.

How Justice Blackmun viewed Sharon represents the dichotomy drawn between good women who get raped and bad women who have rough sex. A reasonable good woman and a reasonable bad woman view a man's sexual overtures differently. Bad women are "asking for it" when they wear provocative clothes, drink alcohol, go to bars alone, or even walk down the street at night, much less go off with men they meet at bus stops. A good woman would rather die than be raped; therefore, a woman who has sex without suffering serious injury from her resistance (more than a few slugs to the face) is per se "bad" and unrapeable, unless the man jumped her from the bushes and brandished a deadly weapon. And some women are viewed as so bad that even the stranger jumping them from the bushes can't rape them. For example, in the 1989 Florida case *State v. Lord,* the defendant kidnapped and raped the twenty-two-year-old victim repeatedly at knifepoint—a classic violent stranger rape. Nonetheless, according to an Associated Press report that ran in the *Chicago Tribune,* the jury acquitted him because "she asked for it . . . she was advertising for sex" and "she was up to no good by the way she was dressed." After his acquittal, the defendant was returned to Georgia to face several rape and assault charges. But because the Florida woman wore a tank top and sheer miniskirt, she was fair game.

Because law is male, it treats many women as unrapeable. This category of unrapeable women probably would have included Sharon had she been an adult. It definitely includes wives and prostitutes. The law of rape presumes that a wife never views sex with her husband as rape—her irrevocable consent to sex with her husband is an implied term of her marriage contract. And a prostitute—the epitome of the bad woman—never experiences sex with anyone as rape. For women who are neither prostitutes nor wives, class and race affect whether they are rapeable. Sharon's poor grammar and her hanging out at a bus stop suggest that she was working-class. This very likely influenced Blackmun's assessment of her rapeability.

Then there are women of color. Race and rape have an especially troubled history. Until recently, if a white woman accused a black man of rape, an almost irrebuttable presumption existed that she *was* raped, regardless of the circumstances. In contrast, black women were unrapeable. As Angela Harris notes in her article "Race and Essentialism in Feminist Legal Theory":

> The experience of rape did not even exist for black women. During slavery, the rape of a black woman by any man, white or black, was simply not a crime. Even after the Civil War, rape laws were seldom used to protect black women against either white or black men, since black women were considered promiscuous by nature. . . . "Rape" . . . was something that only happened to white women; what happened to black women was simply life.

Thus, the dominant group—white upper- and middle-class men—restricts the sexual availability of their "own" women to themselves and creates whole classes of "others" who simply have no right to say no. And the law structures those privileges.

Even for white middle-class women who engage in sex with someone who is not their husband, a continuum of "reasonable" behavior exists. The better a woman knows the man, the more she must actively resist before he can reasonably be expected to recognize her behavior as nonconsent.

How Can You Rape Your Own Wife?

Until recently, in nearly all states the law explicitly excluded a man's rape of his wife from the crime of rape. Although the spousal exception to rape has been eliminated in most states, the burden of proof makes it virtually impossible to obtain a conviction in most states, so the essence of the exception remains. Legal denial of women's rights to bodily integrity, particularly in the marital or quasi-marital context, remains pervasive. Most states' marital rape statutes require that the victim suffer physical injuries (in addition to the rape itself) and that the couple be living apart. Further, the relationship of marriage or quasi-marriage creates an almost insurmountable presumption of consent.

A particularly grotesque example of how hard it can be to convict of marital rape happened in 1992 in North Carolina, less than a year after that state first recognized the crime of marital rape. In that widely publicized case, not only was the woman brutally raped while bound and gagged but her husband-rapist videotaped the act. The jury saw the videotape, heard her testimony, but found him not guilty after a mere hour of deliberation. The videotape showed the woman's arms and legs tied, her mouth and eyes covered with duct tape (an extremely adhesive tape that would rip off skin and hair when removed), obviously struggling and screaming as her husband penetrated her sexually. The woman testified that her husband had hit her and that she was screaming in protest and pain. The man's defense consisted primarily of tapping into stereotypes and gender bias. He said, "No, I didn't rape my wife. How can you rape your wife?" His attorney argued that the woman enjoyed it when her husband slapped her and that her screams were part of a sex game. "Was that a cry of pain and torture? Or was that a cry of pleasure?" the attorney asked as the tape was played.

Similarly, a 1998 case reported by David Cheezum shows that marital rape remains essentially a legal nullity. That case involved a quasi-marital relationship, and a particularly brutal rape:

> [The defendant] had been living with the victim for five years. She had been taking care of the children from his previous marriage . . . while he worked out of town, coming home on most weekends. One time, he came home, and some tension arose. They argued. She ended up tearing out of her house naked, with a broken nose, bruised face and handfuls of hair torn from her scalp. She found refuge in a neighbor's house. The neighbors called the police. When the police officer interviewed her in front of the neighbors, she said he had beaten her. Twenty minutes later, when the police officer interviewed her again in private, she said he had forced anal, oral and vaginal sex upon her.

With this extent of physical injury, and with the neighbors as witnesses, this would seem to be an open-and-shut case of aggravated rape. Unfortunately, it was not. The defendant was charged with three counts of misdemeanor assault, four counts of felonious assault, and one count of tampering with evidence. He was not charged with rape. The defense attorney portrayed the woman as "kinky" and "a conniving gold digger" and focused on slight inconsistencies in her testimony to convince the jury she was lying. The assailant's first trial ended in a hung jury. In the second he was found guilty only of misdemeanor assault. According to an outraged member of the jury in the second trial, one juror in particular kept repeating: "I flat out don't believe her" and "Yeah, well, I'm not saying he didn't do it, but I won't be responsible for sending a guy down the river for that."

However, when a man assaults more than one girlfriend, his conduct may be taken more seriously. It seems that if it happens to more than one woman, then *they* can be believed. A 1999 case reported by Rebekah Denn highlights how the justice system doesn't seem to recognize rape of an intimate (or a prostitute) until and unless the man proves to be an out-of-control menace. In this case, a man was convicted of an October rape and of imprisoning of his girlfriend. The previous June he had been accused of imprisoning another woman—a prostitute—for days and raping her at gunpoint. In the June incident, after a twenty-one-hour standoff, the police arrested the man and discovered marijuana plants, a sawed-off shotgun, and other guns in his home. He was not charged with rape because the June victim disappeared, and, after all, she was a prostitute. He also was not charged with weapons offenses; instead, he was sentenced to fifty-nine days in jail for possession of marijuana.

When released in October, the man "was angry at [his girlfriend] for not visiting him in jail, among other things. He bound, beat and raped her, then threatened to kill her family and then kill her if she told anyone." He pled guilty to rape and was sentenced to eleven years in prison. However, as part of his plea bargain, the prosecutors agreed not to charge him with "other 'strikingly similar' accusations against him, including an 18-year-old acquaintance who told police he had kidnapped, bound and raped her while on the lam after the October attack." One can only wonder how the prosecutors found such compassion and fairness for this violent triple rapist.

The outcome in all the above cases, and in many similar cases, would be radically changed if the standard of behavior was that of a reasonable woman who demands that her autonomy and bodily integrity be respected. It would show that women—wives and girlfriends and even prostitutes—deserve to be treated with a dignity and respect equal to that of men.

"She Asked for It"

In 1993, Donn Esmonde wrote an article about an almost paradigmatic acquaintance rape—paradigmatic except that the young woman pursued the case through trial, and except that she was sure that her no did, in fact, mean no. What happened is typical of date rapes and of how the woman is perceived as "asking for it." As Esmonde described it:

> a group of girls and a group of guys met over a holiday weekend. Cristina and one of the young men were drinking and kissing in a bar, then went outside. After more necking, she told him to stop. She told him again and again, but he didn't.
> . . . In court, the man's attorney said it "was not your classic case of rape, where there's an unknown assailant who . . . jumps out of the bushes." Recently, she told a male friend the story—and he said it was her fault.

Unlike many victims of acquaintance rape, Cristina persisted in saying no throughout the rape and then pursued a rape claim through the court. Nevertheless, the judge found the man not guilty of sexual misconduct, explaining that "sometimes 'no' means 'yes.'" Presumably, because Cristina was affectionate with this man in the bar and went outside with him, she had no further say—like Sharon in *Michael M.*, kissing him meant that she had per se consented to intercourse. However, that is not at all how Cristina and most women in similar situations perceive sex after they say no or stop. For Cristina, what happened outside was completely different from the kissing and hand-holding in the bar. Instead of feeling affectionate, she was scared and angry; his physical strength, not her desires or protests, determined the outcome.

Susan Brownmiller described what she calls the battlefield of rape, and the unevenness of that field, in *Against Our Will: Men, Women, and Rape*:

> The female did not choose this battlefield, this method of warfare, this surprise contestant. Her position, at once, is unprepared and defensive. She cannot win; at best she can escape defeat. Force, or the threat of force, is the method used against her, and a show of force is the prime requisite of masculine behavior that she, as a woman, has been trained from childhood to adjure. She is unfit for the contest. Femininity has trained her to lose. According to the odds, she is three inches shorter and 24 pounds lighter than her male assailant. This works to her disadvantage psychologically as well as physically, but worse than the difference in size is the lifelong difference in mental attitude toward strength. He has been encouraged from childhood to build his muscles and toughen his fists. She has been encouraged to value soft skin, her slender wrist, her smooth, unmuscled thigh and leg.

But even the many women who today pride themselves on their physical strength and toughness are often no match for an unarmed man who decides to rape them. The law does not sufficiently acknowledge a fact that both women and men know: that most unarmed men have the capability of seriously injuring or killing most women. It's *not* a fair fight.

How Many Prostitutes Must He Rape before a Man Is a Rapist?

Guinn attacked his victims between December 1996 and August 1997. The five women said they were raped in the same dirty, abandoned home.

All were tied with a rope that bound their necks and wrists, causing them to choke if they tried to move their hands. Most were blindfolded and gagged. Some were pierced with needles, others burned with lighters or hot wax and most were violated with objects.

The women were robbed after the attacks.

Guinn contended during the trial that the women had agreed to the brutal sex. He said they filed charges only because he hadn't paid them the agreed amount and because he had left them at the house instead of returning them to where he had picked them up.

This October 1998 news article by Hector Castro sketches an ugly picture, albeit with an apparently just outcome. The jury convicted Guinn, the twenty-eight-year-old rapist, of five first-degree rapes, four kidnappings, three robberies, and five assaults, aggravated by his use of a weapon during the crimes, and sentenced him to 237 years in prison. The prosecutors asked for the "exceptional sentence" because Guinn "had subjected his victims to abject terror and incalculable pain." To some extent this could be considered progress, in that prostitutes have generally been considered unrapeable by pimps, by johns, by police, by anyone. However, much is left unsaid in this article.

The article closes with self-congratulatory statements but omits crucial details about when the women came forward and when the investigation began. The prosecutors praised the justice system, saying "good police work and some luck resulted in Guinn being caught before there were more victims." And in fact, Guinn had another woman in the car with him when he was arrested; the report refers to her simply as "a prostitute."

But why did it take so long to arrest him? Guinn kidnapped, raped, assaulted, and robbed these five women between December 1996 and August 1997. Is it "good police work" to find this man, who raped and tortured his victims in "the same dirty, abandoned" house, after nine months and five victims coming forward?

After praising the police work, the prosecutor is quoted in the article as saying, "We do feel like the assaults were escalating both in frequency and violence." That simple statement indicates that the women were not believed, not considered to have been raped, kidnapped, robbed, and assaulted, until enough women reported similar assaults. As all the women were kidnapped, bound at the neck and wrists, raped, pierced or burned, and robbed, it seems *non sequitur* to refer to escalation in the violence of the assaults. How many prostitutes does it take to bring a credible rape charge? Apparently, five.

Getting It Right

Real progress is being made in some jurisdictions. A 1992 New Jersey Supreme Court decision, *State ex rel. M.T.S.*, foreshadows how the reasonable woman might be used positively in rape cases. New Jersey's sexual assault statute criminalizes "sexual penetration using physical force or coercion." In *ex rel. M.T.S.*, there was sexual penetration without consent but no evidence that the defendant used additional force or threats. In many ways this case is the antithesis of *Michael M. v. Superior Court*, in which kissing, described as foreplay, presumed consent to intercourse, even though Michael M. slugged Sharon until she complied. The New Jersey court described the issue as follows:

> The question posed by this appeal is whether the element of "physical force" is met simply by an act of non-consensual penetration involving no more force than necessary to accomplish that result.
> That issue is presented in the context of what is often referred to as "acquaintance rape." The record in the case discloses that the juvenile, a seventeen-year-old boy, engaged in consensual kissing and heavy petting with a fifteen-year-old girl and thereafter engaged in actual sexual penetration of the girl to which she had not consented. There was no evidence or suggestion that the juvenile used any unusual or extra force or threats to accomplish the act of penetration.

The supreme court agreed with the trial court, holding that "physical force in excess of that inherent in the act of sexual penetration is not required for such penetration to be unlawful," and that the physical force element would be satisfied "if the defendant applies any amount of force against another person in the absence of what a reasonable person would believe to be *affirmative and freely-given permission* to the act of sexual penetration" (emphasis added). In reaching this decision, the court relied on an expressly feminist critique of the traditional law of rape, saying:

> Force was identified and determined not as an independent factor but in relation to the response of the victim, which in turn implicated the

victim's own state of mind. . . . Although the terms "non-consent" and "against her will" were often treated as equivalent, under the traditional definition of rape, both formulations squarely placed on the victim the burden of proof and of action. Effectively, a woman who was above the age of consent had actively and affirmatively to withdraw that consent for the intercourse to be against her will. . . .

. . . if the defendant forced himself on a woman, it was her responsibility to fight back, because force was measured in relation to the resistance she put forward. Only if she resisted, causing him to use more force than was necessary to achieve penetration, would his conduct be criminalized.

According to the court's analysis, the New Jersey legislature had amended the law of rape so that it was in conformity with the law of assault and battery, "adopt[ing] the concept of sexual assault as a crime against the bodily integrity of the victim." Because criminal battery is generally defined as "the unlawful application of force to the person of another," and such force is criminal when it results in either a physical injury or an offensive touching, the court stated that, under the revised statute, "permission to engage in sexual penetration must be affirmative and it must be given freely, but that permission may be inferred either from acts or statements reasonably viewed in light of the surrounding circumstances."

The court in *ex rel. M.T.S.* referred to the reformed sexual assault statute as "reflecting an emerging awareness that the definition of rape should correspond fully with the experiences and perspectives of rape victims." We certainly agree with the court about how rape should be defined. In fact, its definition of consent is consistent with the definition we recommend. However, other courts have not followed *ex rel. M.T.S.*, and various commentators, including the *Harvard Law Review* in a note entitled "The Myth of Context in Politics and Law," have criticized the *ex rel. M.T.S.* standard as "requiring men to be mind-readers." We disagree. This standard requires men to pay attention to their partners' desires and wishes, in addition to their own. If mutual desire is lacking, they must stop. This isn't mind reading, but it certainly requires a change in the traditional attitudes about when it's acceptable for men to proceed with having sex.

What Would a Reasonable Woman Do?

Except when raped by a stranger (and sometimes even then), the law holds women responsible for what happens sexually. Tracy Higgins and Deborah Tolman say,

> men's sexuality is defined as natural, urgent, and aggressive and is bounded, both in law and in culture, by the limits of women's consent. Thus even while women's sexuality is denied or problematized, the culture (and the law) tend to assign to women the responsibility for regulating heterosexual sex by resisting male aggression. When women fail in their responsibility to define the boundaries of sexual behavior, including limiting or denying their own sexual desire, they are marginalized or vilified.

This pervasive cultural portrayal of intercourse as conquest and of women as responsible for whether they are conquered grossly distorts sexual relations. Many men still see women as sexual prey, not as equals. Male aggression, violence, and treatment of women as objects are portrayed and perceived as normal and perhaps inevitable. Changing that perception will require a significant shift in the law, a shift whereby the sexual behavior of men is held to a woman's version of the reasonable woman standard.

In *Toward a Feminist Theory of the State*, Catharine MacKinnon argues that because the law of rape embodies the perspective of men, the law concludes that if the man does not consider himself to be a rapist, the act was not rape. We advocate using the reasonable woman standard to measure the behavior of the man, in order to change the law so that it embodies the perspective of women. Thus, if a woman believes she was raped and a reasonable woman would have believed the intercourse was without consent, it was rape.

The law should ask whether the defendant behaved like a person who believed he was engaged in consensual sexual activity and whether a reasonable woman would have behaved similarly. A reasonable woman would not use force, intimidation, or threats of force. A reasonable woman would not believe the sexual activity was consensual if her partner cried, said no, tried to leave, or otherwise resisted intercourse. "No" really does mean "no." In fact, a reasonable woman would want affirmative evidence of consent. Borrowing language from the University of Oregon's Student Conduct Code, we would define rape as a crime committed when a person penetrates another person's vagina or anus without first obtaining explicit consent from that person. We would define explicit consent as "voluntary, non-coerced, and clear communication indicating a willingness to engage in a particular act." Thus, a person accused of rape should be held to a standard that embodies respect for women's autonomy, physical integrity, and right to control their sexuality. Our reasonable woman standard and the accompanying redefinition of rape represent a viable means of rectifying the continuing grave injustice in this most gendered of crimes. By providing women with a law of their own, the adoption of our reasonable woman standard would go far toward providing women with just and equal treatment of their bodily integrity. As human beings, women deserve nothing less.

Postscript

I wish to see women neither heroines nor brutes but reasonable
creatures.   —Mary Wollstonecraft, *A Vindication*
                                  of the Rights of Women, 1792

The words Mary Wollstonecraft penned at the end of the
eighteenth century represent our hopes for women at the beginning of
the twenty-first century. Women aren't better than men, nor are they
worse. But women differ from men in how they perceive and experience certain conduct. As this book has demonstrated, sometimes the
differences between men and women seriously affect how the law
treats perpetrators and victims. For sexual harassment, stalking, domestic homicide, and rape, a male standard excuses conduct as reasonable that a female standard condemns as unreasonable and harmful.

We intend our reasonable woman standard to alter the way in which
the law views certain kinds of behavior. Changing the lens through
which law sees—doing what Katharine Bartlett, in her article "Feminist Legal Methods," calls "asking the woman question"—entails a
paradigm shift that raises the minimum level of legally acceptable behavior for gendered injuries.

Our proposal is radical. The reasonable woman standard, even as
used in the law of sexual harassment, certainly has its critics. Shirley
Robin Letwin in her article "Law and the Reasonable Woman," starts
off by stating, "One of the most insidious threats to our liberties since
World War II has been an attack from within." Letwin goes on to describe how advocating the reasonable woman standard—and feminist
jurisprudence in general—constitutes "an attack on all rational discourse." Aside from the hyperbole, we and others, disagree with
Letwin's claim and instead believe that the reasonable woman is liber-
ating. "Our" liberties must include freedom and dignity for women

and true respect for the perspectives and experiences gendered female in our society. It is neither fascist nor antimale to propose, or to adopt, a legal standard that helps make this possible.

Already some judges, including the former dean of Yale Law School, Judge Guido Calabresi, explicitly apply a reasonable woman standard to men accused of sexually harassing women—but the sky hasn't fallen. Throughout this book we have provided other examples of male judges who clearly understand what a reasonable woman standard demands—and sadly, a few examples of female judges who don't. Over time, as the standard becomes more common and accepted, as what is expected is better understood, most male and female judges and jurors can and will learn to correctly apply the standard. That is, decision makers will routinely apply a woman's version of the reasonable woman standard, not, as in traditional rape law, a man's version.

In this book we have argued that it is time for women to define what is just and fair in certain contexts. Until the law incorporates women's views of what respect for their bodily integrity, autonomy, agency, and self-determination means, women will remain unequal to men. Women should have the right to work without being reviled, objectified, and sexually harassed as "the other." They should have the right to live in their homes free of violence, to leave a relationship safely, and to defend themselves and their children with deadly force if necessary. They should have the right to be free from stalking, to be left alone. And they should have the right to choose whether to engage in sexual activity. A law of her own, a law a reasonable woman would choose, explicitly guarantees these rights. The reasonable woman should become the measure of man so that women can finally be "created equal."

References

BOOKS, JOURNALS, ARTICLES, BRIEFS, AND REPORTS

Abrams, Kathryn. "Gender Discrimination and the Transformation of Workplace Norms." 42 *Vanderbilt Law Review* 1183 (1989).

———. "The New Jurisprudence of Sexual Harassment." 83 *Cornell Law Review* 1170 (1998).

American Law Institute. *Model Penal Code and Commentaries: With Text on Model Penal Code as Adapted at the 1962 Annual Meeting of the American Law Institute at Washington, D.C., May 24, 1962.* Philadelphia: The Institute, 1980–1985.

"Advance Ruling Denied on Scope of Rebuttal: *People of the State of New York v. Gerald Ardito.*" *New York Law Journal* 21 (August 19, 1997).

Anti-Stalking Legislation, 1992. Hearings on S. 2922 before the Senate Judiciary Committee, 102d Cong., 2d sess. 43 (1992).

Associated Press. "Jury: Woman in Rape Case 'Asked for It.'" *Chicago Tribune,* 11C, October 6, 1989.

Bacon-Blood, Littice, and Michael Perlstein. "Estranged Boyfriend Kills Cop, Himself." *New Orleans Times-Picayune,* A1, January 16, 1999.

Bargh, John, Paula Raymond, John Pryor, and Fritz Strack. "Attractiveness of the Underling." 68 *Journal of Personality and Social Psychology* 768 (1995).

Barnard, George W., et al. "Till Death Do Us Part: A Study of Spouse Murder." 10 *Bulletin of the American Academy of Psychiatry and Law* 271 (1982).

Bartlett, Katharine T. "Feminist Legal Methods." 103 *Harvard Law Review* 829 (1990).

———. *Gender and Law: Theory, Doctrine, Commentary.* Boston: Little, Brown, 1993.

Belluck, Pam. "A Woman's Killer Is Very Often Her Partner, a Study Finds." *New York Times,* national ed., A12, March 31, 1997.

Bernstein, Anita. "Treating Sexual Harassment with Respect." 111 *Harvard Law Review* 445 (1997).

Bessent, Alvin E. "D'Amato Blasts Porto Verdict." *Newsday,* 40, May 6, 1988.

Birmingham, Lisa. "Closing the Loophole: Vermont's Legislative Response to Stalking." 18 *Vermont Law Review* 477 (1994).

Blackstone, William. 1 *Commentaries on the Laws of England*. 1602. London: R. Welsh, 1897.

Blackwood, Eileen. "The Reasonable Woman in Sexual Harassment Law and the Case for Subjectivity." 16 *Vermont Law Review* 1005 (1992).

Blalock, Hubert M., Jr., and Paul H. Wilken. *Intergroup Processes: A Micro-Macro Perspective*. New York: Free Press, 1979.

Bograd, Michelle. "Family Systems Approaches to Wife Battering: A Feminist Critique." *American Journal of Orthopsychiatry* 558 (1984).

"Boyfriend Gets Full Six-Year Term in Domestic Killing." *Memphis Commercial Appeal*, B2, November 27, 1997.

"Boyfriend May Get Forty Years in Killing." *New Orleans Times-Picayune*, B1, August 15, 1997.

Bradfield, Jennifer L. "Anti-Stalking Laws: Do They Adequately Protect Stalking Victims?" 21 *Harvard Women's Law Journal* 229 (Spring 1998).

Browne, Angela. *When Battered Women Kill*. New York: Free Press, 1987.

Browne, Angela, and Kirk R. Williams. "Exploring the Effect of Resource Availability and the Likelihood of Female-Perpetrated Homicides." 23 *Law and Society Review* 75 (1989).

Browne, Kingsley. "An Evolutionary Perspective on Sexual Harassment: Seeking Roots in Biology Rather Than Ideology." 8 *Journal of Contemporary Legal Issues* 5 (1997).

Brownmiller, Susan. *Against Our Will: Men, Women, and Rape* 360. New York: Simon & Schuster, 1975.

Burkitt, Janet, and Anne Koch. "Experts Say Leaving Marriage Left Victim at Risk." *Seattle Times*, B3, January 27, 1999.

Castro, Hector. "Man gets 237 Years for Raping Prostitutes: Parkland Resident Had Been Found Guilty of Attacking Five Women." *Tacoma News Tribune*, B1, October 6, 1998.

Chaiken, Jan M. *Violence by Intimates: Analysis of Data on Crimes by Current or Former Spouses, Boyfriends, and Girlfriends*, NCJ-167237. Washington, D.C.: U. S. Department of Justice Bureau of Justice Statistics, March 1998.

Chamallis, Martha. "Feminist Constructions of Objectivity: Multiple Perspectives in Sexual and Racial Harassment Litigation." 1 *Texas Journal of Women and the Law* 95 (1992).

Cheezum, David. "Yes, One Miscreant Can Gum Up the Jury System: Voices from the Community." *Anchorage Daily News*, 8B, May 13, 1998.

Childers, Jolynn. Note. "'Is There a Place for a Reasonable Woman in the Law?' A Discussion of Recent Developments in Hostile Environment Sexual Harassment." 42 *Duke Law Journal* 854 (1993).

Colker, Ruth. "Feminist Consciousness and the State: A Basis for Cautious Optimism." 90 *Columbia Law Review* 1146 (1990).

Crenshaw, Kimberlé. "Demarginalizing the Intersection of Race and Sex: A Black Feminist Critique of Antidiscrimination Doctrine, Feminist Theory, and Antiracist Politics." *University of Chicago Legal Journal* 139 (1989).

———. "Race, Gender, and Sexual Harassment." 65 *Southern California Law Review* 1467 (1992).

Crocker, Phyllis L. "The Meaning of Equality for Battered Women Who Kill Men in Self-Defense." 8 *Harvard Women's Law Journal* 121 (1985).

Daly, Martin, and Margo Wilson. *Homicide*. Hawthorne, N.Y.: A. de Gruyter, 1988.

de Beauvoir, Simone. *The Second Sex*. New York: Bantam Books, 1949.

Denn, Rebekah. "Rapist Sentenced: A Victim Recounts Her Terror." *Seattle Post Intelligencer*, B6, March 12, 1999.

Dobash, R. Emerson, and Russell P. Dobash. "Violence against Women." In *Gender Violence: Interdisciplinary Perspectives*, edited by Laura L. O'Toole and Jessica R. Schiffman. New York: New York University Press, 1997.

Dodge, Mary, and Edith Greene. "Juror and Expert Conceptions of Battered Women." 6 *Violence and Victims* 271 (1991).

Dolkart, Jane. "Hostile Environment Harassment: Equality, Objectivity, and the Shaping of Legal Standards." 43 *Emory Law Journal* 151 (1994).

Dressler, Joshua. *Understanding Criminal Law*. New York: Matthew Bender, 1987.

Dunkelberger, Lloyd. "Former Prosecutor: Killer's Trial Was Fair." *Sarasota Herald-Tribune*, 1B, June 17, 1998.

Duran, Marlys. "Battered Woman Absolved in Slaying; Violence-Scarred Face Convinces Prosecutors Killing Was Self-Defense." *Denver Rocky Mountain News*, 42A, February 15, 1998.

Dutton, Donald G., and Susan K. Golant. *The Batterer: A Psychological Profile*. New York: HarperCollins, 1995.

Dutton, Mary Ann. "Understanding Women's Responses to Domestic Violence: A Redefinition of Battered Woman Syndrome." 21 *Hofstra Law Review* 1191 (1993).

Ehrenreich, Nancy. "Pluralist Myths and Powerless Men: The Ideology of Reasonableness in Sexual Harassment Law." 99 *Yale Law Journal* 1177 (1990).

Equal Employment Opportunity Commission. "Guidelines on Harassment Based on Race, Color, Religion, Gender, National Origin, Age, or Disability." 58 Fed. Reg. 51, 266 (1993). (These proposed rules were never adopted.)

Esmonde, Donn. "She Said 'No' and She Meant It, Despite What Others Think." *Buffalo News*, 1, May 30, 1993.

Estrich, Susan. "Rape." 95 *Yale Law Journal* 1087 (1986).

———. *Real Rape*. Cambridge: Harvard University Press, 1987.

———. "Sex at Work." 43 *Stanford Law Review* 813 (1991).

Ewing, Charles P., and Moss Aubrey. "Battered Women and Public Opinion: Some Realities about the Myth." 2 *Journal of Family Violence* 257 (1987).

Ferguson, Dr. Harry. Letter to the editor. *Irish Times*, 13, August 6, 1996.

Fitzpatrick, Jacki, and Todd Gomez. "Still Caught in a Trap: The Continued Povertization of Women." 12 *Affilia* 318 (Fall 1997).

Forell, Caroline A. "Essentialism, Empathy, and the Reasonable Woman." *University of Illinois Law Review* 769 (1994).

Gibbs, Nancy. "'Til Death Do Us Part." *Time*, 38, January 18, 1993.

Gillespie, Marcia A. "We Speak in Tongues." *Ms.*, 41, January–February 1992.

Gilligan, Carol. *In a Different Voice*. Cambridge: Harvard University Press, 1982.

Gondolf, Edward W., and Ellen R. Fisher. *Battered Women as Survivors: An Alternative to Treating Learned Helplessness*. Lexington, Mass.: Lexington Books, 1988.

Goodman, Ellen. "A Criminal Record or a Wedding Band?" *Boston Globe*, A15, September 12, 1996.

Gregson, Christine B. Comment. "California's Antistalking Statute: The Pivotal Role of Intent." 28 *Golden Gate University Law Review* 221 (1998).

Gutek, Barbara. *Sex and the Workplace*. San Francisco: Jossey-Bass, 1985.

———. "Understanding Sexual Harassment at Work." 6 *Notre Dame Journal of Law, Ethics, and Public Policy* 335 (1992).

Gutek, Barbara, and Maureen O'Connor. "The Empirical Basis for the Reasonable Woman Standard." 51 *Journal of Social Issues* 151 (1995).

Guy, Robert A., Jr. "The Nature and Constitutionality of Stalking Laws." 46 *Vanderbilt Law Review* 991 (1993), citing Marianne W. Zawitz, 2 *Violence between Intimates*. Washington, D.C.: U.S. Department of Justice, 1994.

Hadfield, Gillian K. "Rational Women: A Test for Sex-Based Harassment." 83 *California Law Review* 1151 (1995).

Harmon, Ronnie, Richard Rosner, and Howard Owens. "Sex and Violence in a Forensic Population of Obsessional Harassers." 4 *Psychology, Public Policy, and Law* 236 (1998).

Harris, Angela P. "Race and Essentialism in Feminist Legal Theory." 42 *Stanford Law Review* 581 (1990).

Hart, Barbara. "Beyond the 'Duty to Warn': A Therapist's 'Duty to Protect' Battered Women and Children." In *Feminist Perspectives on Wife Abuse*, edited by Kersti Yllö and Michele Bograd. Newbury Park, Calif.: Sage, 1988.

Hatterly Freetly, Angela J., and Emily Kane. "Men's and Women's Perceptions of Non-Consensual Sexual Intercourse." 33 *Sex Roles* 785–802 (1995).

Higgins, Tracy E., and Deborah L. Tolman. "Law, Cultural Media(tion), and Desire in the Lives of Adolescent Girls." In *Feminism, Media, and the Law*, edited by Martha Fineman and Martha McClusky. New York: Oxford University Press, 1997.

Hill, Anita. Statement to Senate Judiciary Committee. In *Nomination of Judge Clarence Thomas to Be Associate Justice of the Supreme Court of the United States: Hearings before the Senate Committee on the Judiciary.* 102d Cong., 1st sess., 35–37 (1991).

Hoff, Joan. *Law, Gender, and Injustice: A Legal History of U.S. Women.* New York: New York University Press, 1991.

Hoff, Lee Ann. *Battered Women as Survivors.* New York: Routledge, 1990.

Hunter, Rosemary C. "Gender in Evidence: Masculine Norms vs. Feminist Reforms." 19 *Harvard Women's Law Journal* 127 (1996).

Hurston, Zora Neale. "How It Feels to Be Colored Me." In *I Love Myself When I Am Laughing . . . and Then Again When I Am Looking Mean and Impressive,* edited by Alice Walker. New York: Feminist Press, 1979.

Ith, Ian. "Lamson Pleads Guilty—Issaquah-Area Man Faces Rest of Life in Prison." *Seattle Times*, B1, June 17, 1999.

Jacobs, Jerry A. *Revolving Doors: Sex Segregation and Women's Careers.* Stanford: Stanford University Press, 1989.

Jacobson, Neil S., and John M. Gottman. *When Men Batter Women: New Insights into Ending Abusive Relationships.* New York: Simon & Schuster, 1998.

Jimenez, Jose Luis. "Convicted Killer Wins Early Release." *Sarasota Herald-Tribune*, 1A, September 5, 1998.

Jones, Ann. *Next Time, She'll Be Dead: Battering and How to Stop It.* Boston: Beacon Press, 1994.

———. *Women Who Kill.* New York: Holt, Rinehart & Winston, 1980.

Jordon, Emma Coleman. "Race, Gender, and Social Class in the Thomas Sexual Harassment Hearings: The Hidden Fault Lines in Political Discourse." 15 *Harvard Women's Law Journal* 1 (1992).

"Justice has been served." *Lakeland Ledger*, editorial, A6, July 20, 1998.

Kelly, Liz. *Surviving Sexual Violence.* Minneapolis: University of Minnesota Press, 1988.

Koss, Mary P., et al. *No Safe Haven: Male Violence against Women at Home, at Work, and in the Community.* Washington, D.C.: American Psychological Association, 1994.

Koss, Mary P., et al. "Stranger and Acquaintance Rape: Are There Differences in the Victim's Experience?" 21 *Psychology of Women Quarterly* 1 (1988).

LaLonde, Brent. "Police Seek Ex-Boyfriend in North Side Shooting." *Columbus Dispatch*, 6C, September 29, 1996.

Langan, Patrick A., and John M. Dawson. *Spouse Murder Defendants in Large Urban Counties.* Washington, D.C.: U.S. Department of Justice, 1995.

Lardner, George, Jr. "The Stalking of Kristin." *Washington Post,* C1, November 22, 1992.

Letwin, Shirley Robin. "Law and the Unreasonable Woman." *National Review* 34 (November 18, 1991).

Lewin, Tamar. "What Penalty for a Killing in Passion?" *New York Times,* A18, October 21, 1994.

Lloyd, Genevieve. *The Man of Reason: 'Male' and 'Female' in Western Philosophy,* Minneapolis: University of Minnesota Press, 1984.

Lorde, Audre. "Age, Race, Class, and Sex: Women Redefining Difference." *Sister Outsider* 114 (1984).

Lyons, Sheridan. "Slain Woman's Mother Resents Eighteen-Month Term." *Baltimore Sun,* 1B, October 29, 1994.

MacKinnon, Catharine A. "A Conversation." 34 *Buffalo Law Review* 11 (1985).

———. *Feminism Unmodified: Discourses on Life and Law.* Cambridge: Harvard University Press, 1987.

———. *Only Words.* Cambridge: Harvard University Press, 1993.

———. *Sexual Harassment of Working Women.* New Haven: Yale University Press, 1979.

———. *Toward a Feminist Theory of the State.* Cambridge: Harvard University Press, 1989.

———, rep. Amicus Brief of the National Organization of Male Sexual Victimization, et al., in *Oncale v. Sundowner Offshore Services, Inc.* (1997 WL 471814).

Maguigan, Holly. "Battered Women and Self-Defense: Myths and Misconceptions in Current Reform Proposals." 140 *University of Pennsylvania Law Review* 379 (1991).

Mahoney, Martha R. "Legal Images of Battered Women: Redefining the Issue of Separation." 90 *Michigan Law Review* 1 (1991).

———. "Women's Lives, Violence, and Agency." In *The Public Nature of Private Violence,* edited by Martha Albertson Fineman and Roxanne Mykitiuk. New York: Routledge, 1994.

Matsuda, Mari J. "When the First Quail Calls: Multiple Consciousness as Jurisprudential Method." 11 *Women's Rights Law Reporter* 7 (1989).

Matthews, Donna M. "Making the Crucial Connection: A Proposed Threat Hearsay Exception," 27 *Golden Gate Law Review* 117 (1996).

Mayer, Jane, and Jill Bramson. *Strange Justice: The Selling of Clarence Thomas.* Boston: Houghton Mifflin, 1994.

Meloy, J. Reid. "The Clinical Risk Management of Stalking: "Someone Is Watching over Me . . ." 51 *American Journal of Psychotherapy* 174 (Spring 1997).

Mercy, James A., and Linda E. Saltzman. "Fatal Violence among Spouses in the United States, 1976–1985." 79 *American Journal of Public Health* 595 (1989).

Miller, Norman, and Marilynn B. Brewer, eds. *Groups in Contact: The Psychology of Desegregation.* Orlando: Academic Press, 1984.

Minow, Martha. *Making All the Difference: Inclusion, Exclusion, and American Law.* Ithaca, N.Y.: Cornell University Press, 1990.

Moskos, Charles C., and John Sibley Butler. *All That We Can Be: Black Leadership and Racial Integration the Army Way.* New York: Basic Books, 1996.

Note. "The Myth of Context in Politics and Law." 110 *Harvard Law Review* 1292 (1997).

Nourse, Victoria. "Passion's Progress: Modern Law Reform and the Provocation Defense." 106 *Yale Law Journal* 1331 (1997).

O'Neill, Ann W. "Judge Rules Exorcism Death Manslaughter." *Los Angeles Times*, A1, April 17, 1997.

Oxford Dictionary of Quotations. New York: Oxford University Press, 1992.

Patterson, Orlando. "Race, Gender, and Liberal Fallacies." *New York Times*, sec. 4, 15, October 20, 1991.

Ploscowe, Morris. *Sex and the Law.* New York: Prentice-Hall, 1951.

Pontarolo, Mary, and Margaret Hobart. "A Call to Action for Our Murdered Sisters." *Seattle Times*, editorial, B5, February 24, 1999.

Pryor, John, Janet Giedd, and Karen Williams. "A Social Psychological Model for Predicting Sexual Harassment." 51 *Journal of Social Issues* 69 (1995).

Pryor, John, and Lynette Stoller. "Sexual Cognition Processes in Men High in the Likelihood to Sexually Harass." 20 *Personality and Social Psychology Bulletin* 163 (April 1994).

Quindlen, Anna. "Same Old Math," *Baltimore Sun*, editorial, A13, October 25, 1994.

Rainey, L. V. "Killer's Punishment Far Too Small to Fit the Crime." *Eugene Register Guard*, editorial, 10A, February 27, 1990.

Rapaport, Elizabeth. "Capital Murder and the Domestic Discount: A Study of Capital Domestic Murder in the Post-Furman Era." 49 *Southern Methodist University Law Review* 1507 (1996).

Schelong, Katherine M. "Domestic Violence and the State: Responses to and Rationales for Spousal Battering, Marital Rape, and Stalking." 78 *Marquette Law Review* 79 (1994).

Schneider, Elizabeth M. "Describing and Changing: Women's Self-Defense Work and the Problem of Expert Testimony on Battering." 9 *Women's Rights Law Reporter* 195 (1986).

———. "Self-Defense and Relations of Domination: Moral and Legal Perspectives on Battered Women Who Kill: Resistance to Equality." 57 *University of Pittsburg Law Review* 477 (1996).

Schultz, Vicki. "Reconceptualizing Sexual Harassment." 107 *Yale Law Journal* 1683 (1998).

———. "Sex Is the Least of It: Let's Focus Harassment Law on Work, Not Sex." *Nation*, 11, May 25, 1998.

Seigel, Reva. "'The Rule of Love': Wife Beating as Prerogative and Privacy." 105 *Yale Law Journal* 2117 (1996).

"Sexual Assault Called 'Silent Violent Epidemic.'" *Washington Post*, A3, November 6, 1995.

Silverman, Dierdre. "Sexual Harassment: Working Women's Dilemma." *Quest: Feminist Quarterly* (Winter 1976–77).

Smith, J. C. "The Sword and the Shield of Perseus: Some Mythological Dimensions of the Law." 6 *International Journal of Law and Psychiatry* 235 (1984).

Spitko, E. Gary. "He Said, He Said: Same-Sex Sexual Harassment under Title VII and the Reasonable Heterosexist Standard." 18 *Berkeley Journal of Employment and Labor Law* 56 (1997).

Stimpson, C., ed., in conjunction with the Congressional Information Service. *Women and the "Equal Rights" Amendment.* U.S. Senate subcommittee hearings, 91st Congress. New Providence, N.J.: R. R. Bowker, 1972.

Swerdlow, Marian. "Men's Accommodations to Women Entering a Nontraditional Occupation: A Case of Rapid Transit Operatives." *Gender and Society* 373 (September 1989).

Taslitz, Andrew E. *Rape and the Culture of the Courtroom.* New York: New York University Press, 1999.

Taylor, Laurie J. "Provoked Reason in Men and Women: Heat-of-Passion Manslaughter and Imperfect Self-Defense." 33 *UCLA Law Review* 1679 (1986).

Tjaden, Patricia. *The Crime of Stalking: How Big Is the Problem?* Washington, D.C.: National Institute of Justice, U.S. Department of Justice, 1997.

Tjaden, Patricia, Nancy Thoennes, National Institute of Justice, Center for Disease Control and Prevention, and Center for Policy Research. *Stalking in America: Findings for the National Violence against Women Survey.* Washington, D.C.: U.S. Department of Justice, Office of Justice Programs, National Institute of Justice, 1998.

Toobin, Jeffrey. "The Trouble with Sex." *New Yorker*, 48, February 9, 1998.

Tran, Tam B. "Title VII Hostile Work Environment: A Different Perspective." 9 *Journal of Contemporary Legal Issues* 357 (1998).

Unikel, Robert. "'Reasonable Doubts': A Critique of the Reasonable Woman Standard in American Jurisprudence." 87 *Northwestern University Law Review* 326 (1992).

U.S. Department of Justice, Office of Justice Programs, Violence against Women Grants Office. *Domestic Violence and Stalking: Second Annual Re-*

port to Congress under the Violence against Women Act. Washington, D.C.: Violence against Women Grants Office, Office of Justice Programs, U.S. Department of Justice, July 1997.

U.S. Department of Justice, National Institute of Justice. *Domestic Violence, Stalking, and Stalking Legislation: An Annual Report to Congress under the Violence against Women Act.* Washington, D.C.: U.S. Department of Justice, Office of Justice Programs, National Institute of Justice, April 1996.

———. *Project to Develop a Model Anti-Stalking Code for States.* Washington, D.C.: Government Printing Office, 1993.

U.S. Department of Justice, U.S. Department of Health and Human Services, State Justice Institute, and National Association of Women Judges. "Validity of 'Battered Woman Syndrome' in Criminal Cases Involving Battered Women." Washington, D.C.: 1997. Citing R. J. Paterson and R. W. J. Neufeld, "Clear Danger: Situational Determinants of the Appraisal of Threat," 101 (3) *Psychological Bulletin,* 404–16 (1987).

U.S. Department of Labor, Bureau of Statistics. *A Profile of the Working Poor, 1996,* Report 918. Washington, D.C.: Government Printing Office, December 1997. http://stats.bis.gove/cpswp96.htm

Waldo, Craig, Jennifer Berdahl, and Louise Fitzgerald. "Are Men Sexually Harassed? If So, by Whom?" 22 *Law and Behavior* 59 (1998).

Walker, Lenore E. *The Battered Woman.* New York: Harper & Row, 1979.

———. *Terrifying Love: Why Battered Women Kill and How Society Responds.* New York: Harper & Row, 1989.

Weiner, Richard, and Linda Hunt. "Social Sexual Conduct at Work: How Do Workers Know When It Is Harassment and When It Is Not?" 34 *California Western Law Review* 53 (1997).

Weiner, Richard, Linda Hunt, Brenda Russell, Kelley Mannen, and Charles Gasper. "Perceptions of Sexual Harassment: The Effects of Gender, Legal Standard, and Ambivalent Sexism." 21 *Law and Human Behavior* 71 (1995).

Welke, Barbara. "Unreasonable Women: Gender and the Law of Accidental Injury, 1870–1920." *Law and Social Inquiry* 19 (1994).

Wigmore, John H. 3A *Evidence in Trials at Common Law* §924a. Edited by James H. Cadbourn. Boston: Little, Brown, 1983.

Williams, Kimber. "Woman, Son, 15, Stabbed to Death." *Eugene Register Guard,* July 8, 1989.

Williams, Patricia J. *The Alchemy of Race and Rights.* Cambridge: Harvard University Press, 1991.

Wilson, Margo, and Martin Daly. "Spousal Homicide Risk and Estrangement." 8 *Violence and Victims* 3 (1993).

———. "Who Kills Whom in Spouse Killings? On the Exceptional Sex Ratio of Spousal Homicides in the United States." 30 *Criminology* 189 (1992).

Wollstonecraft, Mary. *A Vindication of the Rights of Women, with Strictures of Political and Moral Subjects*. 1792. New Edition. Introduction by Mrs. Henry Fawcett. London: T. F. Unwin, 1891.

Woolf, Virginia. *A Room of One's Own*. New York and Burlingame: Harcourt, Brace & World, 1929.

———. *Three Guineas*. New York: Harcourt, Brace, 1938.

Wrangham, Richard, and Dale Peterson. *Demonic Males: Apes and the Origins of Human Violence*. Boston: Houghton Mifflin, 1996.

Yllö, Kersti, and Michele Bograd, eds. *Feminist Perspectives on Wife Abuse*. Newbury Park, Calif.: Sage, 1988.

Zawitz, Marianne W. *Violence between Intimates*. Washington, D.C.: U.S. Department of Justice, 1994.

Zona, Michael. "A Comparative Study of Erotomanic and Obsessional Subjects in a Forensic Sample." 38 *Journal of Forensic Science* 894 (1993).

Zorza, Joan. "Women Rarely Batter Men Except When Abused Themselves." *New York Times*, national ed., A22, February 17, 1994.

CASES

Andrews v. City of Philadelphia, 895 F.2d 1469 (3d Cir. 1993).

Anthony v. County of Sacramento, 898 F. Supp. 1435 (E.D. Cal. 1995).

Barnes v. Costle, 561 F.2d 983 (D.C. Cir. 1977); *reversing Barnes v. Train*, 13 FEP Cases 123 (D.D.C. 1974).

Baskerville v. Culligan International Co., 50 F.3d 428 (7th Cir. 1995).

Bechtel v. State, 840 P.2d 1 (Okla. Crim. App. 1992).

Bennett v. Corroon & Black Corp., 845 F.2d 104 (5th Cir. 1988).

Bonner v. State, 1998 Ala. Crim. App. LEXIS 42 (1998).

Bouters v. State, 659 So.2d 235 (Fla. 1995).

Bradwell v. Illinois, 83 U.S. (16 Wall.) 130 (1873).

Brooms v. Regal Tube Co., 881 F.2d 412 (7th Cir. 1989).

Burlington Industries, Inc., v. Ellerth, 524 U.S. 742 (1998).

Carreno v. Local Union No. 226, 1990 WL 159199 (D. Kan. 1990), *unreported opinion*.

Commonwealth v. Myers, 609 A.2d 162 (Pa. 1992).

Commonwealth v. Stonehouse, 555 A.2d 772 (Pa. 1989).

Corne & DeVane v. Bausch & Lomb, 390 F. Supp. 233 (D. Ariz. 1975).

DeAngelis v. El Paso Municipal Police Officers Ass'n, 51 F.3d 591 (5th Cir. 1995).

Dellert v. Total Vision, Inc., 875 F. Supp. 506 (N.D. Ill. 1995).

Dillon v. Frank, 1992 WL 5436 (6th Cir. 1992), *unreported opinion*.

Dixon v. United States, 565 A.2d 72 (D.C. Cir. 1989).

Doe v. City of Belleville, Illinois, 119 F.3d 563 (7th Cir. 1996).

Eckroth v. Rockford Products Co., 1996 WL 377170 (N.D. Ill.).

Ellison v. Brady, 924 F.2d 872 (9th Cir. 1991).

Farinas v. State, 569 So.2d 425 (Fla. 1990).

Frontiero v. Richardson, 411 U.S. 677 (1973).

Fuller v. City of Oakland, 47 F.3d 1522 (9th Cir. 1995); *reversing* 1992 U.S. Dist. LEXIS 2536 (February 10, 1992).

Harley v. McCoach , 928 F. Supp. 533 (E.D. Pa. 1996).

Harris v. Forklift Systems, Inc., 510 U.S. 17 (1993).

Hawthorne v. State, 408 So.2d 801 (Fla. Dist. Ct. App. 1982).

Johnson v. Hondo, Inc., 125 F.3d 408 (7th Cir. 1997).

Kortan v. State of California, 5 F. Supp.2d 843 (C.D. Ca. 1998), *unreported opinion.*

McCoy v. Macon Water Authority, 966 F. Supp. 1209 (M.D. Ga. 1997).

Meritor Savings Bank v. Vinson, 477 U.S. 57 (1986).

Michael M. v. Superior Court, 450 U.S. 464 (1981).

Miller v. Bank of America, 418 F. Supp. 233 (N.D. Cal. 1976).

Munday v. Waste Mgmt. of North America, 858 F.Supp. 1364 (D. Md. 1994), *modified*, 126 F.3d 239 (4th Cir. 1997).

Myers v. City of El Paso, 874 F. Supp. 1546 (W.D. Tex. 1995).

Nichols v. Frank, 42 F.3d 503 (9th Cir. 1994).

Oncale v. Sundowner Offshore Services, Inc., 523 U.S. 75 (1998).

People v. Berry, 556 P.2d 777 (Cal. 1976).

People v. Holt, 649 N.E.2d 571 (Ill. App. 1995).

People v. Humphrey, 921 P.2d 1 (Cal. 1996).

People v. May, 213 Cal. App. 3d 118 (1989).

People v. Moye, 489 N.E.2d 736 (N.Y. App. 1985).

People v. Rhoades, 193 Cal.App.3d 1362 (1987).

People v. Rossakis, 605 N.Y.S.2d 825 (Sup. Ct. 1993).

Quick v. Donaldson Co., 895 F. Supp. 1288 (S.D. Iowa 1995).

Rabidue v. Osceola Refining Co., 805 F.2d 611 (6th Cir. 1986); *affirming* 584 F. Supp. 419 (E.D. Mich. 1984).

Reed v. Reed, 404 U.S. 71 (1971).

Robinson v. Jacksonville Shipyards, Inc., 760 F. Supp. 1486 (M.D. Fla. 1991).

Roe v. K-Mart, 1995 WL 316783 (D.S.C. March 28, 1995), *unreported opinion.*

Rushing v. United Airlines, 919 F. Supp. 1101 (N.D. Ill. 1996).

Santos v. State, 591 So.2d 160 (Fla. 1991).

State ex rel. Lawrence, 571 So.2d 133 (La. 1990).

State ex rel. M.T.S., 609 A.2d 1266 (N.J. 1992).

State v. Kelly, 478 A.2d 364, 371 (N.J. 1984).

State v. Necaise, 466 So.2d 660 (La. Ct. App. 1985).

State v. Norman, 378 S.E.2d 8 (N.C. 1989).

State v. Orsello, 554 N.W.2d 70 (Minn. 1996).

State v. Rangel, 977 P.2d 379 (Or. 1999).

State v. Shannon, 514 N.W.2d 790 (Minn. 1994).

State v. Stewart, 763 P.2d 572 (Kan. 1988).

State v. Wanrow, 559 P.2d 548 (Wash. 1977).

Tanner v. Oregon Health Sciences University, 971 P.2d 435 (Or. App. 1998).

Tomkins v. Public Service Electric & Gas Co., 422 F. Supp. 553 (D.N.J. 1976).

Torres v. Pisano, 116 F.3d 625 (2d Cir.), *certeriori denied*, 118 S. Ct. 563 (1997).

United States v. Paul, 37 F.3d 496 (9th Cir. 1994).

Washington v. City of Cleveland, 948 F. Supp. 1301 (N.D. Ohio 1996).

Williams v. Runyon, 881 F. Supp. 359 (N.D. Ill. 1995).

Williams v. Saxbe, 413 F. Supp. 654 (D.D.C. 1976).

STATUTES

Oregon Revised Statutes § 30.866, §§ 163.135(1), 163.730–163.755 (1997).

Texas Penal Code (Vernon 1925), art. 1220 (killing wife's lover justifiable homicide); repealed, 1973 Texas General Laws, chap. 399, § 3(a). Note: Until 1977, Georgia allowed a husband or father to kill the lover of his spouse or child in certain circumstances based on judicial interpretation of a general homicide statute; this interpretation was abrogated in *Burger v. State*, 231 S.E.2d 769 (1977).

Index

About the Authors

Caroline Forell is a professor at the University of Oregon Law School where she writes and teaches about women and the law. Professor Forell is actively involved with community issues concerning domestic violence and sexual assault. Her articles about lawyer-client and faculty-student sexual liaisons have spurred law reform and revision of codes of ethical conduct.

Donna Matthews is an attorney in Oregon, with a practice focusing on women's issues in the areas of family, employment, and civil rights law. Her other work involves writing about women and law, and advocating change to achieve justice.

Both Forell and Matthews are long-time residents of Eugene, Oregon.